Creating
Special Effects
on the Macintosh

*A Ready-to-Run
Library of Effects
for Angling,
Rotating,
Shadowing,
Flipping,
and More*

Creating
Special Effects
on the Macintosh®

DAVID HOLZGANG

Addison-Wesley Publishing Company, Inc.

Reading, Massachusetts • Menlo Park, California • New York
Don Mills, Ontario • Wokingham, England • Amsterdam
Bonn • Sydney • Singapore • Tokyo • Madrid • San Juan
Paris • Seoul • Milan • Mexico City • Taipei

ISBN 0-201-57779-8

Copyright © 1992 by David A. Holzgang

Sponsoring Editor: Rachel Guichard
Project Editor: Joanne Clapp Fullagar
Technical Reviewer: David Blatner
Cover Design: Skolos/Wedell, Inc.
Text Design: Judy Ashkenaz, Total Concept Associates
Indexer: Anne Leach
Set in 11-point Serifa Roman by Total Concept Associates

1 2 3 4 5 6 7 8 9–MW–9594939291

First printing, November 1991

Contents

2 Checkboxes 83

3 Bullets 101

4 Buttons   187

Acknowledgments

Several special circumstances make these acknowledgments particularly necessary and appropriate. This book grew out of the encouragement and creative energy of my acquisitions editor, Rachel Guichard, who had the first idea for this type of effect. She asked if anyone could do printing effects and, if so, could I think up enough of them to fill a book? As it turns out, the answer to both questions was yes. Without her interest and enthusiasm for this concept, I would never have thought to create these effects and put them into a book. I must also acknowledge Scott Knaster, the series editor for my previous book, whose simple comment "Does anyone ever use the PostScript Escape font?" specifically directed me to this approach for general printing effects. With this book, the answer is now "Yes, lots of people!" Thanks for a great idea to both of you.

As an author, I have found that writing a book always involves more people than I ever imagined when I was only a reader. For this book in particular, I have been helped and supported in a variety of ways that have made this book very special. To begin with, Joanne Clapp Fullagar, my editor, has seen this through, in spite of delay, moving, upheavals, and the usual author's tantrums with her customary good grace and sensitive criticism. Without her unfailing support, this book would not only be less accessible, it might not exist at all. Both she and Flo Tumolo at Addison-Wesley have given me invaluable insight into how these effects can be used and how they can be extended; Flo also tested all of the effects in a variety of ways to ensure that they work as advertised. Without her, there would surely be more mistakes and fewer useful hints than there are. I must also thank Shirley Grant, of the Cheshire Group, for testing and tuning all the effects. This was a monumental job, not made any easier by the author's penchant for changing the effects as the book progressed. The technical review was provided by David Blatner of Parallax Productions. Himself a successful author, he offered many valuable suggestions and insights that have improved this book. Many thanks to all for their help. However, as always, if there are any errors or omissions still in the text or the effects, they remain—as they began—my sole responsibility.

As you can imagine, this book has required much more ingenuity in production and design than most; certainly more than any of my previous books, which have been primarily technical in nature. In this case, the graphic content and unusual presentation of the effects required special help from many folks at Addison-Wesley. Mary Cavaliere and Diane Freed have done marvelous work in designing and laying out a book that is both a clear reference and easy to use. In addition, Diane coordinated production and typesetting to make this come out better than I had ever imagined when I started the project.

On the personal side, congratulations to Carole and Yvette—and many thanks: three down and (I hope) more to come. And, always, to Shirley for the tea and lemonade.

Introduction

Creating Special Effects on the Macintosh: A Ready-to-Run Library of Effects for Angling, Rotating, Shadowing, Flipping, and More is about livening up those ordinary, necessary documents you create every day, making them eye-catching and extraordinary instead. And all you need to create better-looking documents is your Macintosh, a word processing application, a LaserWriter or PostScript-compatible printer, and this book—no expensive and complicated drawing or page layout programs to buy.

The enclosed disk contains more than one hundred nifty graphic and text effects you can use to enhance your memos, letters, stationery, newsletters, and other documents. Some of the effects are a bit exotic—I don't suppose that mirror text, for example, is something people need everyday—but, for the most part, these are effects that will be quite useful on a regular basis. You simply copy the effect text from the disk and paste it into your document.

Creating Special Effects on the Macintosh is intended to be fun! It was fun to create and test these effects, and I hope that you will have fun using them. Many of the effects allow you to change variables to create interesting and useful alternatives. You can customize the size, position, combinations, and shading, as well as add numbers, text, and so on. The book illustrates only some of the possibilities; a little creativity, ingenuity, and trial-and-error will give you many more variations. Feel free to explore all of the possibilities. The worst that happens is that your page won't print. If that happens, then you know that you have an error. Don't worry about hurting the printer or causing any major problems. Since these effects are just programs, you are quite safe.

WHAT YOU NEED

The effects themselves consist of text files that draw the desired effect on your printed output. Since these effects are written in the PostScript language, they work with any laser printers or other output devices, such as imagesetters, that understand the PostScript language. Apple's LaserWriter IINT and most other Apple laser printers are such devices. Note, however, that some laser printers, such as the Personal LaserWriter SC, do not understand PostScript, and cannot be used to print these effects. If you are not sure whether your printer supports the PostScript language, check the printer documentation.

The effects don't require any special knowledge or graphics talent to use and they work on all Macintosh systems, even the most basic ones. These are not Encapsulated PostScript (EPS) files and they require no graphics or other special support from your word processing application; they are text files that you can place in any document. The only requirement is that the application must support multiple fonts in a document, as almost all Macintosh applications do. All the effects are text files on the disk that accompanies this book. You copy the effects from this disk onto your system, and then copy and paste the effect text into your document.

Finally, because these are simply text files, you will not see the effects on your screen. The effects only appear when you print your document. Do not expect to paste these effects into your document and see them on the screen; they don't work that way.

HOW TO USE THIS BOOK

The layout of this book is intended to help you find and use effects very easily whether you use these every day or only once or twice over a long period of time. You can use these effects in a cookbook fashion—find the effect you want to prepare and follow the steps. In that sense, you can think of the effects as recipes that you will make. That means that you don't have to understand the details of how the effects work in order to use them, just as a cook doesn't need to know the chemistry and physics of cooking to make a tasty dish. A cook must, however, understand pots and pans and how to combine ingredients correctly to follow even the simplest recipe. In the same way, you need to understand some things about how to create and insert the effect recipes into your document so that they work to create the effect that you want.

Chapter 1 introduces you to the process of creating these effects. It describes, in detail, how to place effects into your document and gives you step-by-step instructions on how to do this, covering each of the four most common word processing applications: Microsoft Word, MacWrite II, WordPerfect, and WriteNow. While the process of cutting and pasting an effect is not difficult, it does require several very precise steps to work correctly. It is important that you read the first chapter and work through the examples in it for your individual word processing application. Once you have done the examples here, you will be ready to place any effects in the book into your documents. Chapter 1 also describes some basic steps that you can take if you have trouble printing the effects.

Each subsequent chapter covers one basic type of effect—checkboxes, bullets, buttons, arrows, text of various kinds, and so on—and begins with step-by-step instructions specific to inserting the effects in that chapter. This is intended as a brief refresher for those who may not have used the effects for some time, or those, like myself, who might otherwise forget one or two critical steps in the middle of the process when they are in a hurry or preoccupied.

Each effect is presented in the same format: The effect is named, and it appears in the margin exactly as it would print if you use the effect directly from the disk. If there are variables associated with the effect, each variable—its name, what it controls, and what values you can put in it—is discussed. Since these effects are all different sizes and shapes, "Size and Position" discusses what you need to know how to place the effect in your document and to control its size. "Using the Effect" illustrates ways to use the effect or shows how the variables change the effect.

You'll find two types of special boxes. "Tip" boxes present little nuggets of interest or advice. "Behind the Scenes" boxes contain additional information, generally of a more technical nature, that you can read if you have an interest in the technology behind the topic being discussed. This information is simply there for background—and, to tell the truth, because sometimes I just want to insert some special, technical information for those interested.

Appendix A tells you, in some detail, how to find and correct errors in your effect. For the technically inclined, Appendix B presents some background information about PostScript and about how the effects work. Appendix C gives you a quick reference, organized by chapter, to all the effects and their variables.

NOTATIONS IN THE EFFECT RECIPES

Just as some recipes require more time and skill to prepare and cook than others, so some of the effects here require more time and skill on your part to insert and use them successfully in a document. A knowledgeable and experienced cook can tell by reading a recipe whether that recipe requires a lot of time and many steps for preparation or only a little. For effects, however, the differences are more difficult to perceive. The knots and hourglasses next to each effect name allow you to tell at a glance when an effect will be easy and when it may require a little more work, or when it will print quickly and when it may take a noticeable time to print.

Knots

Since you can't see these effects on the screen, you will sometimes have to print them to see exactly where they are placed and how they look in your document. For example, background text places a word behind the regular text in your document. To make this work correctly, you have to enter several important parameters: the word itself, the position of the word on the page, the angle for the word, and the color of the word. Because you have to enter all these variables, and because setting some of them may require that you make several trials to get the exact output that you want, this is considered a difficult effect.

The number of knot symbols next to an effect indicates how difficult that effect is to use. If no knot is shown next to an effect, then the effect does not require any special information and should generally work correctly without any test prints. One knot means that the effect requires some input but probably no test prints. Two knots or more means that you either have to enter several items of information for the effect, or that it probably requires test prints, or both.

Hourglasses

Also like cooking recipes, some effects require a lot of time to print, some require almost none, and many fall somewhere between these two extremes. The simplest effects, such as the checkbox effect that is the first example in Chapter 1, add so little time when printing that you cannot tell whether the effect is on the page or not when you print; the time to print is essentially identical in either case. Some effects, however, particularly special text effects, require a long time to create and print. Of course, the amount of time it takes to draw the effect depends on the amount of memory that you have in your printer, what model of printer you use, and other, more esoteric and internal, variables in your printer; therefore, it isn't possible to give exact times for how long an effect will take to print.

The number of hourglass symbols indicates how much time that effect takes to print relative to other effects in the book. If an effect has no hourglass, then it should not add any perceptible time to printing your page of output. If you print an effect with one hourglass, and that adds (say) ten seconds to your printing, then a two-hourglass effect adds two to four times that much time to printing a page, and a three-hourglass effect will multiply that time by five or more.

Of course, even the simplest effects do actually require some time to draw and print. Therefore, if you use multiple effects on a page then you should expect to have the page take a little more time to print than one that has no effects. For example, even though one checkbox is so simple that you won't notice any additional time in printing, a dozen will make a noticeable difference. This obviously is compounded if you have multiple two- or three-hourglass effects on a page.

CUSTOMIZING THE EFFECT RECIPES

You can customize many of the effect recipes in this book by entering information into the variables in the effect text. There are two general points that apply to all of these effects.

First, remember that each variable has a specific format and a specific range of values. The effect recipes have been adjusted and tested to work within the stated range of variable values. If you enter values outside the range, there is a good chance that the effect will not print at all, or will print in some way other than what you had wanted. Of course, you can't "break" your printer, but if you enter values outside the ranges, you're on your own.

The second point is a little more technical, but just as important: Some effects will work only with outline fonts. As you may know, your Macintosh computer works with two types of fonts: bitmapped and outline. Bitmapped fonts create characters by turning dots on and off in the appropriate pattern. Common examples of bitmapped fonts are Geneva, New York, Monaco, and all the other fonts on your system that are named after cities. Outline fonts are created by actually drawing an outline of the character and filling it in. Outline fonts carry the standard font names, such as Helvetica, Times, and Courier.

For most effects in this book, you can use any type of font that you want, although, when you are displaying text, the outline fonts will give you the highest quality output. Some effects however, such as the outline numbered button effect, will not print at all in a bitmapped font. If an effect has this restriction, it is prominently noted in the description of that effect. You can always use any outline font with any effect in this book with no difficulty. If you aren't sure what fonts to use, every PostScript printer contains Helvetica and Times outline fonts.

With all this, let me stress one point. Whatever you do, you will not hurt your document, your application, or the printer. The worst that can happen is that the effect doesn't print. Therefore, if you have a special font that you want to try, by all means try it. If the effect prints, then you know that the font works; if it doesn't, then you know that you can't use that font in that effect. It's as simple as that.

CONCLUSION

You've just read a quick overview of what sort of effects are in this book, how this book is structured, and how you can make best use of the effects presented here. In all of that, there are four points covered in this introduction that I want to emphasize before you move on to the remainder of the book.

- The effects in this book and on its accompanying disk are PostScript text files. You must have a PostScript-equipped printer or other output device to use them.

- These effects are text files; they print but do not show on the screen.

- The complete text of all the effects is on the disk that accompanies this book. You must have the disk to use the effects.

- It is very important that you read Chapter 1 and work through the examples for your word processing application. If you don't, you probably won't be able to get the effects to run.

Last, but not at all least, these effects are fun to use. Experiment, play, adjust, tinker, and have a good time using them. I hope you enjoy using them as much as I enjoyed creating them. And now on to the good stuff!

Setting Up for Effects

1

THIS CHAPTER IS THE KEY THAT YOU USE TO UNLOCK THE effects in the rest of this book. Inserting an effect into your document is, basically, just a matter of cutting and pasting. After all, cooking is, basically, just a matter of applying heat to food. Well, we all know that there's more to a good dinner than that.

The same is true of using the effects in this book. You have to know a thing or two about how to cut and paste these effects to get them to print the way you want. It's not difficult, but it does require some attention and care in the process. This chapter walks you step-by-step through the correct process for inserting each of the several types of effects that you will meet. At the end, you will be able to take any of the effect recipes in this book and use them with full confidence.

First, you'll see a general overview of the process that you will use throughout the book for all the effects. Then, since each major word processing program is slightly different in handling these special effects, you should read the section that applies to your specific word processing program. Before using any of the effects, you must install the special PostScript Escape font. All the steps for using Font/DA mover to install this font are detailed here, as well as the steps required to install the font in System 7.0.

Next, the chapter walks you through four effects. If you use Microsoft Word, read the section titled "Using Effects in Microsoft Word." If you use any other word processor, see the section titled "Using Effects in Other Word Processors." The effects are the same in both sections, but the procedures are quite different.

Working through these effects step-by-step teaches you the process of making and using an effect with your own word processor. Once you have inserted these effects successfully, the rest work exactly alike, using the same basic methods for creating even the most complex effects.

After the examples, the chapter concludes with two sections on reading and using the effect recipes. The first of these sections tells you what to do if you have a problem printing your effect. Generally, if that happens, you have made a slight error in your effect which can easily be corrected by following the instructions in this section. The second section tells you something about how the effects use the PostScript language to create their results.

HOW TO BUILD AN EFFECT

The general process of building an effect follows these four steps:

1. Open the effect with your word processing application.

Note that, except for Microsoft Word, you cannot double-click on the effect and automatically open the application. Since the effects are designed to work with many different applications, they will not open automatically. It's easiest to open the effect as a new document for editing and review.

2. Copy the effect text and paste it into your document where you want the effect to appear.

This may require some special considerations to ensure that the effect is where you want it. See the discussion for each application for specific details.

3. Select all the text—and only the text—that belongs to the effect and change the font to the PostScript Escape font.

This step is the key to the process of creating and using the effect. You make the font change just as you would any other font change. Select the block of text that makes up the effect and then choose the PostScript Escape font from your Font menu.

4. The text for the effect will disappear from the screen display of your document, but the effect will be printed with your ordinary text when you print the document.

The effect disappears because the PostScript Escape font is designed to be invisible on the screen. If the PostScript Escape font were not invisible, it would move all of your remaining text to new positions on the printed page even though the effect text would not print. When you change the effect into the PostScript Escape font, your other text should move back into the position where you want it when it prints.

POSITIONING THE EFFECT

You must set one character—called the *positioning character*—on the line where you want the effect *before* you place the effect. In most word processing programs, you can use either a printing or non-printing character for the positioning character.

Each effect begins at the point where the character immediately in front of it ends and specifically erases that character, on the assumption that the character is being used as a placement character. The effects generally are centered on that point and print both before and after it, extending over the space used for the character. This allows you to use any character, whether it prints or not, to position the effect. A non-printing character, such as Ctrl-Q, shows on your screen as a small hollow rectangle. This sets the correct position for the effect, but won't print anything.

Some word processing programs, however, will not allow you to enter non-printing characters, and some fonts don't have a non-printing character. Also, you might want to use a printing character for placement, so that you can see more clearly where the effect is located. Therefore, you can also use any regular character for placement. For obvious reasons, the effect only erases a small space on the page. If you are using a printing character for placement, you should make it small and compact, like a lower-case 'o', to ensure that it is fully covered by the effect. In particular, you should not use any character that extends below the line of text, such as a 'y', since the lower part of the character is likely to show beneath the effect. Unfortunately for your purposes here, most word processing programs are smart enough to ignore spaces, so the character chosen should not be a space.

BEHIND THE SCENES

You may wonder why a positioning character is required at all. The reason is quite logical once you understand how your word processing application positions text for printing and display. Since the PostScript Escape font has no dimensions, text in that font does not show on your screen. Since it does not appear on the screen, your word processing application does not know how to position the effect text when you print your document. No matter where you place it on the screen before converting to the PostScript Escape font, the effect appears right after the last regular printed character in front of the effect on the page, wherever that was. Thus, for example, placing an effect at the beginning of a line on your screen does not automatically position the effect at the start of that line of text. Instead, the effect will display at the end of the preceding line. This can be quite annoying and a little confusing if you don't expect it. Because of this, a positioning character is essential to place the effect where you want it.

The positioning character also sets the size of the effect. For example, if you want the effect to match some text that comes later on the line, you must set the font and size of the positioning character to match that of the text. The effect will be sized based on the font and size of the positioning character, not on that of any other text.

Some effects, such as rotated text that you will learn about in this chapter, require that you enter a string of characters. For these effects, the positioning character sets both the size and the font of the text used in the effect. You set the positioning character (whether printing or non-printing) to the font and size that you want for your effect. This ensures that the correct font is loaded and available when you print the effect.

WORKING WITH SPECIFIC WORD PROCESSORS

Every application requires a bit of special handling to make sure that the effects will insert and display the way you want. In all cases except Word, the effects will run correctly if you follow the basic directions. However, if you want the precise result that is demonstrated here, you will need to make some small modifications for these programs.

Microsoft Word, on the other hand, requires some special steps to insert and use an effect. It's no more difficult to do than the other applications, but Word has some special features that are used for these effects which require special processing.

If your word processing program isn't described, don't be alarmed. For obvious space reasons, we can't discuss every word processing program on the market. I recommend, in that case, that you read the general instructions and the section on WriteNow, which has a simple, but effective, set of options and tools. Most likely, you will find that the effects can be used in your application in the same way as they are used in WriteNow.

Microsoft Word 4.0

Because Word requires a very different approach to installing and using effects, it is covered separately from the other word processing applications. All Word users should read and work through the examples in "Using Effects in Microsoft Word" to be sure that they understand and can easily use these steps. Special versions of the effects are on the disk that comes with this book in the folder named MS Word Effects.

WriteNow 2.2

WriteNow makes it very easy to insert and place your effect. The only consideration for users of WriteNow is the Font menu. The PostScript Escape font is invisible, so it will not appear if you have set your Font menu to display the font names in the font itself. In this case, you should choose Preferences . . . from the File menu and turn off the checkbox that says Actual Fonts in Font Menu. When this box is not checked, the font names are displayed in the System font, and you will see the PostScript Escape font on your menu.

MacWrite II

Placing your effect in MacWrite II is somewhat more difficult than in other applications for two reasons. First, MacWrite displays font names in its Font menu using characters from the actual font. This is a nice touch for some fonts—in case you don't know how the font looks—but it is not very helpful for the PostScript Escape font. Since the PostScript Escape font is invisible on your screen, the entry on the Font menu is a blank line. However, because the fonts are displayed in alphabetical order, you can easily guess which line is your new PostScript Escape font: It's the blank line that appears where the name PostScript would be alphabetically. You simply select this blank line to select the PostScript Escape font as if you could see the font name on this line. The font still works and still performs the same functions.

The second reason that using MacWrite II is more difficult than other word processing programs is that it is a bit cleverer than the others, with (again) unfortunate consequences for your purposes here. Other word processing programs allow you to key in non-printing characters. If the character doesn't exist in your printer, of course nothing will show on the printed page. On the screen, however, the Macintosh system will automatically display these characters as a hollow rectangle. MacWrite II assumes that you couldn't possibly mean to use a non-printing character, so it will not allow you to type one onto the screen. Therefore, when you are using MacWrite, you will have to use a printing character, such as an 'o', for positioning. MacWrite won't allow any other type of character.

If you have an older version of MacWrite, you may find that you cannot have two documents open at the same time, as recommended when pasting an effect into a document. If that is the case, you will have to close your working document and open the effect. Then you can copy the effect text to the Macintosh clipboard. Once the effect is there, you can close the effect itself and reopen the document. Now you can place the text effect in the document from the clipboard. This is a bit more complex than the standard directions given here, but should not present any problems for you.

WordPerfect 2.01

WordPerfect behaves, for the most part, like WriteNow for using effects. This makes it very easy to insert and place your effect. The only consideration for users of WordPerfect, as it is for users of WriteNow, is the Font menu. The PostScript Escape font is invisible, so that it will not appear if you have set your Font menu to display the font names in the font itself. In this case, you should choose Preferences . . . from the File menu and select Environment. . . . This displays the Environment dialog box. Pull down the Options menu and uncheck the Graphic Font Menu item. When this item is not checked, the font names are displayed in the System font.

There is one additional idiosyncrasy that you must take into account when using these effects in WordPerfect. WordPerfect will not print these effects unless you have Show ¶ enabled in the Edit menu. To use these effects with WordPerfect, make sure that you have Show ¶ set in the Edit menu instead of the more usual Hide ¶ command.

USING THE DISK

This disk is not copy protected. The first thing that you should do is make a copy of the effects disk. This guarantees that you will have a good copy if anything ever happens to your working disk.

Viruses and other problems make having clean, back-up copies of working software imperative. Also, it guarantees that you have the individual effects in an unaltered form. In that way, you can work with the effects and customize those on the working disk without worrying that you might damage the original data. Since these are text files, it's sometimes very useful to be able to go back to the original file when you need a fresh copy.

The effects on the disk are in two files. If you use MS Word, then you will use the effects in the MS Word Effects.sea file; if you use any other word processing program, you will use the effects in the Effects.sea file. The two files contain exactly the same set of effects; the only difference is in the format of the effect text.

Since most people only use one word processing application, I recommend that you expand only the file that corresponds to your program onto your working disk or onto your hard disk, if you have one. This will save you some room and ensures that you won't get the two formats mixed up. Of course, if you do use both Word and another word processing application, then you should copy both sets onto your disk.

Each of these files has been compressed to save space on the distribution disk. You can expand these files to their full size simply by clicking on them.

The files on the effect disk have been individually locked for protection against inadvertent loss or damage. When you are using the effects, you load them into your word processing program. In some cases, you may modify the variables in these effects before you insert them into your document. In the course of doing that, it sometimes happens that the files get saved or closed and saved accidently. By locking the files, you can't accidently write your changed file over the original one. Of course, any copy that you make of the effect is unlocked, and so can be changed if you want. You can unlock the files, or lock your copies of the files, if you want. Simply select the file and choose Get Info from the File menu. This brings up a dialog box that tells you some things about the file. At the top right corner of this dialog is a small checkbox, marked Locked. If this is checked, then the file is locked;

9

if it is empty, then the file is unlocked. To change from one to the other, simply click on this box and close the dialog box. This changes the locking status of the file.

INSTALLING THE POSTSCRIPT ESCAPE FONT

Before you can use any of the effects, you must install the PostScript Escape font. I know that the very name, PostScript Escape font, sounds rather ominous. Unfortunately, this is the exact name that must be used to make these effects work correctly. However, this is just a font, like other fonts such as Geneva and Courier that you have installed in your Macintosh. The difference is that this font allows you to send commands directly to your LaserWriter through your word processing application. The PostScript Escape font is loaded onto the disk that came with this book.

System 7

To install the PostScript Escape font with System 7.0, simply follow these steps:

1. Open the PostScript Escape font by double-clicking on it. This shows you a single font entry, labeled PostScript Escape 12, as shown in Figure 1-1.

2. Drag the font entry into your System file. This automatically copies the font into your system and installs it. That's all there is to installing a font in System 7.0

System 6 and Earlier

If you are running an earlier version of the system software than System 7.0, the process is only slightly more complex.

Simply insert the disk into your Macintosh and install the font as you would any other font. Use the Font/DA Mover program that

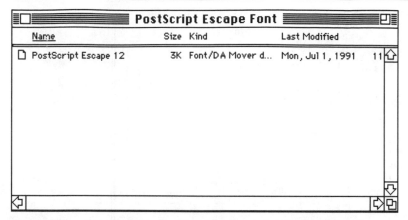

Figure 1-1. Installing the PostScript Escape font in System 7.0

came with your Macintosh, which is usually located on the disk labeled Utilities 2. Remember that, to install a font on your system using the Font/DA Mover, you must turn off MultiFinder if you are running under MultiFinder. Restart your system without MultiFinder and then use Font/DA Mover to install the font.

Follow these steps:

1. Double-click on the font to open it and start the Font/DA Mover program. When you open the font, you should see a window something like Figure 1-2.

2. Click on the Open . . . button under the right display window. This brings up the standard find file display. Go to your System Folder, select the System file, and click on Open. This displays all of your current fonts in the right scroll box.

3. Move back to the left scroll box, which displays only your PostScript Escape font. Select the PostScript Escape font by clicking on it. At this point, your screen should look like Figure 1-3.

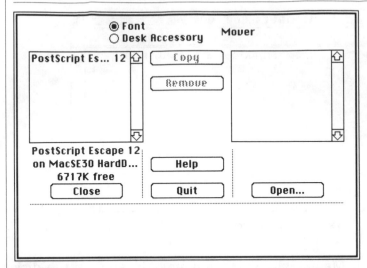

Figure 1-2. Font/DA Mover ready to install the PostScript Escape font

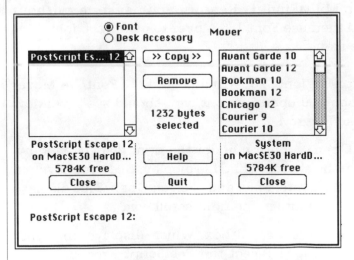

Figure 1-3. Font/DA Mover is now ready to install your PostScript Escape font into your System file

You may notice that the font name, which appears in the bottom of the display window, is not accompanied by a display of text characters, as it would be for other fonts. Don't be alarmed by this. The PostScript Escape font has characters, but these have no width, so they are not visible. As you will see when you use the effects, all the text disappears when you change it to the PostScript Escape font.

4. Click on the Copy button to add the PostScript Escape font to your System file.

5. When the font has been added, click on Quit to end the Font/DA Mover program.

6. Restart your Macintosh to make the new font available to all your applications. When you start an application, you should see the name "PostScript Escape" in the font list. (For WriteNow and MacWrite II, see the application notes in this chapter).

You use the PostScript Escape font just like any other font. The only difference is that any text that you place into the PostScript Escape font will seem to disappear from your document, even though it is still there. This happens because the characters in the PostScript Escape font have no dimensions, so that they cannot be seen on the screen. However, when you print your document on a LaserWriter, this text is sent directly to the LaserWriter for processing.

To view the effect text once you have changed it into the PostScript Escape font, simply select the line of text where the effect is placed and change it to any visible font. Since you can't see the text of the effect, you have to select an entire line. I have found it best to select the last character of the line above the effect and the first character of the line beneath it. This ensures that you have selected all the hidden text. I normally use the Monaco font, since it is a clear and readable bit-mapped screen font that I never use for printing. This makes the effect quite visible in the document and allows me to see what I am doing. Then I just select the effect and change it back to PostScript Escape when I want to print.

USING EFFECTS IN MICROSOFT WORD

Word has a built-in method of using the PostScript style to iden-tify PostScript code and to hide it so that it doesn't print. Although it is not possible to paste an entire effect into Word using the PostScript Escape font, you can still use the effects by using Word's built-in PostScript style. This involves dividing the effect into two parts: one part that you place anywhere on the page, and a sec-ond, shorter part that you change to the PostScript Escape font and place in your document where you want to print the effect. All of the effects in this book come in two versions: one for MS Word, and another for all other word processing applications. In this section, you will learn how to insert the two parts of each Word effect into your Word documents.

BEHIND THE SCENES

Like all Macintosh programs, Microsoft Word has a limitation of 255 char-acters in one output text line. Unlike most other word processing applica-tions, however, Word carries this limit onto its screen display. As a result, Word will only accept 255 characters on one line of screen text. This is an absolute maximum and has no relation to the size of the characters or the font used. As soon as you have placed 255 characters on one line, Word moves down to the next line automatically. This limitation, of course, prevents Word users from pasting an effect into their document where they want it, since the length of the effect will automatically move the following text down one or more lines. None of the effects are less than 255 characters.

Although there are some obvious drawbacks to using this more complex procedure for inserting effects into a Word document, there are some less obvious advantages as well. Adding or changing variable information is easier in the Word effects, since you only change the shorter part of the effect, and you can see the entire effect text as you are working. All text effects must be divided into two sections to work correctly. Since Word effects are already divided, they require no additional special handling for text. In addition, these effects almost never present printing problems, which occur occasionally in other applications, probably because so much of the effect text is translated into a special style that Word recognizes and supports.

Inserting a Simple Effect—Checkbox

With these few preliminaries out of the way, let's place the checkbox effect into a Word document. An example of the checkbox effect, placed next to some text, is shown here in Figure 1-4.

☐ Checkbox test

This is a test in using the PostScript Escape font to create an effect in a document. The idea here is to place a checkbox to the left of the header paragraph. I'm not sure exactly what I have to do to make this work, but we'll see how it goes as we make the attempt.

Figure 1-4.   Printed output from the checkbox effect in Microsoft Word

The page of the document where you will place the effect looks like Figure 1-5.

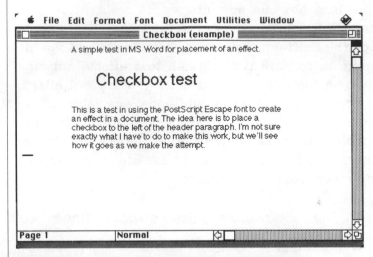

Figure 1-5. Word document for using the checkbox effect

As shown, the checkbox will be inside the body of the text, somewhat to the left of the large text. This is a good example of how a checkbox might be used in a typical document.

As shown here, the text line is set in 24-point Helvetica. The remainder of the text is in 12-point Bookman. You can use any font and any size that you want. The effect works the same way regardless of the font or size selected.

1. Open the file checkbox.w in the MS Word Effects folder on your disk. You should see a document window that looks like Figure 1-6.

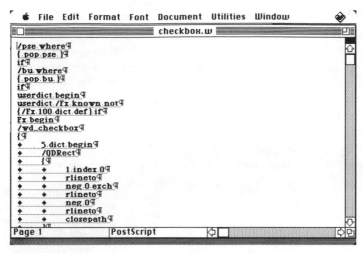

Figure 1-6. The checkbox.w effect for Microsoft Word

If you do not see this, you need to adjust your Preferences . . . settings in the Edit menu. Most of the text for checkbox.w, and for all the .w files for Word effects, is in the PostScript style. The PostScript style is a built-in style in Word that allows you to insert PostScript commands directly into a Word document. However, the automatic PostScript style is Hidden Text that is designed not to be printed all the time with your document and, perhaps, not displayed on the screen as well. If you have set your Preferences . . . in the Edit menu with the Show Hidden Text checkbox off, then the text of the effect disappears from the screen, and you will only see one line of text. The Preferences . . . selection is only shown in the Edit menu if you have Full Menus on, so you may have to turn on Full Menus and then select Preferences . . . before you can see the effect text shown in Figure 1-6.

BEHIND THE SCENES

Although the required part of the effect text in the .w files is already in the PostScript style, you may want at some point to change other text into that style, which usually requires adding the style to your document. To add the PostScript style to your document, simply pull down the Format menu and select Define Styles. When you get the Define Styles dialog box, type in the name PostScript—the capital S in the middle is a required part of the name. Word will warn you that you have selected a built-in (automatic) style and ask if you want to change it. Answer NO. This will automatically add the built-in PostScript style to your document, which you can then use just as you would any other style.

2. Select all of the effect text and copy it from the current document.

3. Open your document and prepare it for the effect. Place your cursor at the beginning of the top line and paste the effect into your document. Your document will now look like Figure 1-7.

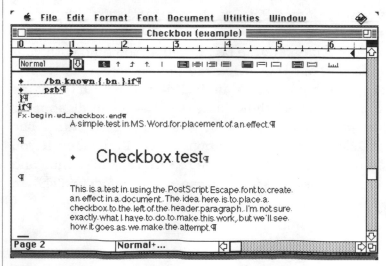

Figure 1-7. Word document with checkbox effect in PostScript style with Hidden Text displayed

Once again, this display depends on having checked the Show Hidden Text box in Preferences . . . . This text moves all of your other text on the page down, but this is only temporary. By changing the Show Hidden Text checkbox, you can return all the text to its previous position.

TIP

It's good practice to always place the text from the .w file in your document at or near the top of the page where you plan to use the effect. Even though Word will automatically reposition the .w file text at the top of the page when it prints, if you place it there yourself, you will always be sure that this part of the effect is on the page when you invoke it to print the effect.

4. Position the effect in your document. Type a positioning character at the point on the page where you want the effect to show. Set the font and size selections for this character to the same ones you used for the rest of the text on that line so the checkbox will match it. Here, 24-point Helvetica was used.

In this case, you want the effect to print to the left of the large line of text. Use spaces or tabs to place the insertion point for the positioning character where you want it, on the same line as the large text. Then type the positioning character—here, a Control-Q (a non-printing character) was used as shown in Figure 1-8.

Figure 1-8 shows the positioning character to the left of the line of text. The position of this character shows where on the page your effect will print. Since a non-printing character looks like a hollow rectangle on the screen, this happens to look a lot like the final printed output. However, that won't be true for most of the other effects in this book. The position of the character will always show you where your effect will print.

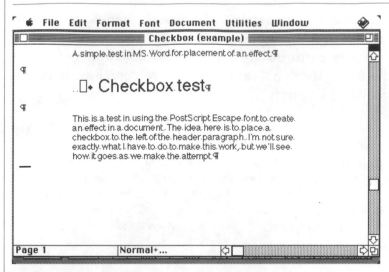

Figure 1-8. Word document prepared for the second part of the effect

TIP

> Notice that I have added two spaces in front of the positioning charac-
> ter. As you can see, the character on the screen is a tall rectangle, not a
> square. However, the checkbox is square. You need to leave some extra
> room on the left side of the positioning character to make the edge of
> the checkbox match up to the paragraph margin. Since you can't actu-
> ally see the effect on the screen, you will sometimes have to make ad-
> justments like this for an effect.

5. Select the last line of the effect text as shown in Figure 1-9,
and cut it out of the effect. This line represents the second part
of the effect and is *not* in the PostScript style, so it is very
noticeable.

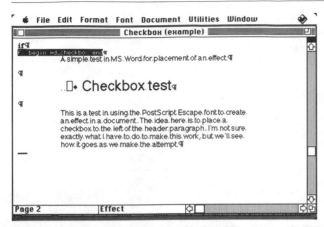

Figure 1-9. Second part of checkbox.w for Microsoft Word

Notice that you don't want to select the final paragraph marker in the text. If you do, the format information from this file will carry over into your document, and you will most likely have to reformat the line that will have the effect on it. This isn't a big problem, but it can be annoying. To avoid it, simply cut the text immediately after the last character of the file. This cuts the effect text without the associated format information. Now you can paste the text into your document without any format changes. then delete the empty line.

6. Place your cursor immediately to the right of the positioning character. Paste the second part of the effect text into position. The result should look something like Figure 1-10.

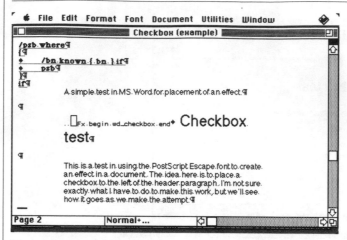

Figure 1-10. Second part of the effect pasted into a Microsoft Word document

This moves the remainder of the text on that line to the right, as you see. Of course, you don't want to print either of these parts of the effect. That's why the PostScript Style is Hidden Text, and why the PostScript Escape font is invisible and dimensionless: so that the real text will return to its correct position when you print.

7. Select all of the second part of the effect text—and only that text. Do *not* select the positioning character and do *not* select the tab or space character(s) that separate the effect text from the printing text that follows. When you have selected the text, your screen will look like Figure 1-11.

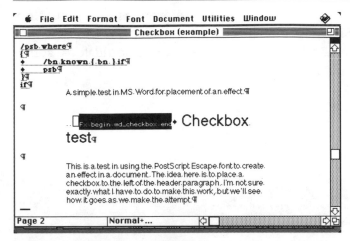

Figure 1-11. Second part of effect text selected and ready for conversion

8. Select the PostScript Escape font. The text for the effect, which you selected in Step 7, will all disappear. The result should look something like Figure 1-12.

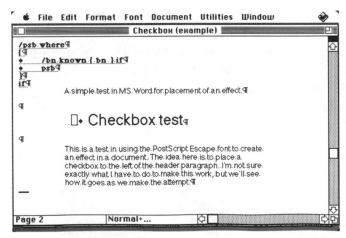

Figure 1-12. Microsoft Word document with second part of effect changed to PostScript Escape font

9. Pull down the Edit menu and select Preferences . . . again. Now uncheck the Show Hidden Text box. The text for the first part of the effect will all disappear. The result should look something like Figure 1-13.

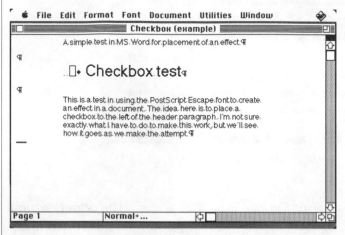

Figure 1-13. Microsoft Word document with Hidden Text not displayed

As you immediately notice, this now looks just like your document did before you pasted in either part of the effect. Of course, that's what you want, since you want the real text to print just where you had it originally. However, now you can't tell if the effect is in your document or not; there is no visible sign of either part of the effect. The only way to see the first part of the effect is to change the Preferences . . . back to show Hidden Text.

TIP

When working with the effects, I have found it very convenient to use Word's Menu function to add Show Hidden Text to the Edit menu. In this way, you can easily switch back and forth between displaying the PostScript text and hiding it.

While the effect will work whether the Hidden Text is displayed on your screen or not, it will not work unless the second part of the effect text is in the PostScript Escape font. If you want to display the second part of the effect text, for editing or any other reason, you must select the line where the text is located, including the positioning character and all, and convert the text to a visible font. Once this part of the effect text is visible, you can easily convert it back into Monaco, or some other distinctive font that will remind you that it is an effect and not part of your ordinary document text. Then change the font back to the PostScript Escape font when you want to print.

TIP

As mentioned earlier, since that part of the effect is invisible in your document, you may have some trouble selecting all of it when you go to convert it into a visible font. If you do have some trouble, the best method to ensure that you have all the text is to select the entire line, plus one character before and one character after the line. This will ensure that all the effect text is included in your selection. Then, after the text is made visible, you can set the fonts as you want them.

10. Choose Print . . . from the File menu. Be sure that the checkbox Print Hidden Text is *not* checked, or the effect won't work. Print the document in the ordinary way. Figure 1-14 shows you the result of printing this document.

Congratulations! You've just printed out your first effect. I know that this may seem a bit complex at first, but once you do it a few times, this entire sequence of steps really becomes second nature. And, once you master it, you will have a complete library of effects at your fingertips—or at least at the drop of a cursor.

☐ Checkbox test

This is a test in using the PostScript Escape font to create an effect in a document. The idea here is to place a checkbox to the left of the header paragraph. I'm not sure exactly what I have to do to make this work, but we'll see how it goes as we make the attempt.

Figure 1-14. Printed output from the checkbox effect in Microsoft Word

Inserting an Effect with a Beginning and End—Textbox

Now that you have completed one effect, let's do another one that requires a few more steps. This effect draws a box around a portion of text in your document. Yes, I know that you can easily do this with the Borders feature of Word. However, many effects in this book, including more advanced boxes presented in later chapters, all require this beginning and ending technique, and a textbox is the clearest and simplest example.

This type of effect requires that you set a point where the effect begins and one where it ends. In this case, the beginning point is in front of the block of text that you want to place in the box, while the ending point is, naturally enough, after the text. All effects that require beginning and ending points, like this one, use the technique demonstrated here. Basically, you insert a special effect text—called begin effect—where you want the effect to start and insert the effect text itself at the ending point.

There are two points that you should note about placing effects that have beginning and ending points. First, as you might expect, in Microsoft Word the effect itself—in this case, the textbox—and the begin effect text are separate effect files. These are both inserted into your document using the following techniques. The second point is to be sure that you place both effects on your document page before you cut and insert the second part of either effect.

The file begin effect.w should be inserted first in your document, followed by the effect that you want to use: in this case, textbox.w. Both of these must be on the same page where you want to print the effect. Once these are inserted on the page, you simply paste the second part of begin effect.w into your document where you want the effect to begin. Then place the second part of the effect text, textbox.w, at the end of the text that you want inside the box.

For this example, let's place the textbox effect into a Word document. Figure 1-15 is an example of the textbox, placed next to some text as shown here.

$$\boxed{\textbf{NOTICE}}$$

This is a test in using the PostScript Escape font insertion into a document. The idea here is to draw a rectangle around the text block at the top of this paragraph. This illustrates marking text within a document with a special rectangle.

Figure 1-15. Printed output from the textbox effect in Microsoft Word.

The page of the document for the effect looks like Figure 1-16.

The intention here is to place the textbox around the line of text in large type, which says NOTICE. This is a good example of how a textbox might be used in a typical document.

As shown here, the text line to be enclosed in the box is set in 24-point Helvetica. The remainder of the text is in 12-point

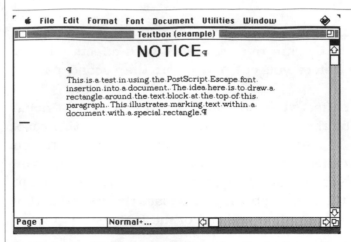

Figure 1-16. Word document for using the textbox effect

Bookman. However, you can use any font and any size that you want. The effect works in the same way regardless of the font or size used.

1. Open the file begin effect.w in the MS Word Effects folder on your disk. You should see a document window that looks like Figure 1-17.

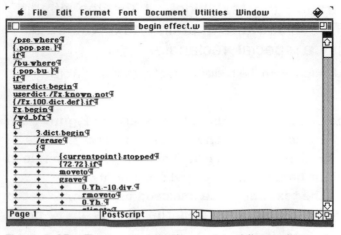

Figure 1-17. The begin effect.w text for Microsoft Word

If you do not see this, you need to adjust your Preferences . . . settings in the Edit menu to Show Hidden Text. See the discussion under the checkbox effect if you have any questions about how to adjust this setting.

2. Select all of the effect text and copy it from the current document.

3. Open your document and prepare it for the effect. Place your cursor at the beginning of the top line and paste the effect into your document. Your document will now look like Figure 1-18.

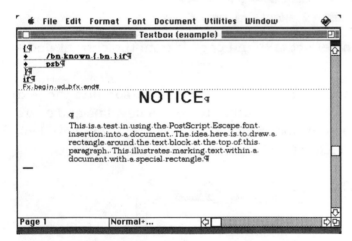

Figure 1-18. Word document with begin effect in PostScript style with Hidden Text displayed

4. Open the file textbox.w in the MS Word Effects folder on your disk. You should see a document window that looks like Figure 1-19.

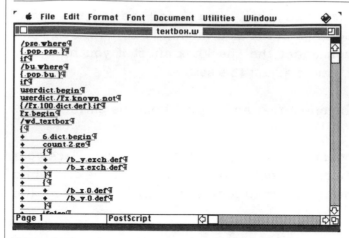

Figure 1-19. The textbox.w effect for Microsoft Word

5. Select all of the effect text and copy it from the current document.

6. Go back to your document and place your cursor after the text from begin effect.w. Press Return to go to a new line and paste the effect into your document. Your document will now look something like Figure 1-20.

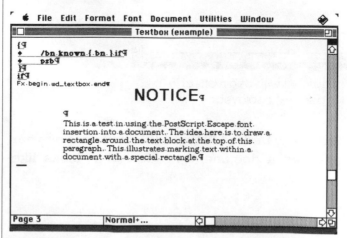

Figure 1-20. Word document with both begin effect and textbox effect in PostScript style with Hidden Text displayed

This combined text moves all of your other text on the page down, possibly onto another page, but this is only temporary. By changing the Show Hidden Text option, you can return all the text to its previous position.

7. Position the effect in your document. Type a positioning character at the point on the page where you want the box to begin. Set the font and size selections for this character to the same ones you used for the rest of the text on that line so the textbox will match it. Here, 24-point Helvetica was used.

In this case, you want the effect to begin to the left of the large line of text that says NOTICE. Type the positioning character—here, a Control-Q (a non-printing character) was used—as shown in Figure 1-21, just to the left of the text to be boxed.

Figure 1-21 shows the positioning character to the left of the line of text. The position of this character shows where on the page your effect will begin.

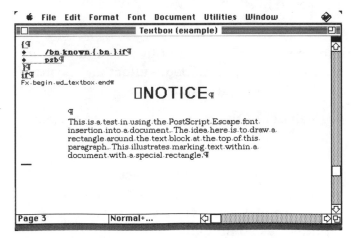

Figure 1-21. Word document prepared for the second part of the effect

8. Select the last line of the begin effect.w text as shown in Figure 1-22, and cut it out of the effect. This line represents the second part of begin effect, and is not in the PostScript style, so it is very noticeable.

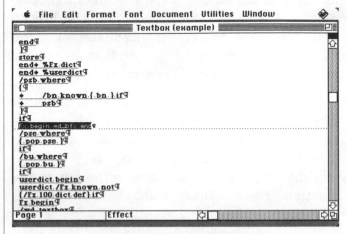

Figure 1-22. Second part of begin effect.w for Microsoft Word

9. Place your cursor immediately to the right of the positioning character. Paste the second part of begin effect into position. The result should look like Figure 1-23

This moves the remainder of the text on that line to the right, as you see.

10. Select all of the second part of the begin effect text—and only that text. Do *not* select the positioning character and do *not* select the tab or space character(s) that separate the effect text from the printing text that follows.

11. Select the PostScript Escape font. The text for the effect, which you selected in Step 10, will all disappear.

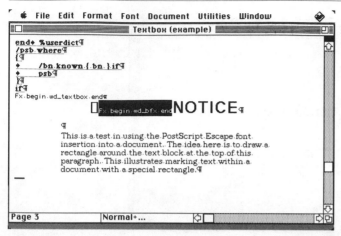

Figure 1-23. Second part of the effect pasted into a Microsoft Word document

This sets the place for the effect to begin in your document. Now you have to set the effect itself at the end of the text that you want to place inside the box.

12. Select the last line of the textbox.w effect text as shown in Figure 1-24, and cut it out of the effect. This line represents the second part of the effect itself, and is not in the PostScript style, so it is very noticeable.

13. Place your cursor immediately to the right of the text that you want to insert into the box. Paste the second part of the textbox effect into that position. The result should look like Figure 1-25.

14. Select all of the second part of the effect text—and only that text. Do *not* select the printing text that precedes the effect and do *not* select the new line, tab, or space character(s) that separate the effect text from the printing text that follows.

15. Select the PostScript Escape font. The text for the effect, which you selected in Step 14, will all disappear.

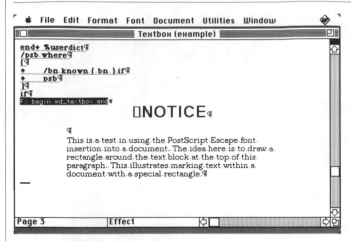

Figure 1-24. Second part of the textbox.w effect for Microsoft Word

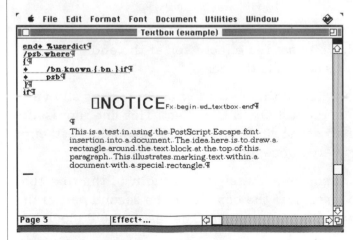

Figure 1-25. Second part of the effect pasted into an Microsoft Word document

16. Pull down the Edit menu and select Preferences . . . again. Now uncheck the Show Hidden Text box. The text for the first part of the effect will all disappear. The result should look something like Figure 1-26.

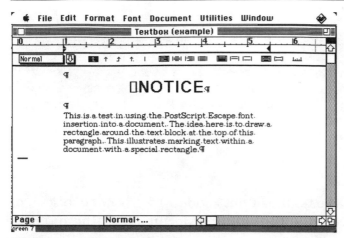

Figure 1-26. Microsoft Word document with first part of effect changed to PostScript Style with Hidden Text not displayed

As you immediately notice, this now looks like your document did before you pasted in any parts of the effect. Of course, that's what you want, since you want the real text to print where you had it originally. However, now you can't tell if the effect is in your document or not; there is no visible sign of any part of the effect. The only way to see the first parts of the effect is to change the Preferences . . . back to Show Hidden Text.

While the effect will work whether the Hidden Text is displayed on your screen or not, it will not work unless the second part of the effect text is in the PostScript Escape font. If you want to display the second part of the effect text, for editing or any other reason, you must select the line where the text is located, including the positioning character, and convert the text to a visible font. Once this part of the effect text is visible, you can easily convert it back into Monaco, or some other distinctive font that will remind you that it is an effect and not part of your ordinary document text. Then change the font back to the PostScript Escape font when you want to print.

TIP

As mentioned earlier, since that part of the effect is invisible in your document, you may have some trouble selecting all of it when you go to convert it into a visible font. If you do have some trouble, the best method to ensure that you have all the text is to select the entire line, plus one character before and one character after the line. This will ensure that all the effect text is included in your selection. Then, after the text is made visible, you can set the fonts as you want them.

17. Be sure that the textbox Print Hidden Text is *not* checked, or the effect won't work. Print the document in the ordinary way. Figure 1-27 shows you the result of printing the document shown here.

NOTICE

This is a test in using the PostScript Escape font insertion into a document. The idea here is to draw a rectangle around the text block at the top of this paragraph. This illustrates marking text within a document with a special rectangle.

Figure 1-27. Printed output from the textbox effect in Microsoft Word

Congratulations! You've just printed out your second effect. This process with its two sets of effect segments is quite complex, but, as you will discover in later chapters, it does allow you to make some very nice text effects, using any font that you have installed into your printer.

Inserting an Effect with Specific Values— Proportioned Checkbox

Any effect that requires you to enter specific values is more difficult than one that does not. As you read in the Introduction, an effect that requires you to enter one or more variables is considered a one-knot effect.

Here is an example of the same checkbox effect presented in the first example, but this time it allows you to enter a variable that defines the width of the box in relation to its height. The resulting output is shown in Figure 1-28.

☐ Checkbox test

This is a test in using the PostScript Escape font to create an effect in a document. The idea here is to place a checkbox to the left of the header paragraph. I'm not sure exactly what I have to do to make this work, but we'll see how it goes as we make the attempt.

Figure 1-28. Printed output from the proportioned checkbox effect

This example uses the same basic document that you used for the checkbox effect, shown in Figure 1-4; you can reuse that one or construct another. The effect for this example is on your disk as proportioned checkbox.w

1. Open the file proportioned checkbox.w in the MS Word Effects folder on your disk. You should see a document window that looks like Figure 1-29.

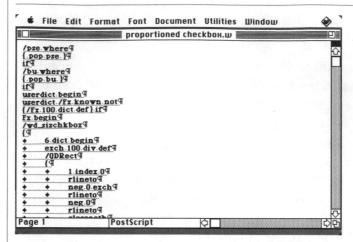

Figure 1-29. The proportioned checkbox.w effect for
Microsoft Word

If you do not see this, you need to adjust your
Preferences . . . settings in the Edit menu to Show Hidden Text.
See the discussion under the checkbox effect if you have any
questions about how to adjust this setting.

2. Select all of the effect text and copy it from the current document.

3. Use the same basic document that you used for the checkbox
effect. Open this document and prepare it for the effect. Place
your cursor at the beginning of the top line and paste the effect
into your document.

This text moves all of your other text on the page down, but
this is only temporary. By changing the Show Hidden Text
checkbox, you can return all the text to its previous position.

4. Position the effect in your document. Type a positioning character at the point on the page where you want the effect to
show. Set the font and size selections for this character to the
same ones you used for the rest of the text on that line so the
checkbox will match it. Here, 24-point Helvetica was used.
Your document will now look something like Figure 1-30.

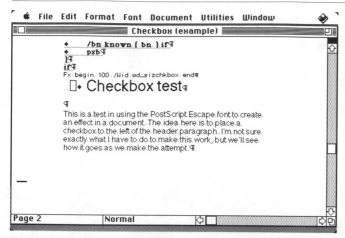

Figure 1-30. Word document with proportioned checkbox effect in PostScript style (Hidden Text displayed) and positioning character in place

In this case, you want the effect to print to the left of the large line of text. Use spaces or tabs to place the insertion point for the positioning character where you want it, on the same line as the large text. Here, a Control-Q (a non-printing character) was used for the positioning character.

5. Move your cursor to the beginning of the last line of the effect text. This line is *not* in the PostScript style, so it is very noticeable. This line represents the second part of the effect. Select all of the text that makes up the second part of the effect from this line, as shown in Figure 1-31, and cut it out of the effect.

6. Place your cursor immediately to the right of the positioning character. Paste the second part of the effect text into position.

This moves the remainder of the text on that line to the right, as you see. Of course, you don't want to print either of these parts of the effect.

7. Change the variable information from 100 to 75.

39

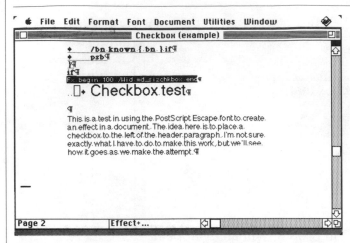

Figure 1-31. Second part of proportioned checkbox.w for Microsoft Word

When you have to insert variable information into Word, the variables will be at the front of the second part of the effect, as shown here:

```
Fx begin 100 /Wid wd_sizchkbox end
```

The number shown in bold at the beginning of the effect is the number that you have to supply. This part of the file is not bold or otherwise specially marked in the file on your disk. It is in bold here so that you can see and identify it very easily. This variable defines the width of the checkbox as a percentage of the height. You set the height of the checkbox by setting the font size for the positioning character, and you set the width by filling in a percentage value at the front of the effect text. The default percentage is 100, which makes the checkbox the same width as its height. A value of 75, for example, would make the checkbox narrower than its height, and a value of 150 would make the checkbox wider. To help you remember the use of this value, the name that comes immediately after the value (/Wid) is deliberately designed to remind you of what the value represents: the width of the resulting checkbox. When you change the default value of 100 to 75 and insert this effect into the document that you used for the first example, you get a result similar to that shown in Figure 1-28.

8. Select all of the second part of the effect text—and only that text. Do *not* select the positioning character and do *not* select the tab or space character(s) that separate the effect text from the printing text that follows.

9. Select the PostScript Escape font. The text for the effect, which you selected in Step 8, will all disappear.

10. Pull down the Edit menu and select Preferences . . . again. Now uncheck the Show Hidden Text box. The text for the first part of the effect will all disappear.

As you immediately notice, this now looks like your document did before you pasted in either part of the effect. Of course, that's what you want, since you want the real text to print where you had it originally. However, now you can't tell if the effect is in your document or not, since there is no visible sign of either part of the effect. The only way to see the first part of the effect is to change the Preferences . . . back to Show Hidden Text.

While the effect will work whether the Hidden Text is displayed on your screen or not, it will not work unless the second part of the effect text is in the PostScript Escape font. If you want to display the second part of the effect text, for editing or any other reason, you must select the line where the text is located, including the positioning character, and convert the text to a visible font. Once this part of the effect text is visible, you can easily convert it back into Monaco, or some other distinctive font that will remind you that it is an effect and not part of your ordinary document text. Then change the font back to the PostScript Escape font when you want to print.

TIP

As mentioned earlier, since that part of the effect is invisible in your document, you may have some trouble selecting all of it when you go to convert it into a visible font. If you do have some trouble, the best method to ensure that you have all the text is to select the entire line, plus one character before and one character after the line. This will ensure that all the effect text is included in your selection. Then, after the text is made visible, you can set the fonts as you want them.

11. Select Print. Be sure that the checkbox Print Hidden Text is *not* checked, or the effect won't work. Print the document in the ordinary way. Figure 1-28 shows you the result of printing this document.

You see that you can make the checkbox larger or smaller than the surrounding type, and you can make it a rectangle instead of a square, by changing the percentage value appropriately.

This is a good example of the type of effect where you have to supply information. The exact type of information required, of course, varies from effect to effect. In some effects you supply a text string for a display. In others, you supply a distance or some other numeric variable. In some effects you may be asked to supply two, three, or more variables. Every effect where you have to supply information provides a short explanation—as you had here—of the type of information required, where it goes in the file, and, if it is a number, what units the number represents. If the effect requires more than one variable, they all appear at the front of the effect, separated by their names which always begin with a slash (/) like the name /Wid in the preceding example. The name of each variable follows the value which is associated with it, as /Wid follows the actual number that is used for the percentage. Notice that the information appears placed in the front of the second part of the effect. This makes it easy for you to modify the effect, even if the text of the effect is quite long and complex.

Inserting an Effect with Variable Text—Rotated Text

Some text effects, like the preceding textbox example, use the text that you type onto your document screen. However, some effects, like rotated text, require that you enter the text to be printed into your effect as a variable. This section shows you how to use this sort of effect. Actually, for Word users, this type of effect is the same as any other effect with variables.

Here is an example of the rotated text effect in a simple document. The resulting output is shown in Figure 1-32.

Next comes the text to place under the rotated headline. Given the headline, I suppose it would be some advertising thing or another. This paragraph might go on for quite a while. You just have to know how much room to allow all around for the rotated text.

Figure 1-32. Printed output from the rotated text effect

This example uses a basic document that you can create quite easily. The rotated text effect is on your disk as rotated text.w.

1. Open the file rotated text.w in the MS Word Effects folder on your disk. You should see a document window that looks like Figure 1-33.

If you do not see this, you need to adjust your Preferences . . . settings in the Edit menu to Show Hidden Text. See the discussion under the checkbox effect if you have any questions about how to adjust this setting.

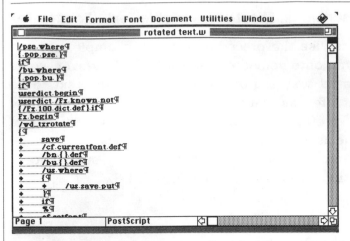

Figure 1-33. The rotated text.w effect for Microsoft Word

2. Select all of the effect text and copy it from the current document.

3. Open your document and prepare it for the effect. Place your cursor at the beginning of the top line of the document and paste the effect text into your document.

Remember that seeing your effect text depends on having checked the Show Hidden Text box in Preferences. . . .

This text moves all of your other text on the page down, but this is only temporary. By changing the Show Hidden Text checkbox, you can return all the text to its previous position.

4. Position the effect in your document. Type a positioning character at the point on the page where you want the effect to show. Set the font and size selections for this character to the ones you want to use for the displayed text. Here, 36-point Palatino was used.

In this case, the rotated text is positioned above the start of the second paragraph, slightly indented to allow for the size and rotation of the text. Place the insertion point for the positioning character where you want it, two lines above the second paragraph. Then type the positioning character—here, a Control-Q (a non-printing character) was used. At this point, your screen should look something like Figure 1-34, depending on where you decide to place the positioning character.

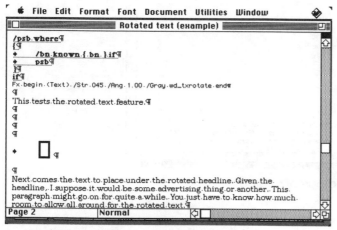

Figure 1-34. The document for the rotated text effect with the positioning character in place

Note that I have left a lot of space between the first and second paragraphs, in this case, 4 lines above the positioning character and 1 line after. This is to allow room for the text to print. The text is large and is rotated at a 45-degree angle to the horizontal line of the normal text. Therefore, the rotated text will take up a lot of room on the page. Since you may have to adjust your spacing, this effect has two knots to warn you that some adjustments may be necessary before you get it to print exactly the way you want.

5. Select the last line of the effect text. This line is *not* in the PostScript style, so it is very noticeable. This line represents the second part of the effect. Select all of the text that makes up the second part of the effect from this line, as shown in Figure 1-35, and cut it out of the effect.

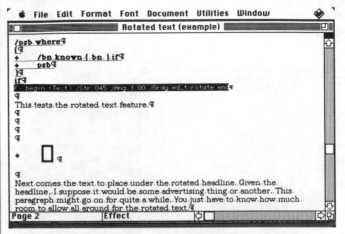

Figure 1-35. Second part of rotated text.w for Microsoft Word

6. Place your cursor immediately to the right of the positioning character. Paste the second part of the effect text into position.

This moves the remainder of the text on that line to the right, as you see. Of course, you don't want to print either of these parts of the effect.

7. Change the variable /Str at the beginning of the file from Text to Sale. Be sure that both the beginning and ending parentheses remain in the file. They are essential.

This file is longer than the second part of the other files that you have seen so far, but it is still quite short. Sometimes this part of the effect has to be longer to accommodate additional variables

or processing issues. When you have to insert variable information into Word, the variables will be at the front of the second part
of the effect, as shown here:

```
Fx begin (Text) /Str 45 /Ang 1.00 /Gray . . .
```

These variables are not bold or otherwise specially marked on
the file on your disk. They are in bold here so that you can see and
identify them easily.

The variables /Str, /Ang, and /Gray each define important information for the rotated text effect. The /Str variable is the string of
text that you want printed on your document. The /Ang variable
is the rotation angle that is used when the string is printed. The
angle is measured counterclockwise from a horizontal line, so text
at 45 degrees slopes up and to the right. The /Gray variable allows you to make the characters in the rotated text any shade of
gray. The uses of all of these variables are described under the
rotated text effect in Chapter 6. For now, you can use the default
values of these effects, except for the /Str variable, where you
define the text to be printed.

To help you remember the use of these variables, the names
that follow the value (/Str, /Ang, and /Gray) are deliberately designed to remind you of what the value represents. When you
change the default value of /Str from Text to Sale and insert this
effect into your document, you get a printed result similar to that
shown in Figure 1-32.

8. Select all of the second part of the effect text—and only that
    text. Do *not* select the positioning character and do *not* select
    the return, tab, or space character(s) that separate the effect
    text from the printing text that follows.

9. Select the PostScript Escape font. The text for the effect, which
    you selected in Step 8, will all disappear.

10. Pull down the Edit menu and select Preferences . . . again. Now uncheck the Show Hidden Text box. The text for the first part of the effect will all disappear.

As you immediately notice, this now looks like your document did before you pasted in either part of the effect. Of course, that's what you want, since you want the real text to print where you had it originally. However, now you can't tell if the effect is in your document or not; there is no visible sign of either part of the effect. The only way to see the first part of the effect is to change the Preferences . . . back to Show Hidden Text.

While the effect will work whether the Hidden Text is displayed on your screen or not, it will not work unless the second part of the effect text is in the PostScript Escape font. If you want to display the second part of the effect text, for editing or any other reason, you must select the line where the text is located, including the positioning character, and convert the text to a visible font. Once this part of the effect text is visible, you can easily convert it back into Monaco, or some other distinctive font that will remind you that it is an effect and not part of your ordinary document text. Then change the font back to the PostScript Escape font when you want to print.

TIP

As mentioned earlier, since that part of the effect is invisible in your document, you may have some trouble selecting all of it when you go to convert it into a visible font. If you do have some trouble, the best method to ensure that you have all the text is to select the entire line, plus one character before and one character after the line. This will ensure that all the effect text is included in your selection. Then, after the text is made visible, you can set the fonts as you want them.

11. Select Print. Be sure that the checkbox Print Hidden Text is *not* checked, or the effect won't work. Print the document in the ordinary way. Figure 1-32 shows you the result of printing this document.

Inserting Multiple Effects on a Page

Once you have gotten used to placing one effect on a page, two major questions naturally arise. One question is whether you can use more than one effect on a page, and the other is whether you can use the same effect more than once on a page. As I hope you anticipated, the answer to both questions is yes.

To use more than one effect on a page, simply paste the first part of each file at the beginning of the page, one right after another, in the same way as you did with the begin effect.w and textbox.w files when you did the textbox example. If several effects use the begin effect.w file, you should only paste that in one time. You don't need to put it in more than once. Then place the positioning characters for your effects where you want the individual effects to print and paste the second part (the last line) of the effect after the positioning character, as you have done in the examples. If you want to place one effect right after another one, be sure that each one has its own positioning character, or the second effect will erase the first one.

To use the same effect several times on one page, simply insert a positioning character at each point on the page where you want the effect to print. Then paste the second part (the last line) of the effect after the positioning character. You only need to insert the first part of the file for any effect one time on any one page of your document. If you are using the same effect on more than one page, insert the first part of the file at the top of each page where the effect is printed.

BEHIND THE SCENES

Actually, it is not always necessary for the effect to be on the page that you are printing. The first portion of the effect remains in the memory of your printer from the first time it is loaded until your job finishes printing. This means that you can use the second part to print the effect again on any subsequent page. There is, however, a catch to this. (Isn't that always the way?) The catch is that you must print the page containing the first part of the file before you print any page, or pages, containing the remainder. Thus, for example, you can't print a range of pages that doesn't include the page with the first part if any pages in the range contain the rest of the effect. If you try to print a page that contains just the second part on it, and the first part has not been loaded, the entire document (NOT just that page—the entire document!) will not print. If you always have both parts of the file on the same page this can't happen. That's why I recommend that the complete file be installed on each page. If you feel comfortable with the restriction on printing, feel free to use the effects on multiple pages without reinstalling the first part of the effect.

USING EFFECTS IN OTHER WORD PROCESSORS

If you are working in any word processor *except* Microsoft Word, follow the instructions in this section to install the checkbox and other types of effects into a document. To illustrate how you use these effects, this section details each step of copying and using effects in your document. The examples here are inserted into a document produced in WriteNow 2.2. As discussed in the section on working with specific word processors, these same techniques are equally applicable to documents created in other word processing programs, except for Microsoft Word which requires the techniques described in the previous section. If you are using any other application, simply make the small corrections to your document noted earlier in the discussion of your specific application.

Inserting a Simple Effect—Checkbox

This effect places a square box, like a checkbox, next to a line of text in your document. An example of the checkbox effect, placed next to some text, is shown in Figure 1-36.

☐ ## Checkbox test

This is a test in using the PostScript Escape font insertion into a document. The idea here is to place a checkbox to the left of the start of the header paragraph. I'm not sure exactly what I have to do to make this work, but we'll see how it goes as we make the attempt.

Figure 1-36. Printed output from the checkbox effect

Let's suppose that you want to place the effect on a page of your document that looks like Figure 1-37.

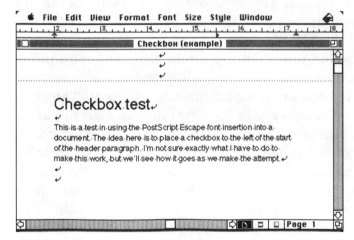

Figure 1-37. Basic document for using the checkbox effect

Of course, your document will look different, depending on what your application is and what you have typed into your document. Note that the document has a line at the top of the paragraph in large type. You will place the checkbox to the left of this line of text. As shown, the headline is the first line of the document and is set in 24-point Helvetica Bold. The remainder of the text is set in 12-point Helvetica regular. You can use any font and size that you want. The effect works the same way regardless of the font or size selected.

1. Prepare your document for the effect by setting the position and size for the effect. Type a positioning character at the point on the page where you want the effect to show. Set the font and size selections for this character to the same ones you used for the rest of the text on that line so the checkbox will match it.

In this case you want the effect to appear to the left of the top line of text in the margin of the page, and you want it sized to the font selection of the headline. Set a hanging indent for the first line of text to position the effect in the margin, then type a printing or non-printing character—here, a Control-Q was used. Be sure that you leave enough room for the effect to print. The positioning character will help you judge how much room is required, since it is in the font and size that you are using for your effect. This effect takes up approximately the same amount of room as the positioning character. (Other effects take more or less room, depending on the effect. Each effect describes any special spacing requirements for using that effect.) If you are familiar with WriteNow, you can see the hanging indent set up in the ruler section at the top of the screen in Figure 1-38. Set the font and size selections for this character to the same ones you used in the headline—here, 24-point Helvetica Bold. Figure 1-38 shows you how this looks.

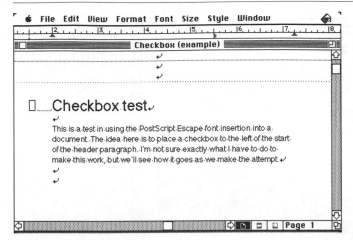

Figure 1-38. Document prepared for the effect

TIP

Figure 1-38 shows you the non-printing character positioned to the left of the first line of text. The position of this character shows you where your effect will print. Since a non-printing character looks like a hollow rectangle on the screen, this happens to look a lot like the final printed output. That won't be true for most of the other effects in this book. The position of the character, however, will always show you where your effect will print.

2. Open the effect file, checkbox, with your application. Note that this is a simple text (ASCII) file. In WriteNow you must set the Type of document to open to Text. When you have opened the file, you will have a document screen that looks something like Figure 1-39.

3. Select all of the effect text and copy it from the effect document.

4. Return to your document and place your cursor immediately to the right of the positioning character. Paste the effect into your document. The result should look something like Figure 1-40.

53

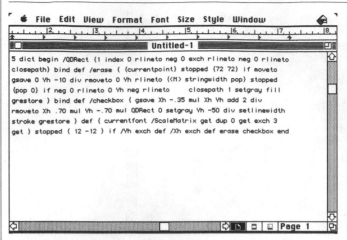

Figure 1-39. Typed version of the checkbox effect from the disk

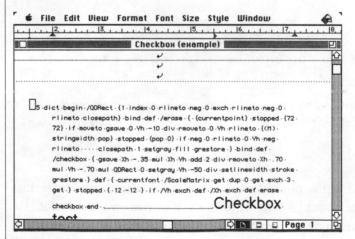

Figure 1-40. Effect text pasted into document

As you can see, this moves all of your other text, including the headline, down the page. Of course, you don't really want to print like this. That's why the PostScript Escape font is invisible and dimensionless: so the real text will go back to its original location.

5. Select all of the effect text—and only the effect text. Do not select the positioning character and do not select the tab that comes before the headline. When you have selected the text, your screen should look something like Figure 1-41.

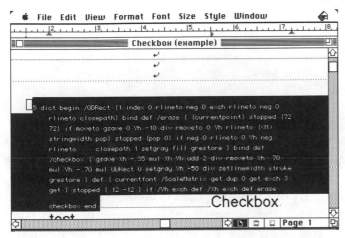

Figure 1-41. Effect text selected and ready for conversion

6. Pull down the Font menu and select the PostScript Escape font. The text for the effect, which you selected in Step 5, will all disappear. The result should look something like Figure 1-42.

As you immediately notice, this looks just like your document did before you pasted in the effect. Of course, that's what you want, since you want the real text to print where you had it originally. If you want to display the effect text, for editing or any other reason, you must select the line where the text is located, including the positioning character, and convert the text to a vis-

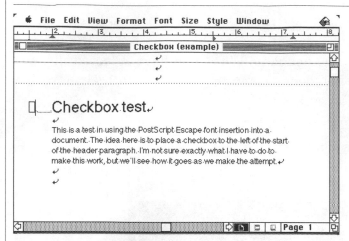

Figure 1-42. Document with effect changed to
PostScript Escape font

ible font. Once this part of the effect text is visible, you can easily
convert it back into Monaco, or some other distinctive font that
will remind you that it is an effect and not part of your ordinary
document text. Then change the font back to the PostScript Escape font when you want to print.

TIP

As mentioned earlier, since the effect is invisible in your document, you
may have some trouble selecting all of it when you go to convert it into a
visible font. If you do have some trouble, the best method to ensure that
you have all the text is to select the entire line, plus one character before
and one character after the line. This will ensure that all the effect text is
included in your selection. Then, after the text is made visible, you can set
the fonts as you want them.

7. Print the document in the ordinary way. Figure 1-43 shows you
the result of printing this document.

☐ Checkbox test

This is a test in using the PostScript Escape font insertion into a document. The idea here is to place a checkbox to the left of the start of the header paragraph. I'm not sure exactly what I have to do to make this work, but we'll see how it goes as we make the attempt.

Figure 1-43. Printed output from the checkbox effect

Congratulations! You've printed your first effect. You have now learned the basic steps for using all the effects in this book. Although this is a simple checkbox, later in the book, you will have examples of this checkbox effect with additional features, such as size controls, a drop shadow behind the effect, and more. For now, this example shows you a simple but useful effect that you can easily insert into your document.

Inserting an Effect with a Beginning and End—Textbox

The checkbox effect is a good example of a simple effect that you place in one position on the page. However, some effects take up more room than one character. A good example of such an effect is the effect that draws a box around some text on your page, as shown in Figure 1-44.

NOTICE

This is a test in using the PostScript Escape font insertion into a document. The idea here is to draw a rectangle around the text block at the top of this paragraph. This illustrates marking text within a document with a special rectangle.

Figure 1-44. Printed output from the textbox effect

When you place an effect like this one, you must specify both beginning and ending points for the effect. Inserting effects that have beginning and ending points into your document is just as easy as inserting effects, such as the checkbox, that only have one position. The following steps show you how to insert the textbox effect in a document. An example of the textbox effect, placed next to some text, is shown in Figure 1-44.

Let's suppose that you want to insert this textbox effect into a document like the one shown in Figure 1-45.

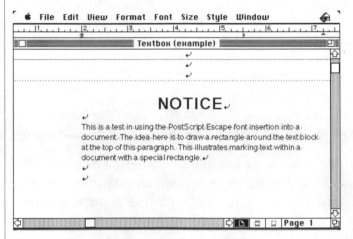

Figure 1-45. Document for the textbox effect

You want to outline the word NOTICE at the top of the page with a box, using the textbox effect.

1. Open your document and insert the positioning character where you want to begin the effect, in this example, right before the word NOTICE. The font and size used for the positioning character should be the same as for the line of text that you want to place inside the box.

Be sure that the positioning character is in the correct font and size for your effect. Although the positioning character will be erased when the effect prints, the textbox effect begins immediately after the positioning character rather than before it. This allows the textbox to wrap around the line of text more closely. Any effect where this positioning is used is clearly noted in the effect recipes.

2. Open the file, begin effect, with your application. When you have opened the file, you will have a document screen that looks something like Figure 1-46.

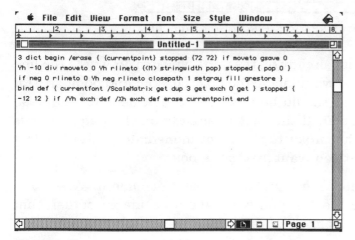

Figure 1-46. begin effect text

3. Select all of the effect text and copy it from the effect document.

4. Return to your document and place your cursor immediately to the right of the positioning character. Paste the effect into your document. The result should look something like Figure 1-47.

The effect file begin effect sets the starting position for your textbox effect. All effects that require a starting position use this same file.

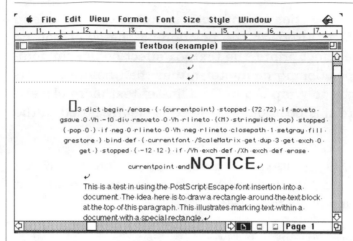

Figure 1-47. begin effect text pasted into document

5. If the text is not already on the page, you can now type the line of text that you want inside the box. The font and point size for this line of text should be identical to that used for the positioning character. If the text is already on the page, as it is here, move the cursor to the point immediately after the last character that you want inside the box.

6. Open the effect file textbox in a new document. When you have opened the file, you will have a document screen that looks something like Figure 1-48.

7. Copy the effect text, and insert it into your document where you want the effect to end, using the same techniques as in steps 2–4. In this example, you will insert the text after the last character in the word NOTICE.

To end an effect, you don't need a positioning character. The effect ends where you set the effect text and begins where you set the begin effect text. Remember that the textbox extends past the actual text enclosed in the box. Therefore, you shouldn't put more text immediately after the text that is to appear in the box. If you do, the first character after the boxed text is likely to

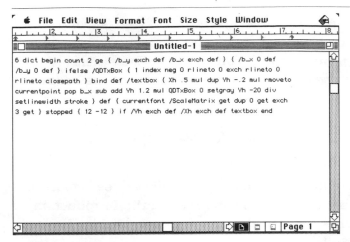

Figure 1-48. Textbox effect text

be wholly or partially erased by the box. If you want to show text after your boxed text, leave some space for the box before you start the new text. Also notice that the box extends slightly above and below the text. This may require that you insert extra spacing to avoid touching the text on the lines above and below your boxed text.

8. Select all of the begin effect text and change it to the PostScript Escape font, which makes this part of the effect disappear. Do not select the text that you want to be visible in the box, which remains in your ordinary font.

9. Select the effect text that comes after the text that you want inside the box and change that to the PostScript escape font. Now only the positioning character and the text that will be inside the box should show in your document.

10. Print the document in the ordinary way. Figure 1-44 above shows you the result of printing the document shown here.

Congratulations! You have just printed your second effect. That's all that you have to do to insert an effect with a beginning and ending point into your document. All effects that require a beginning point use the same special effect to set the beginning: begin effect.

Inserting an Effect with Specific Values—Proportioned Checkbox

Any effect that requires you to enter specific values is more difficult than one that does not. As you read in the Introduction, an effect that requires you to enter one or more variables is considered a one-knot effect.

This is another example of the checkbox effect presented in the first example, but this time you can enter a variable that defines the width of the box in relation to its height. An example of the resulting output is shown in Figure 1-49.

☐ Checkbox test

This is a test in using the PostScript Escape font insertion into a document. The idea here is to place a checkbox to the left of the start of the header paragraph. I'm not sure exactly what I have to do to make this work, but we'll see how it goes as we make the attempt.

Figure 1-49. Printed output from the proportioned checkbox effect

This example uses the same document for the effect as the first example. The document is shown in Figure 1-36. The only difference is that this time you will insert a proportioned checkbox instead of the standard one.

1. Open your document and prepare it for the effect by setting the position and size for the effect. Type a positioning character at the point on the page where you want the effect to show. Set the font and size selections for this character to the same ones you used for the rest of the text on that line so the checkbox will match it.

2. Open the file proportioned checkbox on your disk with your application. Note that this is a simple text (ASCII) file. In WriteNow, you must set the Type of document to open to Text. This brings up the file shown in Figure 1-50.

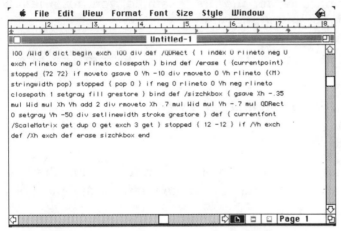

Figure 1-50. Typed version of the proportioned checkbox effect on disk

When you have to insert variable information into an effect, the variables always apppear at the front of the effect text, as shown:

```
100 /Wid 6 dict begin exch def /QDRect { 1 index ...
```

The number in bold, at the beginning of the effect, is the number that you have to supply. Note that this number is not bold or otherwise specially marked on the file on your disk. It is in bold here so that you can see and identify it easily.

63

This defines the width of the checkbox as a percentage of the height. You set the height of the checkbox by setting the font size for the positioning character, and you set the width by filling in a percentage value at the front of the effect text. The default percentage is 100, which makes the checkbox the same width as its height. A value of 75, for example, would make the checkbox narrower than its height, and a value of 150 would make the checkbox wider. To help you remember the use of this value, the name that comes immediately after the value (/Wid) is deliberately designed to remind you of what the value represents. If you change the default value of 100 to 75 and insert this effect into the document that you used for the first example, you get a result similar to that shown in Figure 1-49.

3. Select all of the effect text and copy it from the effect document.

4. Return to your document and place your cursor immediately to the right of the positioning character. Paste the effect into your document.

5. Change the number 100 in the effect text to 75. This changes the /Wid variable to 75 and makes the width of the checkbox 75 percent of its height.

6. Select all of the effect text—and only the effect text. Do *not* select the positioning character and do *not* select the tab that comes before the headline. The result should look something like Figure 1-51.

7. Pull down the Font menu and select the PostScript Escape font. The text for the effect, which you selected in Step 6, will all disappear.

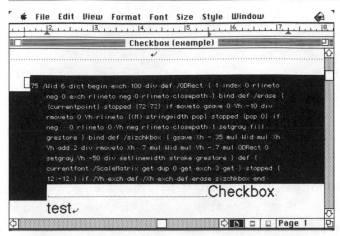

Figure 1-51. Document with effect prepared to be changed to PostScript Escape font

As you immediately notice, the screen looks like your document did before you pasted in the effect. Of course, that's what you want, since you want the real text to print where you had it originally. While the effect will work whether the Hidden Text is displayed on your screen or not, it will not work unless the second part of the effect text is in the PostScript Escape font. If you want to display the second part of the effect text, for editing or any other reason, you must select the line where the text is located, including the positioning character, and convert the text to a visible font. Once this part of the effect text is visible, you can easily convert it back into Monaco, or some other distinctive font that will remind you that it is an effect and not part of your ordinary document text. Then change the font back to the PostScript Escape font when you want to print.

8. Print the document in the ordinary way. Figure 1-49 shows you the result of printing this document.

You see that you can make the checkbox larger or smaller than the surrounding type, and you can make it a rectangle instead of a square, by changing the percentage value appropriately.

This is a good example of the type of effect where you have to supply information. The exact type of information required, of course, varies from effect to effect. In some effects you supply a text string for a display. In others, you supply a number of lines or some other numeric variable. In some effects you may be asked to supply two, three, or more variables. Every effect where you have to supply information provides a short explanation—as you had here—of the type of information required, where it goes in the file, and, if it is a number, what units the number represents. When an effect requires information, the information appears at the front of the effect text, as in this case. If the effect requires more than one variable, they all appear at the front of the effect, separated by their names which always begin with a slash (/) like the name /Wid in the preceding example. The name of each variable follows the value which is associated with it, as /Wid follows the number used for the percentage. This makes it easy for you to modify the effect, even if the text of the effect is quite long and complex.

Inserting an Effect with Variable Text—Rotated Text

Some text effects, like the preceding textbox example, use the text that you type onto your screen. However, some text effects, like rotated text, require that you enter the text to be printed into your effect as a variable. This section shows you how to use this sort of effect.

Here is an example of the rotated text effect in a simple document. The resulting output is shown in Figure 1-52.

This example uses a basic document that you can create quite easily. Figure 1-53 shows you how it might look. The rotated text effect is on your disk as rotated text.

1. Open your document and prepare it for the effect by setting the position and size for the effect. Type a positioning character at the point on the page where you want the effect to

Sale

Next comes the text to place under the rotated headline.
Given the headline, I suppose it would be some advertising
thing or another. This paragraph might go on for quite a
while. You just have to know how much room to allow all
around for the rotated text.

Figure 1-52.   Printed output from the rotated text effect

show. Set the font and size selections for this character to the
same ones that you want to use for the displayed text. Here,
36-point Palatino was used.

In this case, the rotated text is positioned above the start of the
second paragraph, slightly indented to allow for the size and
rotation of the text. Place the insertion point for the positioning
character where you want it, two lines above the second paragraph. Then type the positioning character—here, a Control-Q (a
non-printing character) was used. At this point, your screen should
look something like Figure 1-53, depending on where you decide
to place the positioning character.

Note that I have left a lot of space between the first and second
paragraphs, in this case, 4 lines above the positioning character
and 1 line after. This is to allow room for the text to print. The text
is large, and is rotated at a 45-degree angle to the horizontal line
of the normal text. Therefore, the rotated text will take up a lot of
room on the page. Since you may have to adjust your spacing, this
effect has two knots to warn you that some adjustments may be
necessary before you get it to print exactly the way you want.

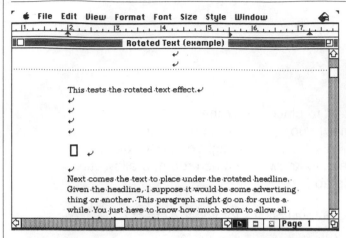

Figure 1-53. The document for the rotated text effect with the positioning character in place

2. Open the file rotated text on your disk with your application. Note that this is a simple text (ASCII) file. In WriteNow you must set the Type of document to open to Text. This brings up the file shown in Figure 1-54.

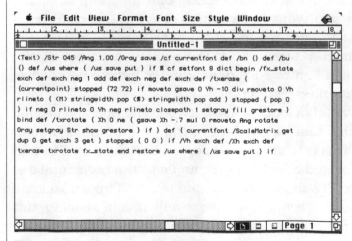

Figure 1-54. Typed version of the rotated text effect on disk

When you have to insert variable information into an effect, the variables will always be at the front of the effect text, as shown:

```
(Text) /Str 45 /Ang 1.00 /Gray save ...
```

The variables for this effect appear here at the beginning of the effect in bold. These variables are not bold or otherwise specially marked on the file on your disk. They are in bold here so that you can see and identify them easily.

The variables /Str, /Ang, and /Gray each define important information for the rotated text effect. The /Str variable is the string of text that you want printed on your document. The /Ang variable is the rotation angle that is used when the string is printed. The angle is measured counterclockwise from a horizontal line, so text at 45 degrees slopes up and to the right. The /Gray variable allows you to make the characters in the rotated text any shade of gray. The uses of all of these variables are described under the rotated text effect in Chapter 6. For now, you can use the default values of these effects, except for the /Str variable where you define the text to be printed.

To help you remember the use of these variables, the names that follow the value (/Str, /Ang, and /Gray) are deliberately designed to remind you of what the value represents. When you change the default value of /Str from (Text) to (Sale) and insert this effect into the document that you used for the first example, you get a printed result similar to that shown in Figure 1-52.

3. Change the variable /Str at the beginning of the file from Text to Sale. Be sure that both the beginning and ending parentheses remain in the file. They are essential. You do not need to change any other variables for this example.

4. Select all of the effect text and copy it from the effect document.

5. Return to your document and place your cursor immediately to the right of the positioning character. Paste the effect into your document.

This is where placing text effects is a little different from the other effects. On the second line of the effect text you will see the following words and characters, about the middle of the line, if your screen is the same size as mine.

```
. . . put } if % cf setfont . . .
```

The % in the middle, shown here in bold—not shown in bold in the disk file, of course—is the critical item for you to identify. In order to properly place and use this type of text effect, you must divide your effect at this point.

6. Select all of the effect text from the beginning of the effect— and only the effect text—up to *but not including* the %. Do *not* select the positioning character and do *not* select the % itself.

7. Select the PostScript Escape font. The text for this part of the effect, which you selected in Step 6, will all disappear. The result should look something like Figure 1-55.

8. Now select all of the effect text from the % *but not including* the % to the end of the effect text. Do *not* select the % and do *not* select the return, tab, or space character(s) that separate the effect text from the printing text that follows it.

9. Select the PostScript Escape font. The text for this part of the effect, which you selected in Step 8, will all disappear. The final result should look something like Figure 1-56.

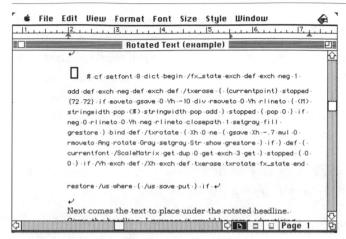

Figure 1-55. Document with first part of rotated text effect changed to PostScript Escape font

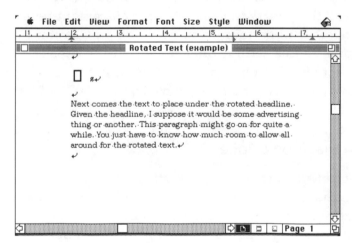

Figure 1-56. Document with all of rotated text effect changed to PostScript Escape font

As you immediately notice, this looks like your document did before you pasted in the effect, except that there is an ampersand right after the positioning character. That's to remind you that this effect is divided into two parts. Don't worry, it doesn't print

71

because the effect itself erases the ampersand when it prints. That's what you want, since you want the real text to print where you had it originally. Although the ampersand signals that the effect is there, the only way to see the effect is to select the line, including the positioning character, and convert the text to a visible font. Then change the font back to the PostScript Escape font when you want to print.

10. Print the document in the ordinary way. Figure 1-52 shows you the result of printing this document.

This is a good example of the type of text effect where you have to divide the effect into two pieces. Certain effects will require this technique. When an effect does require this, it will be clearly noted in the documentation associated with that effect. Generally, you will find all the effects that require this placement technique grouped together in certain chapters, such as Chapter 6. Since every chapter begins with a brief review of the steps required for the effects in that chapter, you will be reminded exactly how to place these advanced text effects by reading the first few pages of the chapter.

Inserting Multiple Effects on a Page

Once you have gotten used to placing one effect on a page, some major questions naturally arise. One question is whether you can use more than one effect on a page, and the other is whether you can use the same effect more than once on a page. As I hope you anticipated, the answer to both questions is yes.

To use more than one effect on a page, or to use multiple effects on a page, simply place the positioning characters for your effects where you want the individual effects to print, and paste the appropriate effect file there, as you have done in the examples. The effects will each print where you have inserted them after the positioning characters. If you want to place one effect right after another one, be sure that each one has its own positioning character, or the second effect will erase the first one.

To use the same effect several times on one page, simply treat them as individual effects. There is no special concern or consideration that you need to take just because the effects are the same.

BITMAPPED VERSUS OUTLINE FONTS

As you may know, there are two types of font on your Macintosh computer: bitmapped fonts and outline fonts (also sometimes called screen fonts and printer fonts, although that's not completely accurate). Bitmapped fonts are fonts where characters are created by turning dots on and off in the appropriate pattern. Generally, bitmapped fonts are created for screen display and are specifically drawn to show well at the low resolutions used on screens. Outline fonts, on the other hand, are created by actually drawing an outline of the character and filling it in. On screen, this doesn't make much visible difference, but when you print, the differences are quite important and often very visible. For most purposes, however, a bitmapped font is quite acceptable except for some loss of quality when you print, and many people use these fonts regularly for all kinds of documents. Common examples of bitmapped fonts are Geneva, New York, Monaco, and all the other fonts on your system that are named after cities.

There is another source of bitmapped fonts when you are printing in the Macintosh system. If you select a font that is not installed in your LaserWriter (or compatible) printer, then the Macintosh system will first try to find the font in outline format on your disk. If it does find the font, it will download the font and use it to print. However, if it does not find the font, it will create a bitmapped version of the font and send that to the printer instead. This is indicated by a dialog box that appears when you print that notifies you that a bitmapped version of the font is being created. For example, suppose that you have two LaserWriter printers connected to your AppleTalk network, one of which has Zapf Chancery built into it and the other one of which does not. When you print a document that uses Zapf Chancery on the printer that has the font in it, then you will use the outline format of the font for printing your document. If you print on the printer that does not have Zapf Chancery, on the other hand, the Macintosh system will build a bitmapped version of the font and send that with your document. Both output documents look very similar, but the difference in the two fonts will be quite evident if you examine the two side-by-side.

Generally, you can use any font that is supported by your word processing application with these effects. Most effects, of course, only use the positioning character for setting the effect size; for such effects, it clearly doesn't matter whether you use a bitmapped or an outline font. However, I strongly urge you to avoid using bitmapped fonts as positioning characters with effects that display text as a part of the effect: numbered bullets, rotated text, and so on. Because of the lower quality of bitmapped fonts, you may see unpleasant mixes of font and effect when you use these fonts. Some effects in fact, such as the outline numbered button effect, will not print at all in a bitmapped font. If an effect has this restriction, it is prominently noted in the description of that effect. Note that you can always use any outline font with any effect in this book with no difficulty. If your regular word processing application can use the font, and there are no messages when you print about creating bitmapped versions of the font, then you can use that font in the effects, both for positioning and for text. If you aren't sure what fonts to use, Helvetica and Times are outline fonts that are available in every PostScript printer.

With all those cautions about fonts, let me stress one point. Whatever you do, you will not hurt your document, your application, or the printer. The main reason to warn you about these issues is to help you avoid the frustration of having an effect work with one document and then fail while you are printing some other document with the same effect. This can be very aggravating, and it may seem as if there is no rhyme or reason to which documents print and which do not. If this happens, you should immediately check the text that describes the effect and see if there is a font restriction for that effect. If so, that may very well be the source of your problem. Check the positioning character, and be sure that you are using an outline font that is actually loaded into your printer.

READING THE EFFECT RECIPES

Each effect is presented as a recipe that you can simply copy and insert into your word processing application. You use the same techniques that you have just practiced. If you have any problems, you can simply return to the steps outlined in the previous sections and retrace them, using the new effect recipe instead of the effect in the example.

If Your Effect Doesn't Print

First of all, don't despair. One of the problems with doing effects in the PostScript Escape font is that when you make a mistake, you aren't likely to see a report of any errors. Sometimes you may get a dialog box that tells you that you have some type of error. Figure 1-57 shows you two common dialogs that you might see.

Don't believe these messages. The problem is that your effect has caused an error during printing. If you remove the error, your document will most likely print just fine. To test this, remove the effect code from your document and print the page that previously contained the effect. If it prints, then the error is in the effect and not in your document. (Conversely, of course, if it still doesn't print, you have some other error in your document—but that's rare.)

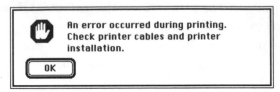

A PostScript error has been generated by the LaserWriter driver;the document is OK but cannot be printed.

An error occurred during printing. Check printer cables and printer installation.

OK

Figure 1-57. Typical document error dialog boxes

Although you may see a dialog box or get some other error indication, most often you simply won't see anything print. If you watch the status lights on your LaserWriter, the processing light (yellow on early models of the LaserWriter and green on later models) blinks a few times, showing that it is receiving and processing data. Then it returns to the waiting state, shown by a steady green light. This indicates that the printer is finished processing and is waiting for the next job, even though it has not printed any output. This also indicates that you have an error in your effect. Appendix A discusses a variety of errors and techniques for finding out what has gone wrong in your effect.

The most common error is to make a small change to the text around the effect while it is in the PostScript Escape font, and therefore invisible. Almost inevitably, in my experience, you may accidentally pick up a small part of the effect text and change or delete that as well. This is especially common if you are changing a string inside an effect, for example, or if you attempt to change or move the positioning character once you have pasted the effect into your document. The best prevention for this is never to work around your effect while it is in the PostScript Escape font. If you need to work around it, make it visible again, so you can be sure that you don't damage the effect text. If you do damage the effect text, the effect will not print. If your effect doesn't print, and you have made any changes on the page with the effect, the first thing to do is to make the effect text visible and make sure that it looks like the effect text on your disk. The easiest way to do that is to repaste the effect text into your document and then try to print again. If you have damaged the effect text, this will solve your problem.

Another common error is to make a typing error in the effect. Many effects in this book, like the checkbox effect, do not require any changes to work correctly. You simply paste them from the disk that comes with this book into your document. These effects, of course, are not subject to typing errors. However, many other effects do require some data. When you type data into the effect, you can make small errors that may cause the effect not to work. Most of these are obvious: If an effect requires a number value, such as 1, and you type a letter, such as l, you will cause an error. Also, some data that you enter must be enclosed in parentheses, like this: (**abc**). In such cases, only replace the bold text characters. If you change or remove either of the parentheses, you will cause an error. If you have entered data into an effect and it doesn't print, try the effect one time with the default data that is supplied with the effect. If it prints, then you know that the data that you entered has somehow caused an error. Review what you entered carefully, then try your effect again.

Sometimes, even after you have checked all the data and everything is perfect, you still can't get the effect to print. In this case, review any variables that you have entered and be sure that they are the correct length and format for your effect. Word processing applications sometimes arbitrarily break words in the PostScript Escape font, which causes an error. If you have changed the length of any variables, this may cause a word to be split, so that the effect doesn't print. Also be sure that you have hyphenation turned off for the part of your document that contains the effect. Your printer won't understand commands split by hyphens. If you continue to have trouble, read through Appendix A and use the tools and techniques described there to decipher your problems.

POSTSCRIPT AND WORD PROCESSING

At this point, you might want to understand a little bit about how you actually produced the effects shown earlier. The answer is in the hidden powers of your Macintosh computer—in particular, in the fact that the Macintosh prints on a LaserWriter or compatible printer by converting the information that you see on the screen into a special language, called PostScript.

You have probably heard about PostScript before, perhaps in articles that you have read in various magazines, or in talking with other Macintosh users. PostScript is a *page-description language,* created by Adobe Systems, which allows applications to describe a page of text and graphics in a compact, device-independent manner. "Device-independent" means that this description can then be transmitted to any device that understands PostScript, such as the LaserWriter, where a special program that resides inside the device, called the *interpreter*, changes these PostScript commands into commands that create the desired output page.

In the Macintosh system, the process that converts the screen data into PostScript is generally performed by the LaserWriter driver software. (That's the file named LaserWriter that you have in your System Folder—or in the Extensions Folder inside the System Folder, if you are running System 7.0.) In fact, all the word processing programs on the Macintosh use the LaserWriter driver to make this conversion. This conversion process allows you to insert the effect text into your word processing documents as you did earlier. Normally, when you type text on the screen in a specific font, the LaserWriter driver translates that text and the associated font into the appropriate PostScript commands to print the text on the page in the font that you have selected. However, when the LaserWriter driver sees information in the PostScript Escape font, it does not make that translation. Instead, it simply passes this information directly through to the LaserWriter printer without any change, where the PostScript interpreter reads this data as commands. These commands can tell the interpreter to draw a box, as you did in the previous examples, or they can tell the interpreter to make any other drawing that you want.

PostScript and Microsoft Word

There is one more point that users of Microsoft Word may wonder about: the PostScript style entry. When you are working in Word, you can access a special style that allows you to enter PostScript commands directly into your documents. At first, you may suppose that you could enter both parts of the effects into Word using the PostScript style, as an alternative to using the PostScript Escape font. Unfortunately, this isn't possible.

There are two major, and several minor, differences between setting an effect into your document using Word's PostScript style and using the PostScript Escape font. The first of these is caused by differences between QuickDraw, the system commands used to draw on your screen, and PostScript, which are the commands used by the printer to create your document output. The Apple LaserWriter driver converts QuickDraw screen commands into PostScript. All the effects presented here are designed to work with the LaserWriter's translation mechanism, so that these effects work with all types of word processing applications. Word's PostScript style, on the other hand, bypasses the LaserWriter driver, so that the effects here will not be correctly translated if you use them in the PostScript style.

The second major difference is that Word automatically places all text on the page that is in the PostScript style at the beginning of the page. This is why the effects must be divided into two segments: one in the PostScript style, to avoid the 255-character line length limit, and the other inserted at the point where the effect is printed. In all, this means that any effect, such as the checkbox, requires special handling to print at a particular point on the page. Word does provide some special, and rather clever, features in the PostScript style that allow PostScript effects to handle positioning in a Word document. Again, however, these features are unique to Word, and are not compatible with the simpler, but more universal, methods used in the effects demonstrated in this book.

All of the effects that are in this book will work in their Word form to produce exactly the same results as they do with other word processing applications. Also, you can still use Word's PostScript style with the effects shown here. This means that you can use any special PostScript effects or code that you may have for Word on pages where you also have placed effects, such as those described in this book, that use the PostScript Escape font. These two processes will coexist quite peacefully on the same page.

CONCLUSION

In this chapter you have learned exactly how to use the effect recipes that are described in this book and are contained on the disk that comes with it. You have seen and gone through the steps necessary to use any of the effects whether you use Microsoft Word or any other word processor

The effects that are used here are quite simple: a checkbox, a variation on the checkbox, and two additional effects. Together, these demonstrate all the major techniques that you will use for placing effects in your document. But all the effects in this book, from the simplest to the most complex, require essentially the same techniques for use in a document. Each effect also has certain special features, which are described with the individual effect, but, overall, once you have successfully placed one effect into a document, you should be able to place any other effect as well.

The chapter ends with a brief section about how these effects work. This is interesting and informative, but by no means essential information. You can easily use all of the effects in this book simply by cutting and pasting as described in this chapter. No further knowledge is assumed or required. On the other hand, some people (myself, for one) always want to know how something works. For such folks I have included the short explanations given here. If these still aren't enough information, you can read Appendix B, which explains in much more detail how these effects are constructed.

In any case, you are now ready to use all of the effects here to enliven your documents and to solve some of the common problems that seem to crop up when you are creating certain types of documents.

IMPORTANT

2

Checkboxes

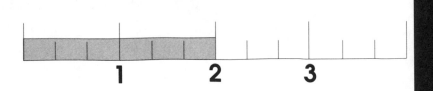

THIS CHAPTER PRESENTS FOUR VARIATIONS OF SIMPLE checkboxes, such as the one presented in the first chapter. Checkboxes are often used in a wide variety of forms for marking or pointing out alternative choices. Checkboxes can also be used as bullets and as decorative elements or delimiters in text blocks. In this use, they resemble the bullets presented in Chapter 3. However, because checkboxes are usually used as selection markers, they are presented here in a separate chapter. Chapter 3 presents an additional section of square bullets. So, if you want to use a checkbox as a bullet and don't find what you want here, look under the square bullet effects for more variations on this theme.

INSERTING CHECKBOXES IN MICROSOFT WORD

1. Open your document. Insert a positioning character at the point in the document where you want to place the effect. The size of the positioning character determines the size of your checkbox.

2. Open the **xxxx**.w file, where **xxxx** represents the name of the desired effect. If you see only one line of text, click on the Show Hidden Text box in the Preferences . . . selection of the Edit menu. Select and copy all the text of the effect and place it at the beginning of your document that will contain the effect. Notice that the major part of the text in this file is in Word's PostScript style. (If you are unclear about how to use this style, review the instructions in Chapter 1.)

3. Cut the text at the end of the .w file that is *not* in the PostScript style from the end of the effect text. This is the second part of the effect.

4. Paste this text into your Word document immediately after (to the right of) the positioning character.

5. Select all of the text, and only the text, from the second part of the effect file that you pasted into your document. Change the font to the PostScript Escape font. This part of the effect text will disappear.

6. Be sure that the Print Hidden Text box in the Print dialog box is not checked. Print your document. The effect will print over the positioning character.

INSERTING CHECKBOXES IN OTHER WORD PROCESSING APPLICATIONS

1. Open your document. Insert a positioning character where you want to place the effect. The size of the positioning character determines the size of your checkbox.

2. Open the effect file and copy the effect text.

3. Paste the effect text into your document immediately after (to the right of) the positioning character.

4. Select all of the effect text, and only the effect text, that you copied into your document, and change it to the PostScript Escape font.

5. Print your document in the ordinary way. The effect will print over the positioning character.

CHECKBOX

checkbox

Description

The checkbox effect simply draws a small square at the place specified by the positioning character. This can be used as a checkbox for forms, tables, or similar applications where you want someone to mark a choice. Or it can be used as a square bullet.

Size and Position

Figure 2-1 shows you different sizes of the checkbox effect. The first three lines show checkboxes created using 12-, 18-, and 24-point fonts. Using a different font does not affect the size or position of the checkbox, as you can see by comparing lines three and four, which display a 24-point checkbox using the Helvetica and Times fonts. In these four examples, the font and size of the positioning character, which governs the size of the checkbox, is identical to that of the font used in the line of text next to the checkbox.

Figure 2-2 shows you how the effect is positioned on the page and the size of the effect. The two bullets above the checkbox

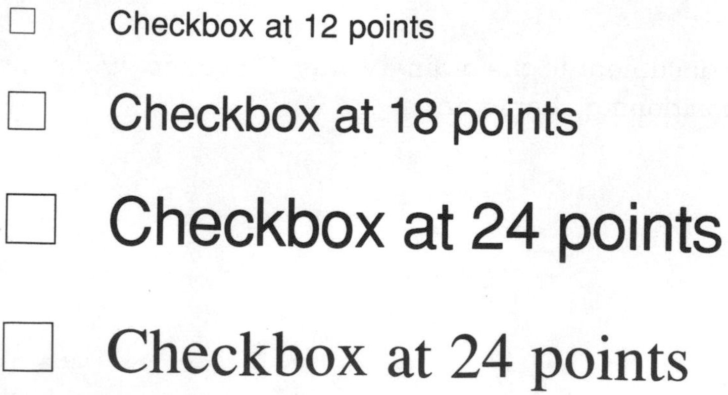

☐   Checkbox at 12 points

☐   Checkbox at 18 points

☐   Checkbox at 24 points

☐   Checkbox at 24 points

Figure 2-1.   Sizing the basic checkbox effect

• •   Positioning and size demonstration:

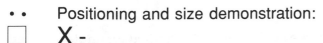

Figure 2-2. Positioning the basic checkbox effect

show roughly the start of the positioning character and the beginning of the checkbox effect code. As you see, the checkbox extends from about the beginning of the positioning character to just past the start of the effect text. This places the center of the checkbox at the point where the positioning character ends. This helps to ensure that there is enough room for the checkbox, even if you have text next to the positioning character.

The second line also demonstrates how the checkbox is sized. The capital X next to the checkbox is in the same font and point size—18-point Helvetica—as the checkbox. As you see, the checkbox is approximately the height of the capital X in the font that you have chosen. Remember that this is the font and size of the *positioning character,* not that of the following text. You can make these match if you want them to match.

TIP

If you place text on both sides of the checkbox, be sure to allow some room both before and after the effect text. As you can see in Figure 2-2, the effect extends both forward and backward from the start of the positioning character to somewhat beyond the start of the effect text. However, since the effect text is invisible in your document, you could print over some text that you want to print if you place the effect too close to it. One way you can avoid this is to place one or two spaces between the effect text and the adjacent word of your text. Another good way to make such placements is to use tab settings for positioning the effect and the text that follows it. This allows you to control more precisely the exact distance between the effect and the beginning of the subsequent text.

Using the Effect

The series of checkboxes in Figure 2-3 is a good example of using tabs to position an effect and its surrounding text. This is a typical use of checkboxes in a text document: to provide a place for readers to indicate a choice among several alternatives. Here I placed the checkbox positioning character by using a tab about where the checkbox effect prints on each line. I followed that with another tab to position the following text. This ensures that both the checkboxes and the associated text line up properly.

Figure 2-3. Examples of the basic checkbox effect

This series of examples also indicates another use for the positioning character size setting. As you read, the checkbox is sized to match a capital X in your chosen font. For these examples, the checkbox positioning character is 14 points, which enlarges the checkbox slightly. This makes the resulting boxes a better match to the following text, which is 12-point Helvetica Bold. If you use 12-point checkboxes, the result looks a little small, even though the boxes are the same height as the text.

TIP

When you are using the checkbox effect, you may want to experiment with different sizes for the boxes and the adjacent text to see how you want them to match up. Because the effects are written in PostScript, you can use any point size that you want. Don't be afraid to use point sizes that are not displayed on your font size menu. If you want a 13-point font, use it— the effect will work just fine.

BEHIND THE SCENES

You may wonder exactly what size the checkbox is when you select a font and size. As you may know, the point size of a font is not the exact size of the characters in the font. Rather it is the distance that must be provided between lines of text to ensure that the ascenders on tall characters, such as 'h', don't run into the descenders of characters, like 'y', from the line above. For most fonts, the capital X is about 70 percent of the actual point size. That is, the capital X in a typical 36-point font is actually between 25 and 26 points high. This changes with the font, with different fonts running slightly more or less than 70 percent, depending on the design of the typeface. Sizes for a capital X range from 56 percent of the font size for Courier to 74 percent for Avant Garde. The text style also affects the actual printed character. Bold characters are often slightly oversized and italic ones slightly undersized (since they're angled). The checkbox effect draws the box at 70 percent of the point size of the font used for the positioning character, regardless of the font, thus approximating the size of a capital X in that font.

PROPORTIONED CHECKBOX

proportioned checkbox

Description

The proportioned checkbox effect is basically the same as the standard checkbox, except that you can control the width of the box independently of its height. The standard checkbox is always the size determined by the point size of the positioning character. Once you have set that, the size of the resulting checkbox is fixed. The proportioned checkbox has one control, called Wid, that allows you to determine the ratio of the width to the height. As with the checkbox, the height of the proportioned checkbox is determined by the point size of the positioning character.

Variables

The single variable, Wid, is located at the front of the proportioned checkbox effect, as follows:

```
75 /Wid 6 dict . . .
```

You must observe the range limits for the variable very strictly.
If you don't, the effect may not print.

Wid   The Wid value represents the width of the checkbox as a
percentage of its height. The height of the checkbox is set by the
size that you use for the positioning character. You can use any
percentage values between 10 and 999 for Wid without trouble.

Size and Position

Figure 2-4 illustrates how the Wid variable works. The percentage shown in the text next to the boxes is the value placed into
each effect for Wid. As you see, the 25 percent box has a width
that is one-quarter of its height, the 50 percent box is half as wide
as it is high, and so on, up to the 200 percent box which is twice
as wide as it is high. Obviously, using 100 percent gives you a
checkbox that is the same as the one produced by the checkbox
effect. Using the Wid variable along with the font size, you can
make your checkbox effect any size you want. Just remember
that the height of the box is set by the size of the positioning
character, just like checkbox, while the width of the box is set by
the Wid variable as a percentage of the height.
The effect is positioned on the page in the same way as the
standard checkbox effect described earlier. The actual space used
by the proportioned checkbox, of course, depends on the setting
of the Wid variable. At 100 Wid, the checkbox extends from about
the beginning of the positioning character to just past the start of
the effect text, thus placing the center of the checkbox at the

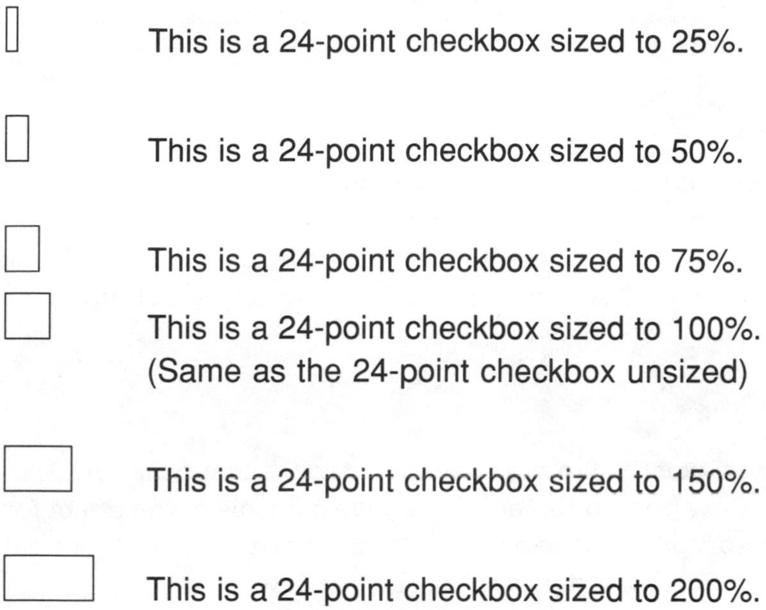

☐ This is a 24-point checkbox sized to 25%.

☐ This is a 24-point checkbox sized to 50%.

☐ This is a 24-point checkbox sized to 75%.

☐ This is a 24-point checkbox sized to 100%.
(Same as the 24-point checkbox unsized)

▭ This is a 24-point checkbox sized to 150%.

▭ This is a 24-point checkbox sized to 200%.

Figure 2-4. Examples of the proportioned checkbox effect

point where the positioning character ends. This helps to ensure that there is enough room for the checkbox, even if you have text next to the positioning character. However, if you place text on both sides of the checkbox, be sure to allow some room either by adding spaces before and after the effect or by using tabs to place the effect.

Using the Effect

This effect is mostly used for making checkboxes that are not square. This can be used for decorative effects or for making boxes where the reader can enter information.

DROP SHADOW CHECKBOX

shadow checkbox

Description

If you look at advertising and other types of circulars, you will notice that some people like to make the checkboxes stand out on the page by placing a shadow behind the box. The shadow checkbox effect allows you to make a shadow behind your checkbox.

Variables

This effect is exactly like the checkbox itself, except that you can place a shadow behind the box. You have controls in the effect for the placement of the shadow in both the horizontal and vertical directions, and for the darkness of the shadow.

The three variables are listed in the front of the shadow checkbox effect, as shown here:

+03 /Xoff **+03** /Yoff **1.00** /Gray 8 dict

Note that you must observe the range and format rules for the variables very strictly. If you don't, the effect may not print.

Xoff/Yoff   You place the shadow behind the box by setting the horizontal distance, called Xoff—an offset in the x, or horizontal, direction. In a similar fashion, the vertical distance for the shadow is called Yoff. Both distances are in points, which are a printer's measure. A point is $1/_{72}$ inch. You can use either positive or negative values for both Xoff and Yoff. Positive values of Xoff move the shadow to the right, while negative values move it to the left. Positive values of Yoff move the shadow down the page, and negative values move it up the page. You must place plus or minus signs in front of the Xoff and Yoff variables, and you must use two digits, as shown. Acceptable values range from ±00 to ±99. Of course, +00 and −00 are identical and give you the same result: no offset in that direction. Examples of shadowed checkbox effects are shown in Figure 2-5.

This is a 24-point checkbox with offsets of +4 and +4. The shadow is .50 gray.

This is a 24-point checkbox with offsets of +4 and -4. The shadow is .50 gray.

This is a 24-point checkbox with offsets of -4 and +4. The shadow is .50 gray.

This is a 24-point checkbox with offsets of -4 and -4. The shadow is .50 gray.

Figure 2-5.   Examples of the drop shadow checkbox effect

Gray   The darkness of the shadow is set by a control named, reasonably enough, Gray. The values of Gray are percentages, with 1.00 being black and 0.01 being almost white. Although you can use a value of 0.00 (white), this may be somewhat misleading. That value actually means that nothing is printed behind the checkbox; it doesn't cause a white spot on colored paper, for example.

The Gray variable may range from 1.00 to .01. You always need to have a decimal point in the value and two digits after the

decimal point, even if you are using exact tenths. For example, use .50 and not .5 as your value. If you don't, the effect may not print.

Size and Position

The shadowed checkbox is sized in the same way as the standard checkbox effect: The positioning character determines the size of the box. The shadow size matches that of the checkbox, as a shadow should. As shown in Figure 2-6, the position of the shadow and the amount of shadow that shows under the checkbox are determined by the Xoff and Yoff variables.

Variations on shadowed checkboxes:

This is a 24-point checkbox with a 0 x offset.

This one, on the other hand, has a 0 y offset.

This is a 24-point checkbox with offsets of -2 and +2 and a black (1.00 gray) shadow.

This is a 24-point shadow with offsets of -8 and +8 and a .25 gray shadow.

You can use checkboxes in a variety of ways:

❑ **RIGHT**
❑ **WRONG**
❑ **MAYBE**

Figure 2-6. Variations of the drop shadow checkbox effect

The four examples in Figure 2-5 show you how changes in the offset values move the shadow effect around the checkbox itself. As you can see, you can get any variation in shadowing by changing the signs of the offset values.

It can be difficult to judge the distance that you want to offset the shadow behind your checkbox. To set it the way you want, you may have to make some tests using different sized offsets in your document. For that reason, this effect has two knots: It contains variables, and it may require test prints to set it exactly the way you want it.

Using the Effect

The examples in Figure 2-6 show you some interesting variations on shadow placement. Basically, if you want a realistic shadow, the values for Xoff and Yoff should be equal and not too large for the box. On the other hand, if you want a special effect, then setting different values can produce some interesting results. For example, notice that by setting the x offset to zero, you can make the shadow appear directly below the checkbox (or on top of the box, if you set the y offset to a negative number). Similarly, the use of a y offset of zero makes the shadow appear to the left or right of the box, depending on the sign of the x offset. Larger boxes will usually require larger offsets, as you might imagine. Notice the examples on lines three and four. These boxes are the same size—24 points—but the shadow is dark and close on one and lighter and further away on the other.

In general, you will find that even the smallest boxes require at least a 2-point offset if you want the shadow to show up clearly. The last three examples show 14-point boxes with 12-point text, and the 1.00 Gray (black) shadow placed 2 points offset in both the horizontal and vertical directions.

This illustrates a common use of shadowed checkboxes. Compare these boxes to the standard checkboxes shown under the checkbox effect. As you can see, these stand out more and, presumably, get the reader's attention more easily. (That's what advertising and public relation types tell me, anyway. . . .)

Anyone, even a professional graphic artist, may find it difficult to visualize the exact shade that a given percentage of gray produces on a page. On a laser printer, this is compounded by the fact that different devices use somewhat different methods to produce grays from what are basically simple black dots. The example in Figure 2-7 gives you some idea of exactly how black

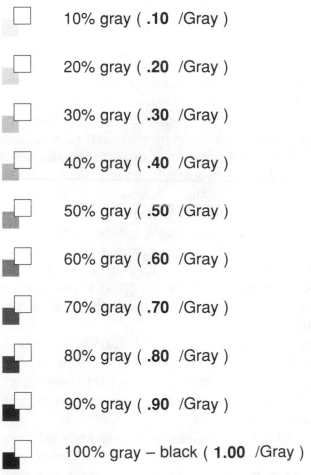

10% gray (**.10** /Gray)

20% gray (**.20** /Gray)

30% gray (**.30** /Gray)

40% gray (**.40** /Gray)

50% gray (**.50** /Gray)

60% gray (**.60** /Gray)

70% gray (**.70** /Gray)

80% gray (**.80** /Gray)

90% gray (**.90** /Gray)

100% gray – black (**1.00** /Gray)

Figure 2-7. Drop shadows showing gray values in 10 percent increments

different percentages of gray appear on an output page. You can use these as a guide when you are setting the Gray variable in this, and other, effects.

TIP

> Readers with color devices may wonder if they can use the Gray variable to get color output. Unfortunately, the answer is no. Although the PostScript language has a very complete set of color operators, using them requires substantially more code in the effect than using black and white. Therefore, effects in this book are restricted to black, white, and shades of gray.

FADED CHECKBOX

faded checkbox

Description

The faded checkbox effect is essentially a fancy variant of the shadowed checkbox. In this case, as shown, it has a longer shadow that changes from white to black over a small distance.

Size and Position

The faded checkbox is sized in the same way as the standard checkbox effect: The positioning character determines the size of the basic checkbox before the faded effect is in place. The faded shadow size is a standard size for all checkboxes. It extends to the left and below the checkbox by a fixed amount and matches the checkbox in width. As illustrated in Figure 2-8, this gives somewhat different results for different-sized checkboxes.

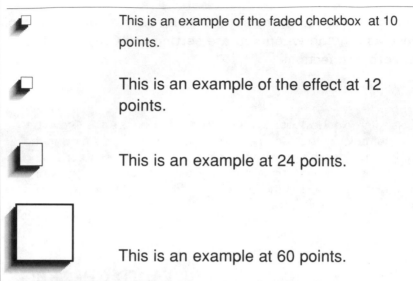

This is an example of the faded checkbox at 10 points.

This is an example of the effect at 12 points.

This is an example at 24 points.

This is an example at 60 points.

Figure 2-8. Examples of the faded checkbox effect

The checkbox itself is placed just where the standard checkbox would appear: centered on the end of the positioning character. If you use the faded checkbox effect with small point size text, be sure to allow enough room below the effect so that the faded shadow does not touch the text below and to the left of the effect.

Using the Effect

Although this effect looks something like the shadow checkbox effect, it has no variables and no controls for shadow placement. Fading a shadow is quite complex and time-consuming, so you don't have alternatives here for shadow placement or coloring. The examples in Figure 2-8 demonstrate how this affects the resulting output. As you can see, smaller point sizes have a faded effect that tails out a great distance relative to the size of the box itself. On the other hand, on large point size boxes the faded background hardly differs from the simple shadow effect. The best results are generally between 18 and 48 points, but you may want larger or smaller boxes for special purposes.

BEHIND THE SCENES

This effect demonstrates the use of a basic fountain fill behind an effect. More examples of this are presented with other effects in later chapters. The effect uses nine 10 percent steps, spread uniformly over a distance of ten points, with one position used to draw the checkbox itself. That is, the x offset and y offset for this effect are both always 10 points. The furthest point of the fade is a 10 percent gray, while the final point (before the actual edge of the box) is 90 percent. The use of such compatible numbers makes the effect quick to calculate and easy to display. This accounts for the fact that larger point sizes have the same size fade as smaller ones.

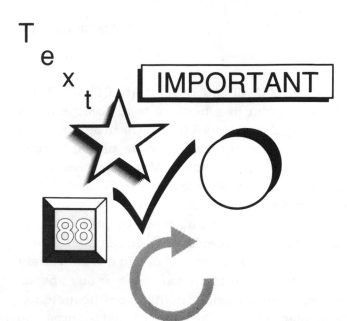

Bullets

3

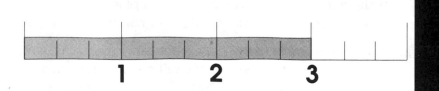

BULLETS ARE COMMONLY USED AS SIMPLE ADDITIONS TO A text document to mark a point in a block of text, to organize a series of text blocks, to highlight a block of text, or to add interest and visual excitement to a line of text. You have probably used bullets often in a variety of ways. Although Macintosh word processing applications generally provide some types of bullets, there are usually some variants that I would like to use that are not easily available. This chapter contains all types of bullets: round and square; filled and outlined; numbered and unnumbered. These form a basic set of bullet types that you can use in a wide variety of situations. They do not require many variables or any special calculations or considerations for using them in your documents.

For convenience, similar types of effects are placed together, so that each type of bullet—round, square, and others—are together. Within each type, the variations on the basic effect are grouped together; that is, all the round bullet effects appear together, and so on. Also, variations that use text follow the basic effect and the variations that don't require text; so, for various types of square bullets for example, bullet effects with no numbers appear before the bullets with numbers in them.

Some of the bullet effects may look very similar. Indeed, some variations on a basic effect look identical at first glance. If you don't see what the differences are, read the discussion that accompanies the effect for an explanation of how one variation differs from the others.

INSERTING BULLETS IN MICROSOFT WORD

1. Open your document. Insert a positioning character at the point in the document where you want to place the effect. The size of the positioning character determines the size of your bullet.

2. Open the xxxx.w file, where xxxx represents the name of the desired effect. If you see only one line of text, click on the Show Hidden Text box in the Preferences . . . selection of the Edit menu.

Select and copy all the text of the effect and place it at the beginning of your document that will contain the effect. Notice that the major part of the text in this file is in Word's PostScript style. (If you are unclear about how to use this style, review the instructions in Chapter 1.)

3. Cut the text at the end of the .w file that is *not* in the PostScript style from the end of the effect text. This is the second part of the effect.

4. Paste this text into your Word document immediately after (to the right of) the positioning character.

5. Select all of the text, and only the text, from the second part of the effect file that you pasted into your document. Change the font to the PostScript Escape font. This part of the effect text will disappear.

6. Be sure that the Print Hidden Text box in the Print dialog box is not checked. Print your document. The effect will print over the positioning character.

INSERTING BULLETS IN OTHER WORD PROCESSING APPLICATIONS

1. Open your document. Insert a positioning character at the point in the document where you want to place the effect. The size of the positioning character determines the basic size of your bullet.

2. Open the effect file, and select and copy the effect text.

3. Paste the effect text into your document immediately after (to the right of) the positioning character.

4. Select all of the effect text, and only the effect text, and change it to the PostScript Escape font.

5. Print your document in the ordinary way. The effect will print over the positioning character.

BULLET

bullet

Description

The bullet effect draws a small open circle at the point specified by the positioning character. In almost every font, the Macintosh also offers a simple black bullet accessed by pressing Option-8. However, this solid bullet is not always sized or positioned correctly for various tasks. The bullet effect is an open circle (the filled bullet effect, later in this chapter, can be filled in with any shade of gray) and can be used in a wide variety of ways, including as an alternative to a regular check box.

Size and Position

Figure 3-1 shows you different sizes of the bullet effect. The first three lines show bullets created using 12-, 18-, and 24-point fonts. Using a different font has no effect on the size or positioning of the bullet, as you can see by comparing lines three and four, which both display a 24-point bullet using the Helvetica and Times fonts. In these four examples, the font and size of the positioning character, which governs the size of the bullet, is identical to the X in the line of text next to the bullet.

The second line also demonstrates how the bullet is sized. The capital X is in the same font and point size—18-point Helvetica—

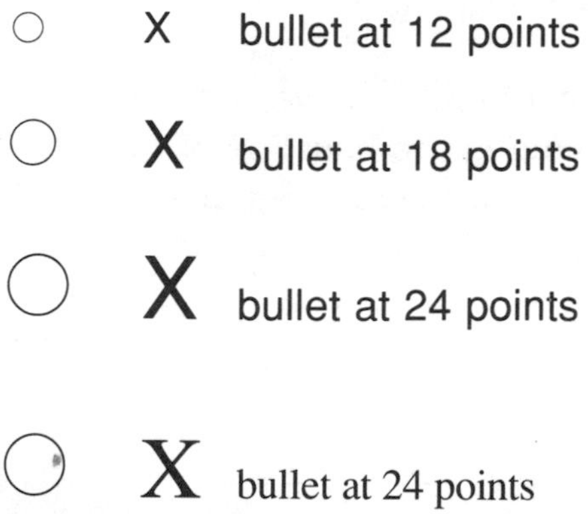

◯   X   bullet at 12 points

◯   **X**   bullet at 18 points

◯   **X**   bullet at 24 points

◯ X bullet at 24 points

Figure 3-1.   Sizing the basic bullet effect

as the bullet. As you see, the bullet is approximately the height of the capital X in the font that you have chosen. Remember that this is the font and size of the *positioning character*, not of the following text. You can ensure that these match if you want them to match.

The bullet effect is positioned on the page with its center at the point where the positioning character ends. The bottom of the bullet lies along the baseline of the text. The size of the bullet ensures that its center is even with the center of the capital X.

TIP

If you place text on both sides of the bullet, be sure to allow some room both before and after the effect text, because the effect extends both forward and backward from the end of the positioning character. Since the effect text is invisible in your document, you could erase or obscure some of the text that you want to print if you place it too close to the effect. One way you can avoid this is to place one or two spaces between the effect text and the adjacent words of your text. Another good way to make such placements is to use tab settings for positioning the effect and the text that follows it. This allows you to control more precisely the exact distance between the effect and the beginning of the subsequent text.

Using the Effect

This bullet effect can be used anywhere you want a full-sized round bullet. Since it is positioned along the baseline of the text, this bullet effect can be used to divide text blocks or to set off specific text items.

SIZED BULLET

sized bullet

Description

In almost every font, the Macintosh offers a simple black bullet accessed by pressing Option-8. However, this solid bullet is not always correctly sized for various tasks. The sized bullet allows you to insert a round bullet, like a small circle, that is sized as you want. This allows you to use various sizes of bullets in lists, for example, without multiple font changes (which slows processing down) and with complete control over size.

Variables

You control the bullet size by setting the Pct variable. The variable is located at the front of the sized bullet effect, as shown here.

`100 /Pct 6 dict . . .`

You must observe the format rules and range limits for the variable very strictly. If you don't, the effect may not print.

Pct The Pct variable allows you to set the ratio of the diameter of the bullet to the font size used for the positioning character. This value represents the diameter of the bullet as a percentage of the font size. You can use any percentage values

106

between 10 and 999 for Pct without trouble. A 100 percent bullet is the same size as a capital X.

Size and Position

The examples in Figure 3-2 illustrate how your bullet is sized. The percentage shown in the text next to the bullets is the value used to set the Pct variable. As you see, the 25 percent bullet is one-quarter the height of the X, the 50 percent bullet is half the height, and so on, up to the 200 percent bullet which is twice the height of the X. Obviously, using 100 percent gives you a bullet that is the same height as the font. Using the Pct variable along with the font size, you can make your bullet effect any size you want.

Figure 3-2 also shows you how the Pct variable affects your bullet. All of the example bullets are based on a 24-point positioning character. The X next to them on the line of text is also 24

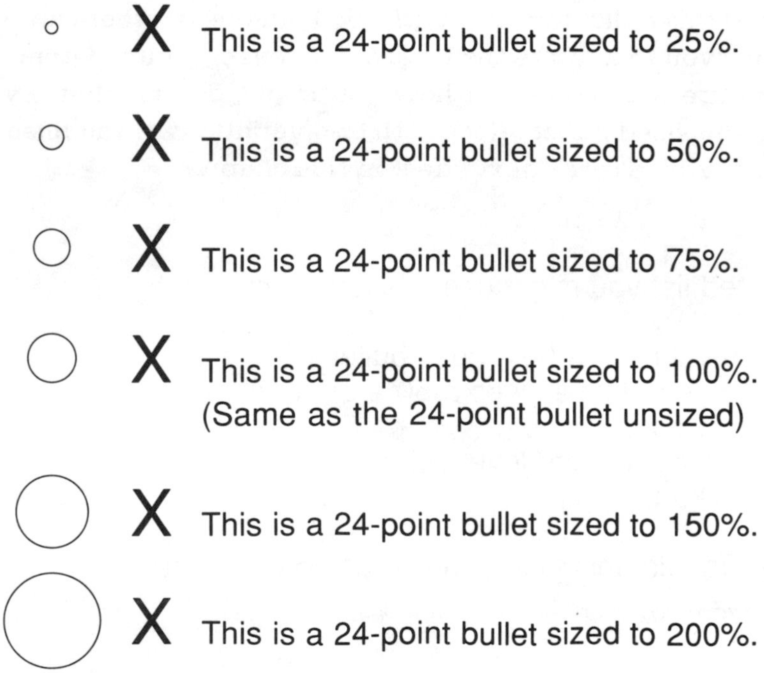

○ **X** This is a 24-point bullet sized to 25%.

○ **X** This is a 24-point bullet sized to 50%.

○ **X** This is a 24-point bullet sized to 75%.

○ **X** This is a 24-point bullet sized to 100%.
(Same as the 24-point bullet unsized)

○ **X** This is a 24-point bullet sized to 150%.

○ **X** This is a 24-point bullet sized to 200%.

Figure 3-2. Examples of the sized-bullet effect

points. As you can see, the bullet is positioned in the center of the line of text, where the two lines of the X cross. The 100 percent bullet also shows you that the bullet, like the checkbox, is the size of a capital X in your designated font.

In the horizontal direction, the bullet is centered, like the checkboxes in Chapter 2, on the point after the positioning character. This allows enough room for most bullets to print without running over the text around them. Remember that the bullets are circles, however. If you use large bullets, particularly if you use large percentage values, then you may have to adjust your text both horizontally and vertically to allow enough room for the bullet to print.

Using the Effect

This bullet effect can be used anywhere that you want a round bullet. In particular it is useful for bulleted lists that have several levels. Using this bullet together with solid bullets (or other variations) allows you to indicate the level of an item or group of items visually. Figure 3-3 shows you how you might do just that, by combining the sized bullet effect with two variations of the filled bullet effect, which is the next effect in this chapter.

For a bulleted list you might use this approach:

- The first level uses a 50% solid bullet
  - The second level uses a 50% open bullet
  - and so on....
    - with the third level using a 25% solid bullet
    - like this

Obviously, any combination you like could be chosen.

Figure 3-3. Examples of bulleted list variations

FILLED BULLET

filled bullet

Description

Although it's nice to have a bullet that you can size, sometimes you may also want to fill the bullet with a shade of gray. The filled bullet effect allows you to add gray fill to your bullets.

Variables

Like the sized bullet, the filled bullet uses a Pct variable to set the size of the bullet. In addition, it adds a Gray variable to allow you to select the color of the bullet. Both variables are located at the beginning of the filled bullet effect, as shown here:

```
1.00 /Gray 100 /Pct 6 dict ...
```

You must observe the format rules and range limits for the variables very strictly. If you don't, the effect may not print.

Gray The darkness of the bullet is set by a control named, reasonably enough, Gray. The values of Gray are percentages, with 1.00 being black and 0.01 being almost white. Although you can use a value of 0.00 (white), this may be somewhat misleading. That value actually means that nothing is printed inside the bullets—it doesn't cause a white spot on colored paper, for example.

The Gray variable may range from 1.00 to .01. You always need to have a decimal point in the value and two digits after the decimal point, even if you are using exact tenths. For example, use .50 and not .5 as your value. If you don't, the effect may not print.

Pct The Pct variable allows you to set the ratio of the diameter of the bullet to the font size used for the positioning character. This value represents the diameter of the bullet as a percentage of the font size. You can use any values between 10 and 999 for Pct without trouble. A 100 percent bullet is the same size as a capital X.

Size and Position

The examples in Figure 3-4 illustrate how your bullet is sized and colored. The text next to the bullets shows both the value placed into each effect for Pct and the value inserted for Gray. As you see, the variations are just what you would expect. Obviously, using 100 percent size (100 /Pct) and 100 percent gray (1.00 /Gray) gives you a bullet that is completely black and the same height as the font.

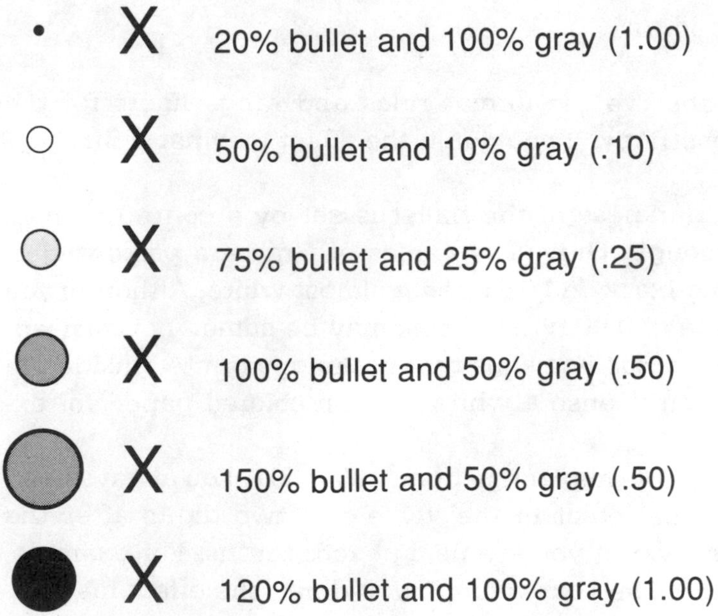

•   X   20% bullet and 100% gray (1.00)

○   X   50% bullet and 10% gray (.10)

◔   X   75% bullet and 25% gray (.25)

●   X   100% bullet and 50% gray (.50)

●   X   150% bullet and 50% gray (.50)

●   X   120% bullet and 100% gray (1.00)

Figure 3-4. Examples of the filled bullet effect

All of the example bullets shown in Figure 3-4 are based on a 24-point positioning character. The X next to them on the line of text is also 24 points. As you can see, the bullet is positioned so that its center is in line with the spot where the two lines of the X cross. The 100 percent bullet also shows you that the bullet, like the checkbox, is the size of a capital X in your designated font.

In the horizontal direction, the bullet is centered on the point after the positioning character. This allows enough room for most bullets to print without running over the text around them. Remember that the bullets are circles, however. If you use large bullets, particularly if you use large percentage values, then you may have to adjust your text both horizontally and vertically to allow enough room for the bullet to print.

Using the Effect

The examples in Figure 3-4 also give you some idea of how this effect can be used. At small percentages or with small point sizes, it can be identical to the standard black bullet, with the additional benefit that it will position itself in the center of a line of text. For other purposes, you may want to use smaller or larger bullets and different shades of gray to mark items in your text. These can also be used to represent any round object, such as punch holes, that you want to place in your document.

TIP

This bullet and the bullets that come from the sized bullet effect are subtly different—aside from the more obvious shading, of course—in that these bullets have heavier lines around them. Visually, bullets that are filled, especially with darker shades of gray, need a heavy line around the edge if the line is going to be visible. For bullets that are white, however, a heavy line makes the bullet too obvious and intrusive. For these reasons, the two effects use different lines around the edge of the bullet.

BEHIND THE SCENES

> The width of the lines in the effects, such as the line around the bullet, is known technically as the *stroke width* of the line. This value is calculated as a percentage of the font size within each effect, so that the lines are darker and heavier for larger versions of an effect and thinner and lighter for smaller ones. Different sizes of lines in different effects are achieved by varying the calculation for that effect to get a heavier or thinner line at all effect sizes, as required.

DROP SHADOW BULLET

shadow bullet

Description

If you want to use a bullet as a decorative enhancement, you may notice that some people make bullets stand out on the page by placing a shadow behind them. The shadow bullet effect allows you to make a shadow behind your bullet.

Variables

This effect is exactly like the sized bullet effect, except that you can place a shadow behind the bullet. You have controls in the effect for the placement of the shadow in both the horizontal and vertical directions, or the darkness of the shadow, and for the size of the bullet. These four variables are listed in the front of the shadow bullet effect, as shown here:

-03 /Xoff **+03** /Yoff **1.00** /Gray **100** /Pct 9 dict begin ...

You must observe the range and format rules for the variables very strictly. If you don't, the effect may not print.

Xoff/Yoff   You place the shadow behind the box by setting the horizontal distance, called Xoff—an offset in the x, or horizontal, direction. In a similar fashion, the vertical distance for the shadow is called Yoff. Both distances are in points, which are a printer's measure. A point is $^1/_{72}$ inch. You can use either positive or negative values for both Xoff and Yoff. Positive values of Xoff move the shadow to the right, while negative values move it to the left. Positive values of Yoff move the shadow down the page, and negative values move it up the page. You must place plus or minus signs in front of the Xoff and Yoff variables, and you must use two digits, as shown. Acceptable values range from ±00 to ±99. Of course, +00 and −00 are identical and give you the same result: no offset in that direction. Examples of shadowed bullet effects are shown in Figure 3-5.

This is a 24-point bullet with offsets of +4 and +4. The shadow is .50 gray.

This is a 24-point bullet with offsets of +4 and -4. The shadow is .50 gray.

This is a-24-point bullet with offsets of -4 and +4. The shadow is .50 gray.

This is a 24-point bullet with offsets of -4 and -4. The shadow is .50 gray.

Figure 3-5.   Examples of the drop shadow bullet effect

Gray   The darkness of the shadow is set by a control named, reasonably enough, Gray. The values of Gray are percentages, with 1.00 being black and 0.01 being almost white. Although you can use a value of 0.00 (white), this may be somewhat misleading. That value actually means that nothing is printed behind the bullets—it doesn't cause a white spot on colored paper, for example.

The Gray variable may range from 1.00 to .01. You always need to have a decimal point in the value and two digits after the decimal point, even if you are using exact tenths. For example, use .50 and not .5 as your value.

Pct   Finally, you have the same Pct variable as you have in the sized bullet effect. This allows you to set the ratio of the height of the bullet to the font size used for the positioning character

You can use any percentage values between 10 and 999 for Pct without trouble. This value represents the height of the bullet as a percentage of the font size. A 100 percent bullet is the same size as a capital X.

Size and Position

The shadowed bullet is sized in the same way as the standard bullet effect: The positioning character and the percentage that you set in the Pct variable together determine the size of the bullet. The shadow size matches that of the bullet, as a shadow should. As illustrated in Figure 3-6, the position of the shadow, and therefore the amount of shadow that shows under the bullet, is determined by the Xoff and Yoff variables.

The four examples in Figure 3-5 show you how changes in the offset values move the shadow effect around the bullet itself. As you can see, you can get any variation in shadowing by changing the signs of the offset values.

This is an 18-point bullet at 50% with offsets of -2 and +2.

This is an 18-point bullet at 100% with offsets of -3 and +3.

This is an 18-point bullet at 150% with offsets of -4 and +4.

This is a 24-point bullet at 100% with offsets of -2 and +2 and a black (1.00 gray) shadow.

This is a 24-point bullet at 100% with offsets of -8 and +8 and a .25 gray shadow.

You can use these bullets in a variety of ways:

NOTICE
SEE SOMETHING SPECIAL
PEEK THROUGH THIS HOLE

Figure 3-6. Variations of the drop shadow bullet effect

It can be very difficult to judge the distance that you want to offset the shadow behind your bullet. To set it the way you want, you may have to make some tests with different sized offsets in your document. For that reason, this effect has two knots: It contains variables, and it may require test prints to produce exactly what you want.

Using the Effect

The examples in Figure 3-6 show you some of the interesting variations that you can achieve using shadow placement and sizing. Notice that at smaller percentages, the offset must also be set smaller in order to prevent the shadow from coming out from behind the bullet entirely. The first three examples illustrate how you can compensate for sizing when positioning the shadows. Larger bullets will usually require larger offsets. Notice the examples on lines four and five. These bullets are the same size—24 points—but the shadow is dark and close on one and lighter and farther away on the other.

The last three examples show 14-point bullets with 12-point text and a 1.00 Gray shadow placed +03 points offset in both the horizontal and vertical directions.

TIP

Normally, you use relatively small values for the offsets. If you keep the offset values the same, the shadow looks most natural when it prints. On the other hand, if you want more of a special effect, you can use different values for the offsets, which makes the shadow look somewhat distorted. Also, if you use very large values, and use different values for the x and y offsets, you can generate an almost "random" pattern of bullets sprinkled over the page.

FADED BULLET

faded bullet

Description

The faded bullet effect is essentially a fancy variant of the shadowed bullet. In this case, as shown, it has a longer shadow that changes from white to black over a short distance.

116

Size and Position

The faded bullet is sized in the same way as the standard bullet effect: The positioning character determines the size of the basic bullet, before the faded effect is in place. The faded shadow size is a standard size for all bullets. It extends to the left and below the bullet by a fixed amount, and matches the bullet in all dimensions. As illustrated in Figure 3-7, this gives somewhat different results for different-sized bullets.

The bullet itself is placed just where the standard bullet would appear: centered on the end of the positioning character. If you use the faded bullet effect with small point size text, be sure to allow enough room below the effect so that the faded shadow does not touch the text below and to the left of the effect.

This is an example of the faded bullet at 10 points.

This is an example of the effect at 12 points.

This is an example at 24 points.

This is an example at 60 points.

Figure 3-7.   Examples of the faded bullet effect

Using the Effect

Although this effect looks something like the shadow bullet effect, it has no variables and no controls for shadow placement. Fading a shadow is quite complex and time-consuming, so you

117

don't have alternatives here for shadow placement or coloring. The examples in Figure 3-7 demonstrate how this affects the resulting output. As you can see, smaller point sizes have a faded effect that tails out a great distance relative to the size of the bullet itself. On the other hand, on very large bullets the faded background hardly differs from the simple shadow effect. The best results are generally between 18 and 48 points, but you may want larger or smaller bullets for special purposes.

NUMBERED BULLET

numbered bullet

Description

One of the things that I often use bullets for is to number lists of items or tasks. The numbered bullet effect allows you to do just that, using any numbers from 0 to 99.

Variables

The numbered bullet requires one variable, called Num, which is located at the beginning of the effect, as shown here

```
(99)  /Num 6 dict . . .
```

You must observe the format rules for the variable very strictly. If you don't, the effect may not print.

Num   The Num variable is the number that you want displayed inside the bullet. Notice that the numbers go *inside* the parentheses. You must place your numbers inside these parentheses, and both the left and right parentheses are required for the effect to work correctly. The numbers may range from 0 (or any single digit with a space in front of it) to 99.

Size and Position

Like the previous bullets, the size of these numbered bullets is based on a percentage of the font size used for positioning. Therefore, the numbers inside the bullet themselves are set somewhat smaller than the font that you select for the position-ing character. However, bullets with two digits are larger than those with only one digit. Only the single-digit bullets are the same size as the unnumbered bullets. This allows you to combine numbered and unnumbered bullets in the same text, as long as the numbers are between 0 and 9. In that case, all of the bullets will be the same size as long as they all have the same size positioning character.

On the other hand, bullets with two-digit numbers inside them will be larger than those with a single digit. As a result, using these bullets mixed with standard unnumbered bullets, all with the same size positioning character, will give you two different sizes of bullet. If you want to mix two-digit numbered bullets with other bullets, you should change the positioning character's size and test to see that the bullets will match. Since the same technique is used for all numbered bullets, you can combine regu-lar numbered bullets and reverse numbered bullets in the same text. All of the numbered bullets will be the same size and font as long as they all have the same positioning character and the same number of digits.

All of the example bullets shown in Figure 3-8 are based on a 14-point positioning character. The X next to them on the line of text is also 14 points. As you can see, the bullet is positioned so that its center is in line with the spot where the two lines of the X cross.

In the horizontal direction, the bullet is centered on the point after the positioning character. This allows enough room for most bullets to print without running over the text around them. Remember that the bullets are circles, however. If you use large bullets, particularly if you use double-digit values, then you may have to adjust your text to allow enough room for the bullet to print.

Using the Effect

The examples in Figure 3-8 illustrate an important point when using the numbered bullet effect. Since the bullets themselves are sized to the numbers that go inside them, bullets with two-digit numbers naturally require more room, and hence are larger, than bullets with single-digit numbers. To allow you to use both single- and double-digit numbers in a series of bullets without having the bullets change sizes unexpectedly as you go from 9 to 10, you must insert the single-digit numbers between the parentheses with a space in front of the number. If we use a 'b' to represent the blank space, then a single-digit number would look like this in the effect: (b4). If you are only using numbers from 0 to 9, then you can simply insert the number that you want inside the parentheses, like this: (4). In that case, the bullets are the same size as an unnumbered bullet. The examples show you how to insert both single- and double-digit numbers into the effect, and what the results look like for each choice.

TIP

The example bullets in Figure 3-8 and the X that follows them are all 14-point type. The examples use 14-point Helvetica Bold, since that gives a nice, clear number that is easily visible. If you use numbered bullets at medium or small point sizes, the bold version of a font is generally more legible than the normal version. In much the same way, sans-serif fonts, like Helvetica, are generally more legible inside bullets than serif fonts, like Times.

0   X for single-digit numbered bullets, for example (0)

9   X to (9), use single characters for numbers

10   X for double-digit numbered bullets, for example, (10)

99   X to (99), use two characters for numbers

1   X to mix single digits with double digits, for example (1)

22   X to (22), use two characters even for single-digit numbers

5   X a space followed by the single digit that you want, like this (5)

Figure 3-8.   Examples of the numbered bullet effect

REVERSE NUMBERED BULLET

 reverse numbered bullet

Description

Numbered bullets are so useful that sometimes you'd like to have them very visible on the page, almost using them for special effects. The reverse numbered bullet provides numbered bullets with more impact, because the numbers are in white against a solid black bullet. This form of printing text is known as *reverse* type and so this effect is named to reflect the fact that the numbers inside the bullet are in reverse type. Other than that, these bullets work exactly like the regular numbered bullets.

Variables

The reverse numbered bullet requires one variable, called Num, which is located at the beginning of the effect, as shown here:

```
(99)  /Num 6 dict . . .
```

Note that you must observe the format rules for the variable very strictly. If you don't, the effect may not print.

Num   The Num variable is the number that you want displayed inside the bullet. Notice that the numbers go *inside* the parentheses. You must place your numbers inside these parentheses, and both the left and right parentheses are required for the effect to work correctly. The numbers may range from 0 (or any single digit with a space in front of it) to 99.

Size and Position

Like the previous numbered bullets, these bullets are sized to the numbers that are inserted into them, and not simply as a percentage of the font size used for positioning. Bullets with two-digit numbers inside them will be larger than those with a single digit. As a result, using these bullets mixed with standard unnumbered bullets, all using the same size of positioning character, will give you two different sizes of bullet if you use two-digit numbers. If you want to mix two-digit numbered bullets with other bullets, you should change the positioning character's size and test to see that the bullets will match. Since the same technique is used for the reverse numbers as is used for the regular numbered bullets, you can combine regular numbered bullets and reverse numbered bullets in the same text. All of the numbered bullets will be the same size and font as long as they all have the same positioning character and the same number of digits.

All of the example bullets shown in Figure 3-9 are based on a 14-point positioning character. The X next to them on the line of text is also 14 points. As you can see, the bullet is positioned so that its center is in line with the spot where the two lines of the X cross.

0 X for single-digit numbered bullets, for example, (0)

9 X to (9), use single characters for numbers

10 X for double-digit numbered bullets, for example, (10)

99 X to (99), use two characters for numbers

1 X to mix single digits with double digits, for example, (1)

22 X to (22), use two characters even for single-digit numbers

5 X a space followed by the single digit that you want, like this (5).

Figure 3-9. Examples of the reverse numbered bullet effect

In the horizontal direction, the bullet is centered on the point after the positioning character. This allows enough room for most bullets to print without running over the text around them. Remember that the bullets are circles, however. If you use large bullets, particularly if you use double-digit values, then you may have to adjust your text to allow enough room for the bullet to print.

Using the Effect

The examples in Figure 3-9 illustrate an important point when using the reverse numbered bullet effect. Since the bullets themselves are sized to the numbers that go inside them, bullets with two-digit numbers naturally require more room, and hence are larger, than bullets with single-digit numbers. To allow you to use both single- and double-digit numbers in a series of bullets without having the bullets change sizes unexpectedly as you go from 9 to 10, you must insert the single-digit numbers between the parentheses with a space in front of the number. If we use a 'b' to represent the blank space, then a single digit number would look like this in the effect: (b4). If you are only using numbers from 0 to 9, then you can simply insert the number that you want inside the parentheses, like this: (4). The examples show you how to insert both single- and double-digit numbers into the effect, and what the results look like for each choice.

TIP

The example bullets in Figure 3-9 and the X that follows them are all 14-point type. The examples use 14-point Helvetica Bold, since that gives a nice, clear number that is easily visible. Even more than regular numbered bullets, it is essential to make your numbers very legible when they are printed in reverse. At almost all point sizes the bold version of a font is more legible than the normal version. In the same way, sans-serif fonts, like Helvetica, are quite a bit more legible inside bullets than serif fonts, like Times. In general, for reverse numbered bullets, I recommend using bold, sans-serif fonts in all cases unless you have some special reason for using other fonts.

PLACED NUMBERED BULLET

placed num bullet

Description

Nice as it is to have numbered bullets, sometimes I want a bullet that is smaller than the font that I am using, like a standard bullet with a small number inside it. The placed numbered bullet effect allows you to choose the point size of the number inside your bullet and then place the bullet in the center of a line of text of a different size.

Variables

The placed numbered bullet effect requires two variables. These two variables occur at the front of the effect text, as shown here:

```
(88) /Num 24 /Ps 7 dict . . .
```

Note that you must observe the range and format rules for the variables very strictly. If you don't, the effect may not print.

Num The first is the Num variable, which sets the number that you will display inside the bullet. Notice that the numbers go *inside* the parentheses. You must place your numbers inside these parentheses, and both the left and right parentheses are required for the effect to work correctly. The numbers may range from 0 (or any single digit with a space in front of it) to 99.

Ps The second is the Ps variable, which is the point size of the font that you want to match with the bullet. The Ps variable controls the placement of the bullet in a vertical plane. The bullet is positioned so that the center of the bullet will be at the center of a capital X of the given point size. Acceptable values for the Ps variable range from 1 to 99 points.

88

125

Size and Position

Like the previous numbered bullets, these bullets are sized to the numbers that are inserted into them, and not simply as a percentage of the font size used for positioning. Bullets with two-digit numbers inside them will be larger than those with a single digit.

The examples in Figure 3-10 illustrate how the bullets are positioned. For each of the first four examples, the positioning character is set in 12-point Helvetica Bold, while the Ps variable is set to the size of the X in the line of text that follows. The result is that the bullet moves up to align its center with the center of the capital X that follows it. As in the other bullet effects, bullets that contain only a single number, like the third bullet in the examples, are slightly smaller than bullets that contain single-digit numbers with a preceding blank, like the second bullet. The fifth example shows you a 9-point bullet centered on a 14-point line of text. As you see, the positioning works the same way for larger point sizes.

In the horizontal direction, the bullet is centered on the point after the positioning character. This allows enough room for most bullets to print without running over the text around them. Remember that the bullets are circles, however. If you use large bullets, particularly if you use double-digit values, then you may have to adjust your text to allow enough room for the bullet to print.

Using the Effect

The examples in Figure 3-10 show you some of the uses for numbered bullets. You should note an important point when using the placed numbered bullet effect. Like the other numbered bullets, the bullets themselves are sized to the numbers that go inside them. Therefore, bullets with two-digit numbers naturally require more room, and hence are larger, than bullets with single-digit numbers. To allow you to use both single- and double-digit numbers in a series of bullets without having the bullets change

(12) **X** 24-point X with 12-point bullet

(8) **X** 18-point X with 12-point bullet—note that the number here is preceded by a blank (8) to make the bullet the same size as the one above

(8) **X** 20-point X with 12-point bullet—note that the number here is *not* preceded by a blank (8) so that the bullet is slightly smaller than the one above

(11) **X** 22-point X with 12-point bullet

(4) **X** 14-point X with 9-point bullet

(**24**) X 12-point X with 24-point bullet

Figure 3-10. Examples of the placed numbered bullet effect

sizes unexpectedly as you go from 9 to 10, you must insert the single-digit numbers between the parentheses with a space in front of the number. If we use a 'b' to represent the blank space, then a single digit number would look like this in the effect: (b4). If you are only using numbers from 0 to 9, then you can simply insert the number that you want inside the parentheses, like this: (4). The examples in Figure 3-8 under the numbered bullet effect show you how to insert both single- and double-digit numbers into the effect, and what the results look like for each choice.

The last example in Figure 3-10 illustrates a use for these placed bullets that might not occur to you offhand. Besides placing small bullets in the middle of a line of larger text, you can also use the variables to place a large bullet in the middle of a line of smaller text. This is often visually more appealing than simply using the numbered bullet with a large point size and following it with smaller text, because the bullet doesn't seem to tower over the text so much.

TIP

The examples in Figure 3-10 use Helvetica Bold for the numbers, since that gives a nice, clear number that is easily visible. Because these bullets are generally smaller than the regular numbered bullets, it is more important to make your numbers legible. At almost all point sizes the bold version of a font is more legible than the normal version. In the same way, sans-serif fonts, like Helvetica, are quite a bit more legible inside bullets than serif fonts, like Times.

PLACED REVERSE NUMBERED BULLET

placed reverse num bullet

Description

The placed reverse numbered bullet has the same relationship to the placed numbered bullet that the reverse numbered bullet has to the numbered bullet: It is the same effect but with the number printed in white on a solid black background.

Variables

The placed reverse numbered bullet effect requires two variables. These two variables occur at the front of the effect text, as shown here:

(88) /Num **24** /Ps 7 dict ...

Note that you must observe the range and format rules for the variables very strictly. If you don't, the effect may not print.

Num   The first is the Num variable, which sets the number that you will display inside the bullet. Notice that the numbers go *inside* the parentheses. You must place your numbers inside these parentheses, and both the left and right parentheses are required for the effect to work correctly. The numbers may range from 0 (or any single digit with a space in front of it) to 99.

Ps   The second is the Ps variable, which is the point size of the font that you want to match with the bullet. The Ps variable controls the placement of the bullet in a vertical plane. The bullet is positioned so that the center of the bullet will be at the center of a capital X of the given point size. Acceptable values for the Ps variable range from 1 to 99 points.

Size and Position

Like the previous numbered bullets, these bullets are sized to the numbers that are inserted into them, and not simply as a percentage of the font size used for positioning. Bullets with two-digit numbers inside them will be larger than those with a single digit.

The examples for this effect illustrate how the bullets are positioned. For each of the first four examples, the positioning character is set in 12-point Helvetica Bold, while the Ps variable is set to the size of the line of text that follows. The result is that the bullet moves up to align its center with the center of the capital X that follows it. As in the other bullet effects, bullets that contain only a single number, like the third bullet in the examples, are slightly smaller than bullets that contain single-digit numbers with a preceding blank, like the second bullet. The fifth example shows you a 9-point bullet centered on a 14-point line of text. As you see, the positioning works the same way for larger point sizes.

In the horizontal direction, the bullet is centered on the point after the positioning character. This allows enough room for most bullets to print without running over the text around them. Remember that the bullets are circles, however. If you use large bullets, particularly if you use double-digit values, then you may have to adjust your text to allow enough room for the bullet to print.

Using the Effect

The examples in Figure 3-11 show you some of the uses for placed reverse numbered bullets. You should note an important point when using the placed reverse numbered bullet effect. Like the other numbered bullets, the bullets themselves are sized to the numbers that go inside them. Therefore, bullets with two-digit numbers naturally require more room, and hence are larger, than bullets with single-digit numbers. To allow you to use both single- and double-digit numbers in a series of bullets without having the bullets change sizes unexpectedly as you go from 9 to 10, you must insert the single-digit numbers between the parentheses with a space in front of the number. If we use a 'b' to represent the blank space, then a single-digit number would look like this in the effect: (b4). If you are only using numbers from 0 to 9, then you can simply insert the number that you want inside the parentheses, like this: (4). See the examples in Figure 3-9 under the reverse numbered bullet effect as an illustration of how to insert single- and double-digit numbers into the effect, and what the results look like for each choice.

The last example in Figure 3-11 illustrates a use for these placed bullets that might not occur to you offhand. Besides placing small bullets in the middle of a line of larger text, you can also use the variables to place a large bullet centered in a line of smaller text. This is often visually more appealing than simply using the numbered bullet with a large point size and following it with smaller text, because the bullet doesn't seem to tower over the text so much.

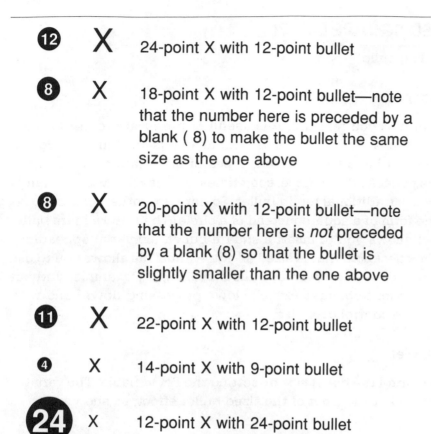

12 X   24-point X with 12-point bullet

8 X   18-point X with 12-point bullet—note that the number here is preceded by a blank (8) to make the bullet the same size as the one above

8 X   20-point X with 12-point bullet—note that the number here is *not* preceded by a blank (8) so that the bullet is slightly smaller than the one above

11 X   22-point X with 12-point bullet

4 X   14-point X with 9-point bullet

24 X   12-point X with 24-point bullet

Figure 3-11. Examples of the placed reverse numbered bullet

TIP

The examples in Figure 3-11 use Helvetica Bold for the numbers, since that gives a nice, clear number that is easily visible. Because sized bullets are generally smaller than the regular numbered bullets, and reverse type is harder to read than normal type, it is essential to make your numbers legible. At almost all point sizes the bold version of a font is more legible than the normal version. In the same way, sans-serif fonts, like Helvetica, are quite a bit more legible inside bullets than serif fonts, like Times, particularly when displayed in reverse.

SIZED SQUARE BULLET

sized sq bullet

Description

Sometimes you find that it is useful or necessary to use two different types of bullets: in lists with headings and subheadings, or when you have two different types of information listed on the same page. And, of course, sometimes you may just want a change from the traditional round bullet. So here is another form of bullet in the form of a square instead of a circle. The sized square bullet effect allows you to insert a square bullet, similar in appearance to the checkbox, that is sized as you want. This allows you to use various sizes and types of bullets in lists, for example, without multiple font changes (which slows processing down) and with complete control over size.

Variables

You control the bullet size by setting the Pct variable. The variable is located at the front of the sized bullet effect, as shown here.

```
100 /Pct 6 dict ...
```

You must observe the format rules and range limits for the variable very strictly. If you don't, the effect may not print.

Pct   The Pct variable allows you to set the ratio of the diameter of the bullet to the font size used for the positioning character. This value represents the size of the bullet as a percentage of the font size. You can use any percentage values between 10 and 999 for Pct without trouble. A 100 percent bullet is the same size as a capital X.

Size and Position

The examples in Figure 3-12 illustrate how your bullet is sized. The percentage shown in the text next to the bullets is the value placed into each effect for Pct. As you see, the 25 percent bullet is one quarter of the height of the line of characters, the 50 percent bullet is half the height, and so on, up to the 200 percent bullet which is twice as high. Obviously, using 100 percent gives you a bullet that is the same height as the font. Using the Pct variable along with the font size, you can make your bullet effect any size you want.

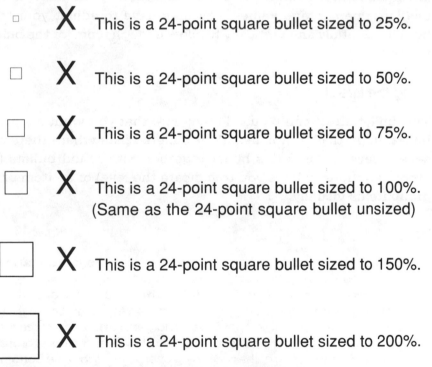

□ X This is a 24-point square bullet sized to 25%.

□ X This is a 24-point square bullet sized to 50%.

□ X This is a 24-point square bullet sized to 75%.

□ X This is a 24-point square bullet sized to 100%. (Same as the 24-point square bullet unsized)

□ X This is a 24-point square bullet sized to 150%.

□ X This is a 24-point square bullet sized to 200%.

Figure 3-12.   Examples of the sized square bullet effect

Figure 3-12 also shows you how the Pct variable affects your bullet. All of the example bullets are based on a 24-point positioning character. The X next to them on the line of text is also 24 points. As you can see, the bullet is positioned so that its center is in line with the spot where the two lines of the X cross. The 100 percent bullet also shows you that the bullet, like the checkbox, is the size of a capital X in your designated font.

In the horizontal direction, the bullet is centered, like the checkboxes in Chapter 2, on the point after the positioning character. This allows enough room for most bullets to print without running over the text around them. Remember that the bullets are squares, however. If you use large bullets, particularly if you use large percentage values, you may have to adjust your text both horizontally and vertically to allow enough room for the bullet to print.

Using the Effect

This bullet effect can be used anywhere that you want a square bullet. In particular, it is useful for bulleted lists where there are several levels. Using this bullet together with round bullets (or other variations) allows you to indicate the level of an item or to group items visually.

TIP

The square bullet can also be used as an alternative to the checkbox effect if you want a checkbox that is sized differently than your text. Notice that there is a difference in how the box is placed. For the checkbox effects, the bottom of the checkbox is always on the same baseline as the following text, even if you have used a larger or smaller point size for the positioning character. For the square bullet, however, the bullet aligns its center with the center of the positioning character, so that the bottom of the box moves above or below the line of text, depending on the percentage that you have set.

FILLED SQUARE BULLET

filled sq bullet

Description

The sized square bullet effect can be used to provide a basic square bullet, but it does not provide all of the variations that are required for a full set of bullets. The filled square bullet effect allows you to use a square bullet that is filled with any shade of gray. Other than being a square, this effect is identical to the filled bullet effect, which draws a round bullet.

Variables

Like the sized square bullet, the filled square bullet uses a Pct variable to set the size of the bullet as a percentage of the font size. It adds a Gray variable to allow you to set the color of your bullet. Both variables are located at the front of the filled bullet effect, as shown here:

1.00 /Gray **100** /Pct 7 dict...

You must observe the format rules and range limits for the variables very strictly. If you don't, the effect may not print.

Gray   The color that fills the effect is set by a control named, reasonably enough, Gray. The values of Gray are percentages, with 1.00 being black and 0.01 being almost white. Although you can use a value of 0.00 (white), this may be somewhat misleading. That value actually means that nothing is printed inside the bullets—it doesn't cause a white spot on colored paper, for example.

The Gray variable may range from 1.00 to .01. You always need to have a decimal point in the value and two digits after the decimal point, even if you are using exact tenths. For example, use .50 and not .5 as your value. If you don't, the effect may not print.

135

Pct   The Pct variable allows you to set the ratio of the diameter of the bullet to the font size used for the positioning character. This value represents the diameter of the bullet as a percentage of the font size. You can use any percentage values between 10 and 999 for Pct without trouble. A 100 percent bullet is the same size as a capital X.

Size and Position

The examples in Figure 3-13 illustrate how your bullet is sized and colored. The text next to the bullets shows both the value placed into each effect for Pct and the value inserted for Gray. As you see, the variations are just what you would expect. Obviously, using 100 percent size (100 /Pct) and 100 percent gray (1.00 /Gray) gives you a bullet that is completely black and the same height as the font.

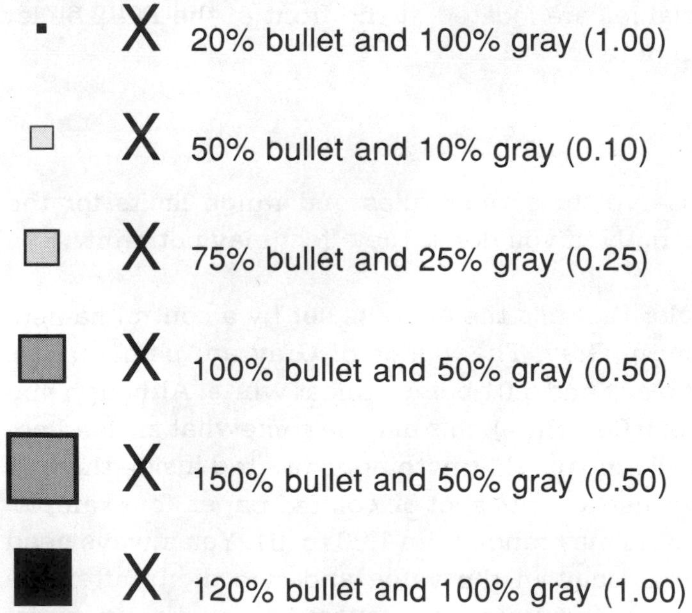

X 20% bullet and 100% gray (1.00)

X 50% bullet and 10% gray (0.10)

X 75% bullet and 25% gray (0.25)

X 100% bullet and 50% gray (0.50)

X 150% bullet and 50% gray (0.50)

X 120% bullet and 100% gray (1.00)

Figure 3-13.   Examples of the filled bullet effect

All of the example bullets shown in Figure 3-13 are based on a 24-point positioning character. The X next to them on the line of text is also 24 points. As you can see, the bullet is positioned so that its center is in line with the spot where the two lines of the X cross. The 100 percent bullet also shows you that the bullet, like the checkbox, is the size of a capital X in your designated font.

In the horizontal direction, the bullet is centered on the point after the positioning character. This allows enough room for most bullets to print without running over the text around them. Remember that the bullets are circles, however. If you use large bullets, particularly if you use large percentage values, then you may have to adjust your text both horizontally and vertically to allow enough room for the bullet to print.

Using the Effect

The examples in Figure 3-13 also give you some idea of how this effect can be used. At small percentages or with small point sizes, it can be used exactly like the standard black bullet, except that it's square and will align its center with the center of the positioning character. For other purposes, you may want to use smaller or larger bullets and different shades of gray to mark items in your text. These can also be used to represent any square object, such as a missing item of information or a box, that you want to place in your document.

DROP SHADOW SQUARE BULLET

shadow sq bullet

Description

If you want to use a bullet as a decorative enhancement, you may notice that some people make a bullet stand out on the page by placing a shadow behind it. The shadow square bullet effect allows you to make a shadow behind a square bullet.

This bullet is almost identical to the shadow checkbox effect in Chapter 2. The difference is that you can control the size of this bullet, where the shadow checkbox is always the same size as the positioning character. Essentially, this bullet bears the same relation to the shadow checkbox as the sized square bullet does to the checkbox. Since checkboxes are mostly intended to match the text around them, while bullets are often smaller than the text, this seemed like the correct place to discuss square bullets.

Variables

This effect is exactly like the bullet effect, except that you can place a shadow behind the bullet. You have controls in the effect for the placement of the shadow in both the horizontal and vertical directions, for the darkness of the shadow, and for the size of the bullet. These four variables are listed in the front of the shadow square bullet effect, as shown here:

```
-03 /Xoff +03 /Yoff 1.00 /Gray 100 /Pct 9 dict begin ...
```

Note that you must observe the range and format rules for the variables very strictly. If you don't, the effect may not print.

Xoff/Yoff   You place the shadow behind the box by setting the horizontal distance, called Xoff—an offset in the x, or horizontal, direction. In a similar fashion, the vertical distance for the shadow is called Yoff. Both distances are in points, which are a printer's measure. A point is $1/72$ inch. You can use either positive or negative values for both Xoff and Yoff. Positive values of Xoff move the shadow to the right, while negative values move it to the left. Positive values of Yoff move the shadow down the page, and negative values move it up the page. You must place plus or minus signs in front of the Xoff and Yoff variables, and you must use two digits, as shown. Acceptable values range from ±00 to ±99. Of course, +00 and − 00 are identical and give you the same result: no offset in that direction. Examples of shadowed square bullet effects are shown in Figure 3-14.

Gray   The darkness of the shadow is set by a control named, reasonably enough, Gray. The values of Gray are percentages, with 1.00 being black and 0.01 being almost white. Although you can use a value of 0.00 (white), this may be somewhat misleading. That value actually means that nothing is printed behind the bullet; it doesn't cause a white spot on colored paper, for example.

The Gray variable may range from 1.00 to .01. You always need to have a decimal point in the value two digits after the decimal point, even if you are using exact tenths. For example, use .50 and not .5 as your value.

Pct   Finally, you have the same Pct variable as you have in the sized square bullet effect. This allows you to set the ratio of the height of the bullet to the font size used for the positioning character.

You can use any percentage values between 10 and 999 for Pct without trouble. This value represents the height of the bullet as a percentage of the font size. A 100 percent bullet is the same size as a capital X.

Size and Position

The shadowed square bullet is sized in the same way as the standard sized bullet effect: The positioning character and the percentage that you set in the Pct variable together determine the size of the bullet. The shadow size matches that of the bullet, as a shadow should. As illustrated in Figure 3-15, the position of the shadow, and therefore the amount of shadow that shows under the bullet, is determined by the Xoff and Yoff variables.

The four examples in Figure 3-14 show you how changes in the offset values move the shadow effect around the bullet itself. As you see, you can get any variation in shadowing by changing the signs of the offset values.

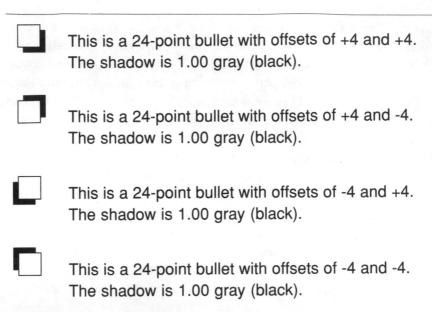

This is a 24-point bullet with offsets of +4 and +4. The shadow is 1.00 gray (black).

This is a 24-point bullet with offsets of +4 and -4. The shadow is 1.00 gray (black).

This is a 24-point bullet with offsets of -4 and +4. The shadow is 1.00 gray (black).

This is a 24-point bullet with offsets of -4 and -4. The shadow is 1.00 gray (black).

Figure 3-14. Examples of the drop shadow square bullet effect

It can be very difficult to judge the distance that you want to offset the shadow behind your bullet. To set it the way you want, you may have to make some tests with different sized offsets in your document. For that reason, this effect has two knots: It contains variables, and it may require test prints to produce exactly what you want.

Using the Effect

The examples in Figure 3-15 show you some of the interesting variations that you can achieve using shadow placement and sizing. Notice that at smaller percentages, the offset must also be set smaller to prevent the shadow from coming out from behind the bullet entirely. The first three examples in Figure 3-15 illustrate how you can compensate for sizing when positioning the shadows. Larger bullets will usually require larger offsets, as you might imagine. Notice the examples on lines four and five. These bullets are the same size—24 points—but the shadow is dark and close on one and lighter and farther away on the other.

This is an 18-point bullet at 50% with offsets of -2 and +2.

This is an 18-point bullet at 100% with offsets of -3 and +3.

This is an 18-point bullet at 150% with offsets of -4 and +4.

This is a 24-point bullet at 100% with offsets of -2 and +2 and a black (1.00 gray) shadow.

This is a 24-point bullet at 100% with offsets of -8 and +8 and a .25 gray shadow.

You can use these bullets in a variety of ways:

NOTICE
SEE SOMETHING SPECIAL
PEEK THROUGH THIS HOLE

Figure 3-15. Variations of the drop shadow square bullet effect

The last three examples show 14-point bullets with 12-point text and the 1.00 Gray shadow placed +03 points offset in both the horizontal and vertical directions.

99

NUMBERED SQUARE BULLET

numbered sq bullet

Description

One of the things that I often use bullets for is to number lists of items or tasks. The numbered square bullet effect allows you to do just that, using any numbers from 0 to 99. Numbered square bullets can also be combined with numbered round bullets to indicate various levels or task structures in lists.

Variables

The numbered square bullet requires one variable, called Num, which is located at the beginning of the effect, as shown here:

```
(99)  /Num 8 dict...
```

Note that you must observe the format rules for the variable very strictly. If you don't, the effect may not print.

Num   The Num variable is the number that you want displayed inside the bullet. Notice that the numbers go *inside* the parentheses. You must place your numbers inside these parentheses, and both the left and right parentheses are required for the effect to work correctly. The numbers may range from 0 (or any single digit with a space in front of it) to 99.

Size and Position

Like the previous bullets, the size of these numbered square bullets is based on a percentage of the font size used for positioning. Therefore, the numbers inside the bullet themselves are set somewhat smaller than the font that you select for the positioning character. However, bullets with two digits are larger than those with only one digit. Only the single-digit bullets are the same size as the unnumbered square bullets. This allows you to combine numbered and unnumbered bullets in the same text, as long as the numbers are between 0 and 9. In that case, all of the bullets will be the same size as long as they all have the same size positioning character.

On the other hand, bullets with two-digit numbers inside them will be larger than those with a single digit. As a result, using these bullets mixed with standard unnumbered bullets, all using the same size of positioning character, will give you two different sizes of bullet if you use two-digit numbers. If you want to mix two-digit numbered bullets with other bullets, you should change the positioning character's size and test to see that the bullets will match. Since the same technique is used for all numbered bullets, you can combine both round and square numbered bullets and reverse numbered bullets in the same text. All of the numbers inside the bullets will be the same size and font as long as they all have the same positioning character and the same number of digits.

All of the example bullets in Figure 3-16 below are based on a 14-point positioning character. The X next to them on the line of text is also 14 points. As you can see, the bullet is positioned so that its center is in line with the spot where the two lines of the X cross.

In the horizontal direction, the bullet is centered on the point after the positioning character. This allows enough room for most bullets to print without running over the text around them. Remember that the bullets are squares, however. If you use large bullets, particularly if you use large percentage values, then you may have to adjust your text both horizontally and vertically to allow enough room for the bullet to print.

0	X	for single-digit numbered bullets; for example, (0)
9	X	to (9), use single characters for numbers
10	X	for double-digit numbered bullets; for example, (10)
99	X	to (99), use two characters for numbers
1	X	to mix single digits with double digits; for example, (1)
22	X	to (22), use two characters even for single-digit numbers
5	X	a space followed by the single digit that you want, like this (5).

Figure 3-16. Examples of the numbered square bullet effect

Using the Effect

The examples in Figure 3-16 illustrate an important point when using the numbered square bullet effect. Since the bullets themselves are sized to the numbers that go inside them, bullets with two-digit numbers naturally require more room, and hence are larger, than bullets with single-digit numbers. To allow you to use both single- and double-digit numbers in a series of bullets without having the bullets change sizes unexpectedly as you go from 9 to 10, you must insert the single-digit numbers between the parentheses with a space in front of the number. If we use a 'b' to represent the blank space, then a single digit number would look like this in the effect: (b4). If you are only using numbers from

0 to 9, then you can simply insert the number that you want inside the parentheses, like this: (4). The examples show you how to insert both single- and double-digit numbers into the effect, and what the results look like for each choice.

TIP

The examples use 14-point Helvetica Bold for the positioning character, since that gives a nice, clear number that is easily visible. If you use numbered bullets at medium or small point sizes, the bold version of a font is generally more legible than the normal version. In much the same way, sans-serif fonts, like Helvetica, are generally more legible inside bullets than serif fonts, like Times.

REVERSE NUMBERED SQUARE BULLET

reverse num sq bullet

Description

Numbered bullets are so useful that sometimes you'd like to have them very visible on the page. The reverse numbered square bullet provides numbered bullets with more impact, because the numbers are in white against a solid black bullet. Other than that, these bullets work exactly like the regular numbered square bullets.

Variables

The reverse numbered square bullet requires one variable, called Num, which is located at the beginning of the effect, as shown here:

```
(99) /Num 8 dict . . .
```

Note that you must observe the format rules for the variable very strictly. If you don't, the effect may not print.

Num   The Num variable is the number that you want displayed inside the bullet. Notice that the numbers go *inside* the parentheses. You must place your numbers inside these parentheses, and both the left and right parentheses are required for the effect to work correctly. The numbers may range from 0 (or any single digit with a space in front of it) to 99.

Size and Position

Like the previous bullets, the size of these reverse numbered square bullets is based on a percentage of the font size used for positioning. Therefore, the numbers inside the bullet themselves are set somewhat smaller than the font that you select for the positioning character. However, bullets with two digits are larger than those with only one digit. Only the single-digit bullets are the same size as the unnumbered bullets. This allows you to combine numbered and unnumbered bullets in the same text, as long as the numbers are between 0 and 9. In that case, all of the bullets will be the same size as long as they all have the same size positioning character.

On the other hand, bullets with two-digit numbers inside them will be larger than those with a single digit. As a result, using these bullets mixed with standard unnumbered bullets, all with the same size positioning character, will give you two different sizes of bullet if you use two-digit numbers. If you want to mix two-digit numbered bullets with other bullets, you should change the positioning character's size and test to see that the bullets will match. Since the same technique is used for all numbered bullets, you can combine both square and round numbered bullets and reverse numbered bullets in the same text. All of the numbers inside the bullets will be the same size and font as long as they all have the same positioning character and the same number of digits.

All of the example bullets in Figure 3-17 are based on a 14-point positioning character. The X next to them on the line of text is also 14 points. As you can see, the bullet is positioned so that its center is in line with the spot where the two lines of the X cross.

In the horizontal direction, the bullet is centered on the point after the positioning character. This allows enough room for most bullets to print without running over the text around them. Remember that the bullets are squares, however. If you use large bullets, particularly if you use large percentage values, then you may have to adjust your text both horizontally and vertically to allow enough room for the bullet to print.

0   X   for single-digit numbered bullets; for example, (0)

9   X   to (9), use single characters for numbers

10   X   for double-digit numbered bullets; for example, (10)

99   X   to (99), use two characters for numbers

1   X   to mix single digits with double digits; for example, (1)

22   X   to (22), use two characters even for single-digit numbers

5   X   a space followed by the single digit that you want, like this (5).

Figure 3-17. Examples of the reverse numbered square bullet effect

Using the Effect

The examples in Figure 3-17 illustrate an important point when using the reverse numbered square bullet effect. Since the bullets themselves are sized to the numbers that go inside them, bullets with two-digit numbers naturally require more room, and hence are larger, than bullets with single-digit numbers. To allow you to use both single- and double-digit numbers in a series of bullets without having the bullets change sizes unexpectedly as you go from 9 to 10, you must insert the single-digit numbers between the parentheses with a space in front of the number. If we use a 'b' to represent the blank space, then a single digit number would look like this in the effect: (b4). If you are only using numbers from 0 to 9, then you can simply insert the number that you want inside the parentheses, like this: (4). The examples show you both how to insert single- and double-digit numbers into the effect, and what the results look like for each choice.

TIP

The positioning characters for the example bullets in Figure 3-17 use 14-point Helvetica Bold, since that gives a nice, clear number that is easily visible. Even more than regular numbered bullets, it is essential to make your numbers very legible when they are printed in reverse. At almost all point sizes the bold version of a font is more legible than the normal version. In the same way, sans-serif fonts, like Helvetica, are quite a bit more legible inside bullets than serif fonts, like Times. In general, for reverse numbered bullets, I recommend using bold, sans-serif fonts in all cases unless you have some special reason for using other types of fonts.

PLACED NUMBERED SQUARE BULLET

placed num sq bullet

Description

Nice as it is to have numbered bullets, sometimes I want a bullet that is smaller than the font that I am using, more like a standard bullet but with a small number inside it. The placed numbered square bullet effect allows you to choose the point size of the number inside your bullet and then align the center of the bullet in the center of the positioning character. This effect is essentially identical to the placed numbered bullet effect, except the bullet is square instead of round.

Variables

The placed numbered square bullet effect requires two variables. These two variables occur at the front of the effect text, as shown here:

```
(88)  /Num 24 /Ps 7 dict ...
```

Note that you must observe the range and format rules for the variables very strictly. If you don't, the effect may not print.

Num   The first is the Num variable, which sets the number that you will display inside the bullet. Notice that the numbers go *inside* the parentheses. You must place your numbers inside these parentheses, and both the left and right parentheses are required for the effect to work correctly. The numbers may range from 0 (or any single digit with a space in front of it, as you will see in the example text and discussion that follow) to 99.

Ps   The second is the Ps variable, which is the point size of the font that you want to match with the bullet. The Ps variable controls the placement of the bullet in a vertical plane. The bullet is positioned so that the center of the bullet will be at the center of a capital X of the given point size. Acceptable values for the Ps variable range from 1 to 99 points.

Size and Position

Like numbered bullets, these bullets are sized to the numbers that are inserted into them, and not simply as a percentage of the font size used for positioning. Bullets with two-digit numbers inside them will be larger than those with a single digit.

The examples in Figure 3-18 illustrate how the bullets are positioned. For each of the first four examples, the positioning character is set in 14-point Helvetica Bold, while the Ps variable is set to the size of the X in the line of text that follows. The result is that the bullet moves up to align its center with the center of the capital X. As in the other bullet effects, bullets that contain only a single number, like the third bullet in the examples, are slightly smaller than bullets that contain single-digit numbers with a preceding blank, like the second bullet. The fifth example shows you a 10-point bullet centered on a 14-point X. As you can see, the positioning works the same way for larger point sizes.

14   X   24 point with 14 pt bullet

5   X   18 point with 14 pt bullet

4   X   20 point with 14 pt bullet

10   X   22 point with 14 pt bullet

8   X   14 point with 10 pt bullet

Figure 3-18. Examples of the placed numbered square bullet effect

In the horizontal direction, the bullet is centered on the point after the positioning character. This allows enough room for most bullets to print without running over the text around them. Remember that the bullets are squares, however. If you use large bullets, particularly if you use double-digit values, then you may have to adjust your text to allow enough room for the bullet to print.

Using the Effect

You should note an important point when using the placed numbered square bullet effect. Like the other numbered bullets, the bullets themselves are sized to the numbers that go inside them. Therefore, bullets with two-digit numbers naturally require more room, and hence are larger, than bullets with single-digit numbers. To allow you to use both single- and double-digit numbers in a series of bullets without having the bullets change sizes unexpectedly as you go from 9 to 10, you must insert the single-digit numbers between the parentheses with a space in front of the number. If we use a 'b' to represent the blank space, then a single-digit number would look like this in the effect: (b4). If you are only using numbers from 0 to 9, then you can simply insert the number that you want inside the parentheses, like this: (4). See the examples in Figure 3-16 under the numbered square bullet effect as an illustration of how to insert single- and double-digit numbers into the effect, and what the results look like for each choice.

TIP

The examples in Figure 3-16 use Helvetica Bold for the numbers, since that gives a nice, clear number that is easily visible. Because placed bullets are generally smaller than the regular numbered bullets, it is more important to make your numbers very legible. At almost all point sizes the bold version of a font is more legible than the normal version. In the same way, sans-serif fonts, like Helvetica, are quite a bit more legible inside bullets than serif fonts, like Times.

88

PLACED REVERSE NUMBERED SQUARE BULLET

placed reverse num sq bullet

Description

The placed reverse numbered square bullet has the same relationship to the placed numbered square bullet that the reverse numbered bullet has to the numbered square bullet: It is the same effect but with the number printed in white on a solid black background.

Variables

The placed reverse numbered square bullet effect requires two variables. These two variables occur at the front of the effect text, as shown here:

```
(88) /Num 24 /Ps 7 dict ...
```

Note that you must observe the range and format rules for the variables very strictly, If you don't, the effect may not print.

Num   The first is the Num variable, which sets the number that you will display inside the bullet. Notice that the numbers go *inside* the parentheses. Both the left and right parentheses are required for the effect to work correctly. The numbers may range from 0 (or any single digit with a space in front of it, as you will see in the example text and discussion that follow) to 99.

Ps   The second is the Ps variable, which is the point size of the font that you want to match with the bullet. The Ps variable controls the placement of the bullet in a vertical plane. The bullet is positioned so that the center of the bullet will be at the center of a capital X of the given point size. Acceptable values for the Ps variable range from 1 to 99 points.

Size and Position

Like the previous numbered bullets, these bullets are sized to the numbers that are inserted into them, and not simply as a percentage of the font size used for positioning. Bullets with two-digit numbers inside them will be larger than those with a single digit.

The examples in Figure 3-19 for this effect illustrate how the bullets are positioned. For each of the first four examples, the positioning character is set in 12-point Helvetica Bold, while the Ps variable is set to the size of the X in the line of text that follows. The result is that the bullet moves up to align its center with the center of the capital X. As in the other bullet effects, bullets that contain only a single number, like the third bullet in the examples, are slightly smaller than bullets that contain single-digit numbers with a preceding blank, like the second bullet. The fifth example shows you a 10-point bullet centered on a 14-point X. As you see, the positioning works the same way for larger point sizes.

In the horizontal direction, the bullet is centered on the point after the positioning character. This allows enough room for most bullets to print without running over the text around them. Remember that the bullets are squares, however. If you use large bullets, particularly if you use double-digit values, then you may have to adjust your text to allow enough room for the bullet to print.

Using the Effect

The examples in Figure 3-19 show you some of the uses for placed reverse numbered square bullets. You should note an important point when using the placed reverse numbered square bullet effect. Like the other numbered square bullets, the bullets themselves are sized to the numbers that go inside them. Therefore, bullets with two-digit numbers naturally require more room, and

[99]   **X**   24-point X with 12-point bullet

[2]   **X**   18-point X with 12-point bullet—note that the number here is preceded by a blank (2) to make the bullet the same size as the one above

[4]   **X**   20-point X with 12-point bullet—note that the number here is *not* preceded by a blank (4) so that the bullet is slightly smaller than the one above

[38]   **X**   22-point X with 12-point bullet

[9]   **X**   14-point with 10-point bullet

Figure 3-19. Examples of the placed reverse numbered square bullet

hence are larger, than bullets with single-digit numbers. To allow you to use both single- and double-digit numbers in a series of bullets without having the bullets change sizes unexpectedly as you go from 9 to 10, you must insert the single-digit numbers between the parentheses with a space in front of the number. If we use a 'b' to represent the blank space, then a single-digit number would look like this in the effect: (b4). If you are only using numbers from 0 to 9, then you can simply insert the number that you want inside the parentheses, like this: (4). See the examples in Figure 3-11 under the reverse numbered bullet effect as an illustration of how to insert single- and double-digit numbers into the effect, and what the results look like for each choice.

TIP

The examples in Figure 3-19 use Helvetica Bold for the numbers, since that gives a nice, clear number that is easily visible. Because placed bullets are generally smaller than the regular numbered bullets, and reverse type is harder to read than normal type, it is essential to make your numbers very legible. At almost all point sizes the bold version of a font is more legible than the normal version. In the same way, sans-serif fonts, like Helvetica, are quite a bit more legible inside bullets than serif fonts, like Times, particularly when displayed in reverse.

RR BULLET

rr bullet

Description

There are times when I want to use a bullet to mark a special point or to use as a signal for action. The rr bullet effect—so called because it contains an 'x', like the signs at railroad crossings—is an example of such a bullet effect.

Variables

You control the bullet size by setting the Pct variable. The variable is located at the front of the rr bullet effect, as shown here:

```
100 /Pct 6 dict . . .
```

You must observe the format rules and range limits for the effect very strictly. If you don't, the effect may not print.

Pct   The Pct variable allows you to set the ratio of the diameter of the bullet to the font size used for the positioning character. This value represents the diameter of the bullet as a percentage of the font size. You can use any percentage values between

10 and 999 for Pct without trouble. A 100 percent bullet is the same size as a capital X.

Size and Position

The examples in Figure 3-20 illustrate how your bullet is sized. The percentage shown in the text next to the bullets is the value placed into each effect for Pct. As you see, the 25 percent bullet is one quarter of the height of the X, the 50 percent bullet is half the height, and so on, up to the 150 percent bullet which is one-and-a-half times as high. Obviously, using 100 percent gives you a bullet that is the same height as the font. Using the Pct variable along with the font size, you can make your bullet effect any size you want.

Figure 3-20 also shows you how the Pct variable affects your bullet. All of the example bullets are based on a 24-point positioning character. The X next to them on the line of text is also 24

Figure 3-20. Examples of the rr bullet effect

points. The 100 percent bullet shows you that the bullet, like the other bullet effects, is the size of a capital X in your designated font.

In the horizontal direction, the bullet is centered on the point after the positioning character. This allows enough room for most bullets to print without running over the text around them. Remember that the bullets are circles, however. If you use large bullets, particularly if you use large percentage values, then you may have to adjust your text both horizontally and vertically to allow enough room for the bullet to print.

Using the Effect

As you can see in Figure 3-20, the bullet is designed so that the center of the bullet is aligned with the center of a capital X of the same size as the positioning character. This works in exactly the same way as the sized bullet effect and allows you to mix the rr bullet with sized bullets and filled bullets in a line either vertically or horizontally without any problems. If you use a percentage value greater than 100 percent, as shown in the last example, then the bullet will be larger than the text but still centered on the line of text.

STOP BULLET

stop bullet

Description

The stop bullet effect produces another special form of round bullet: one with a single line across the bullet. Because this bullet looks something like the signs that show that a function or activity is prohibited, this is referred to as a stop bullet.

Variables

You control the bullet size by setting the Pct variable. The variable is located at the front of the stop bullet effect, as shown here:

```
100 /Pct 6 dict . . .
```

You must observe the format rules and range limits for the variable very strictly. If you don't, the effect may not print.

Pct   The Pct variable allows you to set the ratio of the diameter of the bullet to the font size used for the positioning character. This value represents the diameter of the bullet as a percentage of the font size. You can use any percentage values between 10 and 999 for Pct without trouble. A 100 percent bullet is the same size as a capital X.

Size and Position

The examples in Figure 3-21 illustrate how your bullet is sized. The percentage shown in the text next to the bullets is the value placed into each effect for Pct. As you see, the 25 percent bullet is one-quarter of the height of the X, the 50 percent bullet is half the height, and so on, up to the 150 percent bullet which is one-and-a-half times as high. Obviously, using 100 percent gives you a bullet that is the same height as the font. Using the Pct variable along with the font size, you can make your bullet effect any size you want.

Figure 3-21 also shows you how the Pct variable affects your bullet. All of the example bullets are based on a 24-point positioning character. The X next to them on the line of text is also 24 points. The 100 percent bullet shows you that the bullet, like the other bullet effects, is sized to match the size of a capital X in your designated font.

In the horizontal direction, the bullet is centered on the point after the positioning character. This allows enough room for most bullets to print without running over the text around them

⊘   **X**   25% bullet

⊘   **X**   50% bullet

⊘   **X**   75% bullet

⊘   **X**   100% bullet

⊘   **X**   150% bullet

Figure 3-21. Examples of the stop bullet effect

Remember that the bullets are circles, however. If you use large bullets, particularly if you use large percentage values, then you may have to adjust your text both horizontally and vertically to allow enough room for the bullet to print.

Using the Effect

As you can see in Figure 3-21, the bullet is designed so that the center of the bullet aligns with the center of a capital X of the same size as the positioning character. This works in exactly the same way as the sized bullet effect and allows you to mix the stop bullet with other bullets, such as the rr bullets, sized bullets, and filled bullets, in a line either vertically or horizontally without any problems. If you use a percentage value greater than 100 percent, as shown in the last example, then the bullet will be larger than the text but still centered on the line of text.

Figure 3-22 gives you an example of one way that you might combine these effects in a project chart.

As you can see, each of the types of bullet—rr, stop, sized, and filled—are used in the chart to give immediate visual feedback on

159

Project Status Report

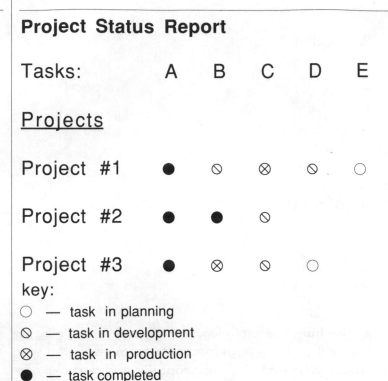

Tasks: A   B   C   D   E

<u>Pro</u>jects

Project #1   ●   ⊘   ⊗   ⊘ .   ○

Project #2   ●   ●   ⊘

Project #3   ●   ⊗   ⊘   ○

key:
○ — task in planning
⊘ — task in development
⊗ — task in production
● — task completed

Figure 3-22. Bullet effects used in a project status chart

the status of several projects with multiple tasks. This can be very useful if you produce this type of report on a regular basis.

STAR

star

Description

The star effect simply draws a five-pointed star at the position specified by the positioning character. The star effect is an open star (the filled star effect, later in this chapter, can be filled in with

160

any shade of gray) and can be used in a wide variety of ways, including as an alternative to ordinary bullets.

Size and Position

The examples in Figure 3-23 show you different sizes of the star effect. The first three lines show stars created using 12-, 18-, and 24-point fonts. Using a different font has no effect on the size or positioning of the star, as you can see by comparing lines three and four, which both display a 24-point star, using the Helvetica and Times fonts. In these four examples, the font and size of the positioning character, which governs the size of the star, is identical to that of the font used in the line of text next to the star.

The second line also demonstrates how the star is sized. The capital X next to the star is in the same font and point size—18-point Helvetica—as the star. As you see, the star is approximately the height of the capital X in the font that you have chosen. Remember that this is the font and size of the *positioning character,* not that of the following text. It's up to you to ensure that these match if you want them to.

The star effect is positioned on the page with the center of the star at the point where the positioning character ends and even with the center of the capital X in height.

☆   X   star bullet at 12 points

☆ X   star bullet at 18 points

☆X   star bullet at 24 points

☆X   star bullet at 24 points

Figure 3-23.   Sizing the basic star effect

If you place text on both sides of the star, be sure to allow some room both before and after the effect text. The effect extends both forward and backward from the end of the positioning character. Since the effect text is invisible in your document, you could erase or obscure some of the text that you want to print if you place it too close to the effect. One way to avoid this is to place one or two spaces between the effect text and the adjacent word of your text. Another good way to make such placements is to use tab settings for placing the effect and the text that follows an effect. This allows you to control more precisely the exact distance between the effect and the beginning of the subsequent text.

Using the Effect

This star effect can be used anywhere that you want a full-sized star. It can also be used to divide text blocks or to set off specific text items. A line or border of small stars is quite eye-catching.

SIZED STAR

sized star

Description

The sized star effect draws a simple, five-pointed star, at the given point. This is one more variant of bullet, which you can use as a replacement for, or in addition to, regular bullets.

Variables

The star has one control, called Pct, which allows you to determine the height of the star in relation to the point size of the font selected by the positioning character. You control the star size by setting the Pct variable. The variable is located at the front of the sized star effect, as shown here:

```
100 /Pct 6 dict . . .
```

You must observe the format rules and range limits for the variable very strictly. If you don't, the effect may not print.

Pct   The Pct variable allows you to set the ratio of the height of the star to the font size used for the positioning character. This value represents the height of the star as a percentage of the font size. You can use any percentage values between 10 and 999 for Pct without trouble. A 100 percent star is the same size as a capital X.

Size and Position

The examples in Figure 3-24 illustrate how your star is sized. The percentage shown in the text next to the star bullets is the value placed into each effect for Pct. As you see, the 25 percent star is one-quarter of the height of the X, the 50 percent star is half the height, and so on, up to the 200 percent star which is twice as high. Obviously, using 100 percent gives you a star that is the same height as the font. Using the Pct variable along with the font size, you can make your star effect any size you want.

Figure 3-24 also shows you how the Pct variable affects your star. All of the example stars are based on a 24-point positioning character. The X next to them on the line of text is also 24 points. As you can see, the center of the star is aligned with the center of the positioning character, where the two lines of the X cross. The 100 percent star also shows you that the star, like the other bullets, is the size of a capital X in your designated font.

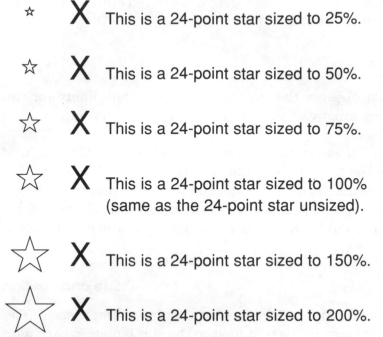

✭   **X** This is a 24-point star sized to 25%.

☆   **X** This is a 24-point star sized to 50%.

☆   **X** This is a 24-point star sized to 75%.

☆   **X** This is a 24-point star sized to 100% (same as the 24-point star unsized).

☆   **X** This is a 24-point star sized to 150%.

☆   **X** This is a 24-point star sized to 200%.

Figure 3-24.   Examples of the sized star effect

In the horizontal direction, the star is centered on the point after the positioning character. This allows enough room for most star bullets to print without running over the text around them. If you use large stars, however, particularly if you use large percentage values when drawing them, then you may have to adjust your text both horizontally and vertically to allow enough room for the star to print.

Using the Effect

This effect can be used anywhere that you would otherwise use standard bullets. In my opinion, the star gives a different feeling to a bulleted list and makes the list and its entries stand out clearly. Stars, particularly at large sizes, can be used as a decorative element in text, to mark an item of special importance, or to decorate a page. A line of stars can also be used to delimit sections of a page. For example, a line of stars might be used to set off a special section of your text that you want the reader to notice or act upon.

FILLED STAR

filled star

Description

Although it's nice to have a star that you can size, sometimes you want to fill the star with a shade of gray. The filled star effect allows you to add gray to your stars.

Variables

Like the sized star, the filled star uses a Pct variable to set the size of the star as a percentage of the font size. It adds a Gray variable to allow you to set the color of your star. Both variables are located at the front of the filled star effect, as shown here:

`1.00 /Gray 100 /Pct 6 dict . . .`

You must observe the format rules and range limits for the variables very strictly. Values outside of these ranges may cause the effect not to print.

Gray   The Gray variable may be anything from 1.00 (black) to .01. Always have a decimal point in the value, and always have two digits after the decimal point, even if you are using exact tenths. For example, use .50 and not .5 as your value.

Pct   The Pct variable allows you to set the ratio of the height of the star to the font size used for the positioning character. This value represents the height of the star as a percentage of the font size. You can use any percentage values between 10 and 999 for Pct without trouble. A 100 percent star is the same size as a capital X.

Size and Position

The examples in Figure 3-25 illustrate how your star is sized and colored. The text next to the stars shows both the value placed into each effect for Pct and the value inserted for Gray. As you see, the variations are just what you would expect. Obviously, using 100 percent size (100 /Pct) and 100 percent gray (1.00 /Gray) gives you a star that is completely black and the same height as the font.

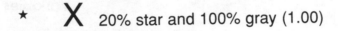

★   X 20% star and 100% gray (1.00)

☆   X 50% star and 10% gray (0.10)

☆   X 75% star and 25% gray (0.25)

★   X 100% star and 50% gray (0.50)

★   X 150% star and 50% gray (0.50)

★   X 120% star and 100% gray (1.00)

Figure 3-25.   Examples of the filled star effect

All of the example stars shown in Figure 3-25 are based on a 24-point positioning character. The X next to them on the line of text is also 24 points. As you can see, the star is positioned so that its center is in line with the spot where the two lines of the X cross. The 100 percent star also shows you that the star, like the checkbox, is the size of a capital X in your designated font.

In the horizontal direction, the star is centered on the point after the positioning character. This allows enough room for most stars to print without running over the text around them. If you use large stars, particularly if you use large percentage values, then you may have to adjust your text both horizontally and vertically to allow enough room for the star to print.

Using the Effect

The examples in Figure 3-25 also give you some idea of how this effect can be used. You may want to use smaller or larger stars and different shades of gray to mark items in your text. Various shades of fill can also be used in a decorative way to indicate sections of a document or to mark completed and uncompleted items, for example.

DROP SHADOW STAR

shadow star

Description

If you want to use the star as a decorative enhancement, you may notice that some people make a star stand out on the page by placing a shadow behind it. The drop shadow star effect allows you to make a shadow behind your star.

Variables

This effect is exactly like the star effect, except that you can place a shadow behind the star. You have controls in the effect for the placement of the shadow in both the horizontal and vertical directions, for the darkness of the shadow, and for the height of the star. These four variables are listed in the front of the shadow bullet effect, as shown here:

```
-03 /Xoff +03 /Yoff 1.00 /Gray 100 /Pct 9 dict begin . . .
```

Note that you must observe the range and format rules for the variables very strictly. If you don't, the effect may not print.

Xoff/Yoff   You place the shadow behind the star by setting the horizontal distance, called Xoff—an offset in the x, or horizontal, direction. In a similar fashion, the vertical distance for the shadow is called Yoff. Both distances are in points, which is a printer's measure. A point is $^1/_{72}$ inch. You can use either positive or negative values for both Xoff and Yoff. Positive values of Xoff move the shadow to the right, while negative values move it to the left. Positive values of Yoff move the shadow down the page, and negative values move it up the page. You must place plus or minus signs in front of the Xoff and Yoff variables, and you must use two digits, as shown. Acceptable values range from ±00 to ±99. Of course, +00 and – 00 are identical and give you the same result: no offset in that direction.

Gray   The darkness of the shadow is set by a control named, reasonably enough, Gray. The values of Gray are percentages, with 1.00 being black and 0.01 being almost white. Although you can use a value of 0.00 (white), this may be somewhat misleading. That value actually means that nothing is printed behind the star; it doesn't cause a white spot on colored paper, for example.

The Gray variable may range from 1.00 to .01. You always need to have a decimal point in the value and two digits after the decimal point, even if you are using exact tenths. For example, use .50 and not .5 as your value.

Pct   Finally, you have the same Pct variable as you have in the sized star effect. This allows you to set the ratio of the height of the star to the font size used for the positioning character.

You can use any percentage values between 10 and 999 for Pct without trouble. This value represents the height of the star as a percentage of the font size. A 100 percent star is the same size as a capital X.

Size and Position

The shadowed star is sized in the same way as the sized star effect: The positioning character and the percentage that you set in the Pct variable together determine the size of the star. The shadow size matches that of the star, as a shadow should. As illustrated in Figure 3-27, the position of the shadow, and therefore the amount of shadow that shows under the star, is determined by the Xoff and Yoff variables.

The four examples in Figure 3-26 show you how changes in the offset values move the shadow effect around the star itself. As you can see, you can get any variation in shadowing by changing the signs of the offset values.

It can be very difficult to judge the distance that you want to offset the shadow behind your star. To set it the way you want, you may have to make some tests with different sized offsets in your document. For that reason, this effect has two knots: It contains variables, and it may require test prints to produce exactly what you want.

This is a 24-point star with offsets of +4 and +4.
The shadow is 1.00 gray (black).

 This is a 24-point star with offsets of +4 and -4.
The shadow is 1.00 gray (black).

 This is a 24-point star with offsets of -4 and +4.
The shadow is 1.00 gray (black).

 This is a 24-point star with offsets of -4 and -4.
The shadow is 1.00 gray (black).

Figure 3-26. Examples of the drop shadow star effect

Using the Effect

The examples in Figure 3-27 show you some of the interesting variations that you can achieve using shadow placement and sizing. Notice that at smaller percentages, the offset must also be set smaller to prevent the shadow from coming out from behind the star entirely. The first three examples illustrate how you can compensate for sizing when positioning the shadows. Larger bullets will usually require larger offsets, as you might imagine. Notice the examples on lines four and five. These stars are the same size—24 points—but the shadow is dark and close on one and lighter and farther away on the other.

The last three examples show 14-point stars with 12-point text and the 1.00 Gray shadow placed +03 points offset in both the horizontal and vertical directions.

This is an 18-point star at 50% with offsets of -2 and +2 and a .80 gray shadow.

This is an 18-point star at 100% with offsets of -3 and +3 and a .80 gray shadow.

This is an 18-point star at 150% with offsets of -4 and +4 and a .80 gray shadow.

This is a 24-point star at 100% with offsets of -2 and +2 and a 1.00 gray (black) shadow.

This is a 24-point star at 100% with offsets of -8 and +8 and a .25 gray shadow.

You can use star bullets in a variety of ways:

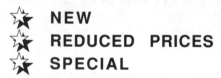

NEW
REDUCED PRICES
SPECIAL

Figure 3-27. Variations of the drop shadow star effect

FADED STAR

faded star

Description

The faded star effect is essentially a fancy variant of the shadowed star. In this case it has a longer shadow that changes from white to black over a small distance.

Size and Position

The faded star is sized in the same way as the basic star effect: The positioning character determines the size of the basic star, before the faded effect is in place. The faded shadow size is a standard size for all stars. It extends to the left and below the star by a fixed amount and matches the star in all dimensions. As illustrated in Figure 3-28, this gives somewhat different results for different-sized stars.

 This is an example of the faded star at 10 points.

 This is an example of the effect at 12 points.

 This is an example at 24 points.

 This is an example at 60 points.

Figure 3-28. Examples of the faded star effect

The star itself is placed just where the standard star would appear: centered on the end of the positioning character. If you use the faded star effect with small point size text, be sure to allow enough room below the effect so that the faded shadow does not touch the text below and to the left of the effect.

Using the Effect

Although this effect looks something like the shadow star effect, it has no variables and no controls for shadow placement. Fading a shadow is quite complex and time-consuming, so you don't have alternatives here for shadow placement or coloring. The examples in Figure 3-28 demonstrate how this affects the resulting output. As you can see, smaller point sizes have a faded effect that tails out a great distance relative to the size of the star itself. On the other hand, on very large point size stars the faded background hardly differs from the simple shadow effect. The best results are generally between 18 and 48 points, but you may want larger or smaller stars for special purposes.

TRIANGLE

triangle

Description

The triangle effect simply draws a triangle at the position specified by the positioning character. The triangle effect is an open triangle (the filled triangle effect, later in this chapter, can be filled in with any shade of gray) and can be used in a wide variety of ways, including as an alternative to ordinary bullets.

Size and Position

The examples in Figure 3-29 show you different sizes of the triangle effect. The first three lines show triangles created using 12-, 18-, and 24-point fonts. Using a different font has no effect on the size or positioning of the triangle, as you can see by comparing lines three and four, which both display a 24-point triangle, using the Helvetica and Times fonts. In these four examples, the font and size of the positioning character, which governs the size of the triangle, is identical to that of the font used for the X next to the triangle.

The second line also demonstrates how the triangle is sized. The capital X next to the triangle is in the same font and point size—18-point Helvetica—as the triangle. As you see, the triangle matches, approximately, the height of the capital X in the font that you have chosen. Remember that this is the font and size of the *positioning character*, not that of the following text. It's up to you to ensure that these match if you want them to.

The triangle effect is positioned on the page with the center of the triangle at the point where the positioning character ends and even with the center of the capital X in height.

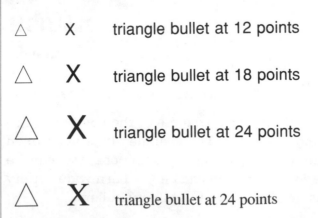

Figure 3-29. Sizing the basic triangle effect

If you place text on both sides of the triangle, be sure to allow some room both before and after the effect text. The effect extends both forward and backward from the end of the positioning character. Since the effect text is invisible in your document, you could erase or obscure some of the text that you want to print if you place it too close to the effect. One way to avoid this is to place one or two spaces between the effect text and the adjacent word of your text. Another good way to make such placements is to use tab settings for placing the effect and the text that follows an effect. This allows you to control more precisely the exact distance between the effect and the beginning of the subsequent text.

Using the Effect

This triangle effect can be used anywhere that you want a full-sized triangle. It can also be used to divide text blocks or to set off specific text items. A line or border of small triangles is quite eye-catching.

SIZED TRIANGLE

sized triangle

Description

The sized triangle effect draws a triangle, at the given point. This is one more variant of bullet, which you can use as a replacement for, or in addition to, regular bullets.

Variables

The triangle has one control, called Pct, which allows you to determine the height of the triangle to the point size of the font selected by the positioning character. You control the triangle size by setting the Pct variable. The variable is located at the front of the sized triangle effect, as shown here:

```
100 /Pct 6 dict . . .
```

You must observe the format rules and range limits for the variable very strictly. If you don't, the effect may not print.

Pct   The Pct variable allows you to set the ratio of the height of the triangle to the font size used for the positioning character. This value represents the height of the triangle as a percentage of the font size. You can use any percentage values between 10 and 999 for Pct without trouble. A 100 percent triangle is the same size as a capital X.

Size and Position

The examples in Figure 3-30 illustrate how your triangle is sized. The percentage shown in the text next to the triangle bullets is the value placed into each effect for Pct. As you see, the 25 percent triangle is one-quarter of the height of the X, the 50 percent triangle is half the height, and so on, up to the 200 percent triangle which is twice as high. Obviously, using 100 percent gives you a triangle that is the same height as the font. Using the Pct variable along with the font size, you can make your triangle effect any size you want.

Figure 3-30 also shows you how the Pct variable affects your triangle. All of the example triangles are based on a 24-point positioning character. The X next to them on the line of text is also 24 points. As you can see, the center of the triangle is aligned with the center of the positioning character, where the two lines of the X cross. The 100 percent triangle also shows you that the triangle, like the other bullets, is the size of a capital X in your designated font.

△ **X** This is a 24-point triangle sized to 25%

△ **X** This is a 24-point triangle sized to 50%

△ **X** This is a 24-point triangle sized to 75%

△ **X** This is a 24-point triangle sized to 100%
(Same as the 24-point triangle unsized)

△ **X** This is a 24-point triangle sized to 150%

△ **X** This is a 24-point triangle sized to 200%

Figure 3-30. Examples of the sized triangle effect

In the horizontal direction, the triangle is centered on the point after the positioning character. This allows enough room for most triangle bullets to print without running over the text around them. If you use large triangles, however, particularly if you use large percentage values when drawing them, then you may have to adjust your text both horizontally and vertically to allow enough room for the triangle to print.

Using the Effect

This effect can be used anywhere that you would otherwise use standard bullets. In my opinion, the triangle gives a different feeling to a bulleted list and makes the list and its entries stand out clearly. Triangles, particularly at large sizes, can be used as a decorative element in text, to mark an item of special importance, or to decorate a page. A line of triangles can also be used to delimit sections of a page. For example, a line of triangles might be used to set off a special section of your text that you want the reader to notice or act upon.

FILLED TRIANGLE

filled triangle

Description

Although it's nice to have a triangle that you can size, sometimes you want to fill the triangle with a shade of gray. The filled triangle effect allows you to add gray to your triangles.

Variables

Like the sized triangle, the filled triangle uses a Pct variable to set the size of the triangle as a percentage of the font size. It adds a Gray variable to allow you to set the color of your triangle. Both variables are located at the front of the filled triangle effect, as shown here:

1.00 /Gray **100** /Pct 6 dict . . .

You must observe the format rules and range limits for the variables very strictly. If you don't, the effect may not print.

Gray The Gray variable may be anything from 1.00 (black) to .01. Always have a decimal point in the value, and always have two digits after the decimal point, even if you are using exact tenths. For example, use .50 and not .5 as your value.

Pct   The Pct variable allows you to set the ratio of the height of the triangle to the font size used for the positioning character. This value represents the height of the triangle as a percentage of the font size. You can use any percentage values between 10 and 999 for Pct without trouble. A 100 percent triangle is the same size as a capital X.

Size and Position

The examples in Figure 3-31 illustrate how your triangle is sized and colored. The text next to the triangles shows both the value placed into each effect for Pct and the value inserted for Gray. As you see, the variations are just what you would expect. Obviously, using 100 percent size (100 /Pct) and 100 percent gray (1.00 /Gray) gives you a triangle that is completely black and the same height as the font.

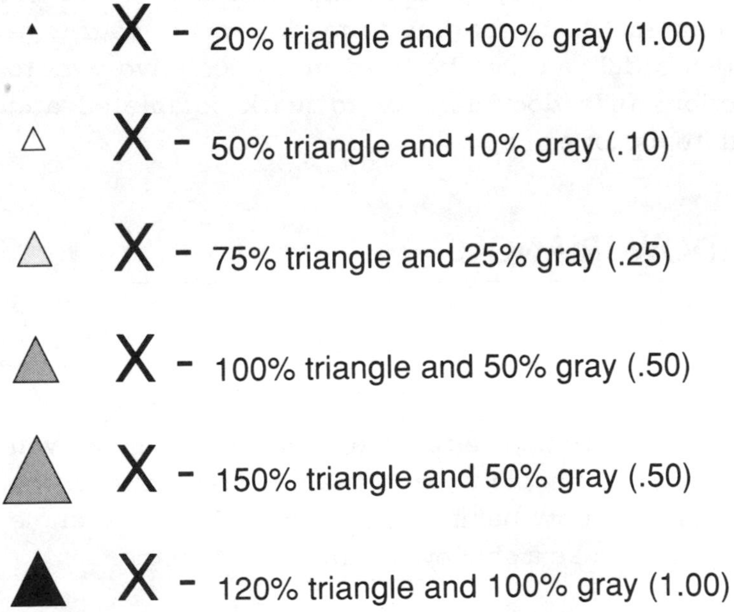

X - 20% triangle and 100% gray (1.00)

X - 50% triangle and 10% gray (.10)

X - 75% triangle and 25% gray (.25)

X - 100% triangle and 50% gray (.50)

X - 150% triangle and 50% gray (.50)

X - 120% triangle and 100% gray (1.00)

Figure 3-31.   Examples of the filled triangle effect

All of the example triangles shown in Figure 3-31 are based on a 24-point positioning character. The X next to them on the line of text is also 24 points. As you can see, the triangle is positioned so that its center is in line with the point where the two lines of the X cross. The 100 percent triangle also shows you that the triangle, like the checkbox, is the size of a capital X in your designated font.

In the horizontal direction, the triangle is centered on the point after the positioning character. This allows enough room for most triangles to print without running over the text around them. If you use large triangles, particularly if you use large percentage values, then you may have to adjust your text both horizontally and vertically to allow enough room for the triangle to print.

Using the Effect

The examples in Figure 3-31 also give you some idea of how this effect can be used. You may want to use smaller or larger triangles and different shades of gray to mark items in your text. Various shades of fill can also be used in a decorative way to indicate sections of a document or to mark completed and uncompleted items, for example.

DROP SHADOW TRIANGLE

shadow triangle

Description

If you want to use the triangle as a decorative enhancement, you may notice that some people make a triangle stand out on the page by placing a shadow behind it. The drop shadow triangle effect allows you to make a shadow behind your triangle.

Variables

This effect is exactly like the triangle effect, except that you can place a shadow behind the triangle. You have controls in the effect for the placement of the shadow in both the horizontal and vertical directions, for the darkness of the shadow, and for the height of the triangle. These four variables are listed in the front of the shadow bullet effect, as shown here.

```
-03 /Xoff +03 /Yoff 1.00 /Gray 100 /Pct 9 dict begin . . .
```

Note that you must observe the range and format rules for the variables very strictly. If you don't, the effect may not print.

Xoff/Yoff You place the shadow behind the triangle by setting the horizontal distance, called Xoff—an offset in the x, or horizontal, direction. In a similar fashion, the vertical distance for the shadow is called Yoff. Both distances are in points, which are a printer's measure. A point is $^1/_{72}$ inch. You can use either positive or negative values for both Xoff and Yoff.

Positive values of Xoff move the shadow to the right, while negative values move it to the left. Positive values of Yoff move the shadow down the page, and negative values move it up the page.

You must place plus or minus signs in front of the Xoff and Yoff variables, and you must use two digits, as shown. Acceptable values range from ±00 to ±99. Of course, +00 and – 00 are identical and give you the same result: no offset in that direction.

Gray The darkness of the shadow is set by a control named, reasonably enough, Gray. The values of Gray are percentages, with 1.00 being black and 0.01 being almost white. Although you can use a value of 0.00 (white), this may be somewhat misleading. That value actually means that nothing is printed behind the triangle—it won't make a white spot on colored paper, for example.

The Gray variable may range from 1.00 to .01. You always need to have a decimal point in the value, and two digits after the decimal point, even if you are using exact tenths. For example, use .50 and not .5 as your value.

Pct   Finally, you have the same Pct variable as you have in the sized triangle effect. This allows you to set the ratio of the height of the triangle to the font size used for the positioning character.

You can use any percentage values between 10 and 999 for Pct without trouble. This value represents the height of the triangle as a percentage of the font size. A 100 percent triangle is the same size as a capital X.

Size and Position

The shadowed triangle is sized in the same way as the standard triangle effect: The positioning character and the percentage that you set in the Pct variable together determine the size of the triangle. The shadow size matches that of the triangle, as a shadow should. As illustrated in Figure 3-32, the position of the shadow, and therefore the amount of shadow that shows under the triangle, is determined by the Xoff and Yoff variables.

The four examples in Figure 3-32 show you how changes in the offset values move the shadow effect around the triangle itself. As you can see, you can get any variation in shadowing by changing the signs of the offset values.

It can be very difficult to judge the distance that you want to offset the shadow behind your triangle. To set it the way you want, you may have to make some tests with different-sized offsets in your document. For that reason, this effect has two knots: It contains variables, and it may require test prints to produce exactly what you want.

This is a 24-point triangle with offsets of +4 and +4. The shadow is .50 gray.

 This is a 24-point triangle with offsets of +4 and -4. The shadow is .50 gray.

 This is a 24-point triangle with offsets of -4 and +4. The shadow is .50 gray.

 This is a 24-point triangle with offsets of -4 and -4. The shadow is .50 gray.

Figure 3-32. Examples of the drop shadow triangle effect

Using the Effect

The examples in Figure 3-33 show you some of the interesting variations that you can achieve using shadow placement and sizing. Notice that at smaller percentages, the offset must also be set smaller to prevent the shadow from coming out from behind the triangle entirely. The first three examples illustrate how you can compensate for sizing when positioning the shadows. Larger bullets will usually require larger offsets. Notice the examples on lines four and five. These triangles are the same size—24 points— but the shadow is dark and close on one and lighter and farther away on the other.

The last three examples show 14-point triangles with 12-point text and the 1.00 Gray shadow placed +03 points offset in both the horizontal and vertical directions.

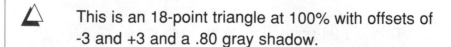 This is an 18-point triangle at 50% with offsets of -2 and +2 and a .80 gray shadow.

This is an 18-point triangle at 100% with offsets of -3 and +3 and a .80 gray shadow.

This is an 18-point triangle at 150% with offsets of -4 and +4 and a .80 gray shadow.

This is a 24-point triangle at 100% with offsets of -2 and +2 and a black (1.00 gray) shadow.

This is a 24-point triangle at 100% with offsets of -8 and +8 and a .25 gray shadow.

You can use these triangles in a variety of ways:

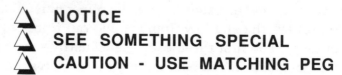 **NOTICE**

SEE SOMETHING SPECIAL

CAUTION - USE MATCHING PEG

Figure 3-33.   Variations of the drop shadow triangle effect

FADED TRIANGLE

faded triangle

Description

The faded triangle effect is essentially a fancy variant of the shadowed triangle. In this case, it has a longer shadow that changes from white to black over a small distance.

Size and Position

The faded triangle is sized in the same way as the basic triangle effect: The positioning character determines the size of the basic triangle, before the faded effect is in place. The faded shadow size is a standard size for all triangles. It extends to the left and below the triangle by a fixed amount and matches the triangle in all dimensions. As illustrated in Figure 3-34, this gives somewhat different results for different-sized triangles.

 This is an example of the faded triangle at 10 points.

 This is an example of the effect at 12 points.

 This is an example at 24 points.

 This is an example at 60 points.

Figure 3-34. Examples of the faded triangle effect

The triangle itself is placed just where the standard triangle would appear: centered on the end of the positioning character. If you use the faded triangle effect with small point size text, be sure to allow enough room below the effect so that the faded shadow does not touch the text below and to the left of the effect.

Using the Effect

Although this effect looks something like the shadow triangle effect, it has no variables and no controls for shadow placement. Fading a shadow is quite complex and time-consuming, so you don't have alternatives here for shadow placement or coloring. The examples in Figure 3-34 demonstrate how this affects the resulting output. As you can see, smaller point sizes have a faded effect that tails out a great distance relative to the size of the triangle itself. On the other hand, on very large point size triangles the faded background hardly differs from the simple shadow effect. The best results are generally between 18 and 48 points, but you may want larger or smaller triangles for special purposes.

T
e
x
t

IMPORTANT

88

Buttons

4

4   5   6

BUTTONS, LIKE CHECKBOXES, ARE A SPECIAL TYPE OF bullet. Buttons have a specific use in many computer-related texts, where they are used to represent keys on the keyboard or button images on the screen. The buttons in this chapter are all of the same basic format: a rectangular button face, with four sides drawn around the button. To give the button effect a three-dimensional look, each side can be shaded. You choose the sides to shade in the effect by setting a variable.

The buttons in this chapter are all standard in their placement and usage. One type of button, the button with text on it, is not presented in this chapter because it requires additional steps for placement and handling due to the insertion of text on the button. Buttons with text on them are included in Chapter 9, which covers text effects on various backgrounds.

INSERTING BUTTONS IN MICROSOFT WORD

1. Open your document. Insert a positioning character at the point in the document where you want to place the effect. The size of the positioning character determines the basic size of your button.

2. Open the xxxx.w file, where xxxx represents the name of the desired effect. If you see only one line of text, click on the Show Hidden Text box in the Preferences . . . selection of the Edit menu. Select and copy all the text of the effect and place it at the beginning of the page of your document that will contain the effect. Notice that the major part of the text in this file is in Word's PostScript style. (If you are unclear about how to use this style, review the instructions in Chapter 1.)

3. Cut the text at the end of the .w file that is *not* in the PostScript style. This is the second part of the effect.

4. Paste this text into your Word document immediately after (to the right of) the positioning character.

5. Select all of the text, and only the text, from the second part of the effect file that you pasted into your document. Change the font to the PostScript Escape font. This part of the effect text will disappear.

6. Be sure that the Print Hidden Text box in the Print dialog box is not checked. Print your document. The effect will print over the positioning character.

INSERTING BUTTONS IN OTHER WORD PROCESSING APPLICATIONS

1. Open your document. Insert a positioning character where you want to place the effect. The size of the positioning character determines the basic size of your effect.

2. Open the effect file and copy the effect text.

3. Paste the effect text into your document immediately after (to the right of) the positioning character.

4. Select all of the effect text, and only the effect text, that you inserted into your document and change it to the PostScript Escape font.

5. Print your document in the ordinary way. The effect will print over the positioning character.

BUTTON

Description

The button effect draws a simple button at the point set by the positioning character. The button is a square with four sloping sides drawn around it, giving the basic button a three-dimensional appearance. Each of the four sides can be shaded individually to give the appearance of shadowing, as you require. The result is an effect that can be used as a button symbol in text where that is required or that can be used as a fancy substitute for a standard bullet.

Variables

You can control the shading of the sides of the button by setting the variable TRBLSideColor. The variable is located at the front of the effect text, as shown here:

```
[0 0 1 1] /TRBLSideColor 9 dict begin . . .
```

You must observe the format rules and range limits for the variable very strictly. Values outside of these ranges may cause the effect not to print.

TRBLSideColor   I know that the name, TRBLSideColor, is quite long, but it is intended to help you remember how the variable is used. As you see, the variable consists of four numbers, 0 or 1, enclosed within brackets. This arrangement is called an *array*. These numbers control whether each side of the button is shaded or clear. Each number controls one side, in this order: Top, Right, Bottom, Left. This order corresponds to the initials in the variable's name, which should help you remember how they are set. (Another way to remember this is that the sides are set in clockwise order from the top.) Each side is shaded like this: If the corresponding number is a 0, then the side is clear; if the number is 1, then the side is shaded 50 percent gray. For example, the default settings [0 0 1 1] mean that the top and right sides are clear, while the bottom and left sides are shaded. Conversely, if you want to shade the top and right sides, and not the bottom and left, then you would use [1 1 0 0]. Figure 4-1 shows you some of the possible shadings. The text next to each example shows you how the array was set for that effect.

□ X button at 12 points, array [0 0 1 1]

□ X button at 18 points, array [0 1 1 0]

□ X button at 24 points, array [1 1 0 0]

□ X button at 24 points, array [1 0 0 1]

Figure 4-1. Sizing and shading the basic button effect

You can only use the values 0 or 1 in this array. Using any other numbers will result in possible errors. Also, you must set four numbers, one number for each of the four sides, and have no more than four numbers.

Size and Position

The examples in Figure 4-1 show you different sizes of the button effect. The first three lines show buttons created using 12-, 18-, and 24-point fonts. Using a different font does not affect the size or position of the button, as you can see by comparing lines three and four, which display a 24-point button using the Helvetica and Times fonts. In these four examples, the font and size of the positioning character, which governs the size of the button, is identical to that of the font used in the X next to the button.

The second line also demonstrates how the button is sized. The capital X is in the same font and point size—18-point Helvetica—as the button. As you see, the center square inside of the button is approximately the height of the capital X in the font that you have chosen. This makes the center of the button the same size as a square bullet or checkbox that has the same positioning character. Since the edges take up some additional room, the overall button size is slightly larger than a capital X. Remember that this is the font and size of the *positioning character*, not that of the following text. You can ensure that these match if you wish.

The button effect is positioned on the page with the center of the button at the point where the positioning character ends, and even with the center of the capital X in height.

TIP

> If you place text on both sides of the button, be sure to allow some room both before and after the effect text. The effect extends both forward and backward from the end of the positioning character. Since the effect text is invisible in your document, you could erase or obscure some of the text that you want to print if you place it too close to the effect. One way you can avoid this is to place one or two spaces between the effect text and the adjacent words of your regular text. Another good way to make such placements is to use tab settings for positioning the effect and the text that follows it. This allows you to control more precisely the exact distance between the effect and the beginning of the subsequent text.

Using the Effect

You use this effect in two ways. First, you can use it wherever you want to show a button in your text. Text about computers, for example, often includes a discussion of keys or options that you want to illustrate with a button. Second, the button can be used as a fancy type of bullet. This is particularly useful for a sequence of steps or some other bulleted list where a button metaphor is appropriate or suggestive.

PROPORTIONED BUTTON

proportioned button

Description

The proportioned button effect is basically the same as the standard button, except that you can control the width of the button independently of its height. The standard button is always a square, with the size determined by the point size of the positioning character. Once you have set that, the size of the resulting button is fixed. The proportioned button, on the other hand, has a Wid control variable that allows you to determine the ratio of the width to the height. The height of the button is set by the size of the positioning character, just like the standard button. The effect enables you to make rectangular buttons as well as square ones.

Variables

The Wid variable sets the width of the button as a percentage of the height. The TRBLSideColor variable controls the shading for the sides of the button. These two variables are located at the front of the proportioned button effect, as shown here:

```
100 /Wid [0 0 1 1] /TRBLSideColor 10 dict begin...
```

You must observe the format rules and range limits for the variables very strictly. Values outside of these ranges may cause the effect not to print.

Wid   The Wid value represents the width of the button as a percentage of its height. The height of the button is set by the size that you use for the positioning character. You can use any percentage values between 10 and 999 for Wid without trouble.

TRBLSideColor   The name, TRBLSideColor, is quite long because it is intended to help you remember how the variable is used. As you see, the variable consists of four numbers, 0 or 1, enclosed within brackets. This arrangement is called an *array*. These numbers control whether each side of the button is shaded or clear. Each number controls one side, in this order: Top, Right, Bottom, Left. This order corresponds to the initials in the variable's name, which should help you remember how they are set. (Another way to remember this is that the sides are set in clockwise order from the top.) Each side is shaded like this: If the corresponding number is a 0, then the side is clear; if the number is 1, then the side is shaded 50 percent gray. For example, the default settings [0 0 1 1] mean that the top and right sides are clear, while the bottom and left sides are shaded. Conversely, if you want to shade the top and right sides, and not the bottom and left, then you would use [1 1 0 0], and so on. You can only use the values 0 or 1 in this array. Using any other numbers will result in possible errors. Also, you must set four numbers, one number for each of the four sides, and have no more than four numbers.

Size and Position

These examples illustrate how the Wid variable works. The percentage shown in the text next to the boxes is the value placed into each effect for Wid. As you see, the 50 percent button is half as wide as it is high, and so on, up to the 400 percent button which is four times as wide as it is high. Obviously, using 100 percent gives you a button that is the same as the one produced by the standard button effect. Using the Wid variable along with the font size, you can make your button any size you want. Just remember that the height of the box is set by the font, just like the standard button, while the width of the box is set by the Wid variable as a percentage of the height.

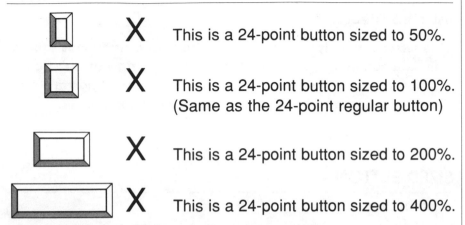

X   This is a 24-point button sized to 50%.

X   This is a 24-point button sized to 100%.
     (Same as the 24-point regular button)

X   This is a 24-point button sized to 200%.

X   This is a 24-point button sized to 400%.

Figure 4-2. Examples of the proportioned button effect

The effect is positioned on the page in the same way as the standard button effect described earlier. The actual space used by the proportioned button, of course, depends on the setting of the Wid variable. At all values of Wid, the center of the button is at the point where the positioning character ends. This is clearly illustrated in Figure 4-2, where you can see that all the buttons are centered on the same point. This helps to ensure that there is enough room for the button, even if you have text on both sides of the positioning character. However, if you place text on both sides of the button, be sure to allow some room either by adding spaces before and after the effect or by using tabs to place the effect.

If you use large values for Wid, such as the 400 in the example, then you have to allow enough room on both sides of the positioning character for the effect to print. For large values, the effect extends quite a bit further than the positioning character itself. This may require some trial and error to get the correct spacing if you have text on both sides of the effect.

Using the Effect

This effect is mostly used for making buttons that are not square. This is a common requirement when displaying buttons from a computer screen, for example, since many buttons portrayed on the screen, in dialog boxes and so on, are rectangular.

SIZED BUTTON

sized button

Description

Both the standard button and the proportioned button are designed to match the baseline of the line of text where they are used. This is true even if the positioning character is a different size than the other text in the same line. However, sometimes you want a button that is smaller or larger than the line of text, and that is centered on the line. For these situations, you can use the sized button effect, which allows you to shrink or expand the button uniformly. The result is always centered on the positioning character, which can then be set to match your line of text.

Variables

You control the button size by setting the Pct variable and you control the shading on the sides by setting TRBLSideColor. These variables are located at the front of the sized button effect, as shown here:

100 /Pct [**0 0 1 1**] /TRBLSideColor 10 dict begin . . .

You must observe the format rules and range limits for the variables very strictly. Values outside of these ranges may cause the effect not to print.

Pct   The Pct variable allows you to set the ratio of the size of the button to the font size used for the positioning character. This value represents the size of the button as a percentage of the font size. You can use any values between 10 and 999 for Pct without trouble. A 100 percent button is the same size as a standard button.

TRBLSideColor   The name, TRBLSideColor, is quite long because it is intended to help you remember how the variable is used. As you see, the variable consists of four numbers, 0 or 1, enclosed within brackets. This arrangement is called an *array*. These numbers control whether each side of the button is shaded or clear. Each number controls one side, in this order: Top, Right, Bottom, Left. This corresponds to the initials in the variable's name, which should help you remember how they are set. (Another way to remember this is that the sides are set in clockwise order from the top.) Each side is shaded like this: If the corresponding number is a 0, then the side is clear; if the number is 1, then the side is shaded 50 percent gray. For example, the default settings [0 0 1 1] mean that the top and right sides are clear, while the bottom and left sides are shaded. Conversely, if you want to shade the top and right sides, and not the bottom and left, then you would use [1 1 0 0], and so on. You can only use the values 0 or 1 in this array. Using any other numbers will result in possible errors. Also, you must set four numbers, one number for each of the four sides, and have no more than four numbers.

Size and Position

The examples in Figure 4-3 illustrate how your button is sized. The percentage shown in the text next to the buttons is the value placed into each effect for Pct. As you see, the 50 percent button is half the height of the X, and so on, up to the 200 percent button which is twice as high. Obviously, using 100 percent gives you a button that is the same height as the font. Using the Pct variable along with the font size, you can make your button effect any size you want and still keep the button centered on your line of text.

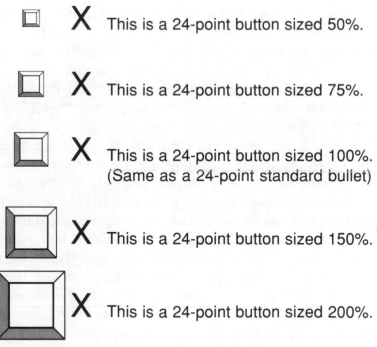

Figure 4-3.   Examples of the sized button effect

The examples also show you how the Pct variable affects your button. All of the example buttons are based on a 24-point positioning character. The X next to them on the line of text is also 24 points. As you can see, the button is positioned so that its center is in line with the spot where the two lines of the X cross. The 100 percent button also shows you that the button, like the other button effects, is the size of a capital X in your designated font.

In the horizontal direction the button is centered on the point after the positioning character. This allows enough room for most buttons to print without running over the text around them. Remember that the buttons are squares, however. If you use large buttons, particularly if you use large percentage values, then you may have to adjust your text both horizontally and vertically to allow enough room for the button to print.

Using the Effect

This button can be used anywhere that you need a larger or smaller button image than that provided by the standard button. This can be especially helpful if you want to use oversized buttons with text, since the buttons are centered on the line of text, instead of towering over the line.

NUMBERED BUTTON

numbered button

Description

Sometimes you require a button with a number on it to indicate a choice or to illustrate a specific type of button. In addition, buttons, like bullets, can also be used to number lists of items or tasks. The numbered button effect allows you to do just that, using any numbers from 0 to 99. The numbered button is more dramatic and visible than most numbered bullets. Numbered buttons can also be combined with other numbered bullets to indicate various levels or task structures in a list.

Variables

You determine the number in the button by setting the Num variable, and you control the shading on the sides by setting TRBLSideColor. These variables are located at the front of the numbered button effect, as shown here:

```
(99) /Num [0 0 1 1] /TRBLSideColor save 16 dict begin . . .
```

You must observe the format rules and range limits for the variables very strictly. Values outside of these ranges may cause the effect not to print.

Num   The Num variable is the number that you want displayed inside the bullet. You must place your numbers inside the parentheses; both the left and right parentheses are required for the effect to work correctly. The numbers may range from 0 (or any single digit with a space in front of it) to 99.

TRBLSideColor   The name, TRBLSideColor, is quite long because it is intended to help you remember how the variable is used. As you see, the variable consists of four numbers, 0 or 1, enclosed within brackets. This arrangement is called an *array*. These numbers control whether each side of the button is shaded or clear. Each number controls one side, in this order: Top, Right, Bottom, Left. This corresponds to the initials in the variable's name, which should help you remember how they are set. (Another way to remember this is that the sides are set in clockwise order from the top.) Each side is shaded like this: If the corresponding number is a 0, then the side is clear; if the number is 1, then the side is shaded 50 percent gray. For example, the default settings [0 0 1 1] mean that the top and right sides are clear, while the bottom and left sides are shaded. Conversely, if you want to shade the top and right sides, and not the bottom and left, then you would use [1 1 0 0], and so on. You can only use the values 0 or 1 in this array. Using any other numbers will result in possible errors. Also, you must set four numbers, one number for each of the four sides, and have no more than four numbers.

Size and Position

Like the previous buttons, these buttons are sized as a percentage of the font size used for positioning. Therefore, the numbers inside the buttons themselves are set somewhat smaller than the font that you select for the positioning character. This allows you to combine numbered and unnumbered buttons in the same text. All of the buttons will be the same size as long as they all have the same size positioning character.

In a similar way, the numbers inside the buttons are the same size as the numbers inside a comparable numbered bullet effect. Obviously, the effects themselves are different, but the numbers inside are the same size and font as long as the same positioning character is used for all of them. This allows you to mix numbered bullets and numbered buttons in the same list, for example.

All of the example buttons in Figure 4-4 are based on an 18-point positioning character. The X next to them on the line of text is also 18 points. As you can see, the button is positioned so that its center is in line with the spot where the two lines of the X cross.

In the horizontal direction, the button is centered on the point after the positioning character. This allows enough room for most buttons to print without running over the text around them.

Using the Effect

The examples in Figure 4-4 illustrate an important point when using the numbered button effect. Since the buttons themselves are sized to the numbers that go inside them, buttons with two-digit numbers naturally require more room, and hence are larger, than buttons with single-digit numbers. To allow you to use both

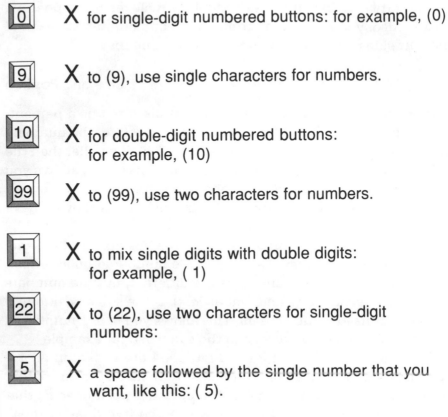

X for single-digit numbered buttons: for example, (0)

X to (9), use single characters for numbers.

X for double-digit numbered buttons:
for example, (10)

X to (99), use two characters for numbers.

X to mix single digits with double digits:
for example, (1)

X to (22), use two characters for single-digit
numbers:

X a space followed by the single number that you
want, like this: (5).

Figure 4-4. Examples of the numbered button effect

single- and double-digit numbers in a series of buttons without
having the buttons change sizes unexpectedly as you go from 9 to
10, you must insert the single-digit numbers between the parentheses with a space in front of the number. If we use a 'b' to
represent the blank space, then a single-digit number would look
like this in the effect: (b4). If you are only using numbers from 0 to
9, then you can simply insert the number that you want inside the
parentheses, like this: (4). The examples in Figure 4-4 show you
how to insert both single- and double-digit numbers into the effect,
and what the results look like for each choice.

TIP

The examples use 18-point Helvetica Bold for the positioning character, since that gives a nice, clear number that is easily visible. If you use numbered buttons at medium or small point sizes, the bold version of a font is generally more legible than the normal version. In much the same way, sans-serif fonts, like Helvetica, are generally more legible inside buttons than serif fonts, like Times.

OUTLINE NUMBERED BUTTON

outline num button

Description

Numbered buttons are so useful that sometimes you'd like to have them very visible on the page, almost using them for special effects. In addition, some forms of buttons in real life have white printing on a dark background. The outline numbered button can be used in both of these cases, because the numbers are drawn in white with a black outline against a gray button. This form of printing text is known as *outline* and so this effect is named to reflect the fact that the numbers inside the button are outlined. Other than that, these buttons work exactly like the regular numbered buttons. For this effect, you must not use bitmapped fonts. Bitmapped fonts cannot print in the outline format used here.

Variables

You determine the number in the button by setting the Num variable, and you control the shading on the sides by setting TRBLSideColor. These variables are located at the front of the numbered button effect, as shown here:

`(99) /Num [0 0 1 1] /TRBLSideColor save 16 dict begin...`   **203**

You must observe the format rules and range limits for the variables very strictly. Values outside of these ranges may cause the effect not to print.

Num   The Num variable is the number that you want displayed inside the bullet. You must place your numbers inside the parentheses; both the left and right parentheses are required for the effect to work correctly. The numbers may range from 0 (or any single digit with a space in front of it) to 99.

TRBLSideColor   The name, TRBLSideColor, is quite long because it is intended to help you remember how the variable is used. As you see, the variable consists of four numbers, 0 or 1, enclosed within brackets. This arrangement is called an *array*. These numbers control whether each side of the button is shaded or clear. Each number controls one side, in this order: Top, Right, Bottom, Left. As you see, this corresponds to the initials in the variable's name, which should help you remember how these are set. (Another way to remember this is that the sides are set in clockwise order from the top.) Each side is shaded like this: If the corresponding number is a 0, then the side is clear; if the number is 1, then the side is shaded 50 percent gray. For example, the default settings [0 0 1 1] mean that the top and right sides are clear, while the bottom and left sides are shaded. Conversely, if you want to shade the top and right sides, and not the bottom and left, then you would use [1 1 0 0], and so on. You can only use the values 0 or 1 in this array. Using any other numbers will result in possible errors. Also, you must set four numbers, one number for each of the four sides, and have no more than four numbers.

Size and Position

Like the previous buttons, these buttons are sized as a percentage of the font size used for positioning. Therefore, the numbers inside the buttons themselves are set somewhat smaller than the font that you select for the positioning character. This allows you to combine numbered and unnumbered buttons in the same text. All of the buttons will be the same size as long as they all have the same size positioning character.

In a similar way, the numbers inside the buttons are the same size as the numbers inside a comparable numbered bullet effect. Obviously, the effects themselves are different, but the numbers inside are the same size and font as long as the same positioning character is used for all of them. This allows you to mix numbered bullets and numbered buttons in the same list, for example.

All of the example buttons shown in Figure 4-5 are based on an 18-point positioning character. The X next to them on the line of text is also 18 points. As you can see, the button is positioned so that its center is in line with the spot where the two lines of the X cross.

In the horizontal direction, the button is centered on the point after the positioning character. This allows enough room for most buttons to print without running over the text around them.

Using the Effect

The examples in Figure 4-5 illustrate an important point when using the outline numbered button effect. Since the buttons themselves are sized to the numbers that go inside them, buttons with two-digit numbers naturally require more room, and hence are larger, than buttons with single-digit numbers. To allow you to use both single- and double-digit numbers in a series of buttons without having the buttons change sizes unexpectedly as you go from 9 to 10, you must insert the single-digit numbers between the parentheses with a space in front of the number. If we use a 'b' to represent the blank space, then a single-digit number would look like this in the effect: (b4). If you are only using numbers from 0 to 9, then you can simply insert the number that you want inside the parentheses, like this: (4). The examples in Figure 4-5 show you how to insert both single- and double-digit numbers into the effect, and what the results look like for each choice.

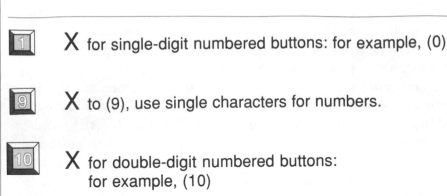

X for single-digit numbered buttons: for example, (0)

X to (9), use single characters for numbers.

X for double-digit numbered buttons:
for example, (10)

X to (99), use two characters for numbers.

X to mix single digits with double digits:
for example, (1)

X to (22), use two characters for single-digit
numbers:

X a space followed by the single number that you
want, like this: (5).

Figure 4-5. Examples of the outline numbered button effect

TIP

The example buttons in Figure 4-5 and the X that follows them are all 18-point type. The examples use 18-point Helvetica Bold, since that gives a nice, clear number that is easily visible. Even more than regular numbered buttons, it is essential to make your numbers very legible when they are printed in outline. At almost all point sizes the bold version of a font is more legible than the normal version. In the same way, sans-serif fonts, like Helvetica, are quite a bit more legible inside buttons than serif fonts, like Times. In general, for outline numbered buttons, I recommend using bold, sans-serif fonts in all cases unless you have some special reason for using other fonts. Also remember that bitmapped fonts, like Geneva and Monaco, will not print in the outline format required by the button effect.

BEHIND THE SCENES

You may wonder why this effect, and other similar effects that use text, cannot use the bitmapped versions of your fonts. The answer lies in how such fonts are created in PostScript. Most PostScript fonts are based on character outlines, which are essentially little drawings of a character. When using these fonts, the effect can draw the character, fill it with white, and then stroke it in black, giving you the desired outline. A bitmapped font, however, has no lines. It consists simply of a number of black dots that make up each character. In that case, there is no way to get the outline of the character to generate an outline image.

PLACED NUMBERED BUTTON

placed num button

Description

Although numbered bullets are nice, sometimes you may want a bullet that is larger than the font that you are using for additional visibility, or you may want one smaller if you are using the button as a form of bullet. The placed numbered button effect allows you either of these options, since it allows you to choose the point size of the number inside your bullet and then place the bullet in the center of a line of text of a different size.

Variables

The placed numbered button effect requires three variables. These three variables occur at the front of the effect text, as shown here:

```
(88) /Num 12 /Ps [0 0 1 1] /TRBLSideColor save . . .
```

Note that you must observe the range and format rules for the variables very strictly. If you don't, the effect may not print.

Num The Num variable is the number that you want displayed inside the bullet. You must place your numbers inside the parentheses; both the left and right parentheses are required for the effect to work correctly. The numbers may range from 0 (or any single digit with a space in front of it) to 99.

Ps The second variable is the Ps variable, which is the point size of the font that you want to match with the bullet. The Ps variable controls the placement of the bullet in a vertical plane. The bullet is positioned so that the center of the bullet will be at the center of a capital X of the given point size. Acceptable values for the Ps variable range from 1 to 99 points.

TRBLSideColor The name, TRBLSideColor, is quite long because it is intended to help you remember how the variable is used. As you see, the variable consists of four numbers, 0 or 1, enclosed within brackets. This arrangement is called an *array.* These numbers control whether each side of the button is shaded or clear. Each number controls one side, in this order: Top, Right, Bottom, Left. This corresponds to the initials in the variable's name, which should help you remember how these are set. (Another way to remember this is that the sides are set in clockwise order from the top.) Each side is shaded like this: If the corresponding number is a 0, then the side is clear; if the number is 1, then the side is shaded 50 percent gray. For example, the default settings [0 0 1 1] mean that the top and right sides are clear, while the bottom and left sides are shaded. Conversely, if you want to shade the top and right sides, and not the bottom and left, then you would use [1 1 0 0], and so on. You can only use the values 0 or 1 in this array. Using any other numbers will result in possible errors. Also, you must set four numbers, one number for each of the four sides, and have no more than four numbers.

Size and Position

Like the previous buttons, these buttons are sized as a percentage of the font size used for positioning. Therefore, the numbers inside the buttons themselves are set somewhat smaller than the font that you select for the positioning character. This allows you to combine numbered and unnumbered buttons in the same text. All of the buttons will be the same size as long as they all have the same size positioning character.

In a similar way, the numbers inside the buttons are the same size as the numbers inside a comparable numbered bullet effect. Obviously, the effects themselves are different, but the numbers inside are the same size and font as long as the same positioning character is used for all of them. This allows you to mix numbered bullets and numbered buttons in the same list, for example.

The examples in Figure 4-6 illustrate how you can mix text and button sizes. The text in each example tells you what the size of the button and the associated text line are for that example. As you can see, the button is positioned with its center in line with the point where the two lines of the X cross.

In the horizontal direction, the button is centered on the point after the positioning character. This allows enough room for most buttons to print without running over the text around them.

Using the Effect

The examples in Figure 4-6 show you some of the uses for numbered buttons. You should note an important point when using the placed numbered button effect. Like the other numbered buttons, the buttons themselves are sized to the numbers that go inside them. Therefore, buttons with two-digit numbers naturally require more room, and hence are larger, than buttons with single-digit numbers. To allow you to use both single- and double-digit numbers in a series of buttons without having the buttons change size unexpectedly as you go from 9 to 10, you must insert the single-digit numbers between the parentheses with a space in front of the number. If we use a 'b' to represent the blank space,

X   24-point text with
14-point button

X   18-point text with 14-point
button

X   20-point text with 14-point
button

X   22-point text with 14-point
button

X   14-point text with 24-point button

Figure 4-6. Examples of the placed numbered button effect

then a single-digit number would look like this in the effect: (b4).
If you are only using numbers from 0 to 9, then you can simply
insert the number that you want inside the parentheses, like this:
(4). The examples in Figure 4-4 under the numbered button effect
show you how to insert both single- and double-digit numbers
into the effect, and what the results look like for each choice.

The last example in Figure 4-6 illustrates a use for these placed
buttons that might not occur to you offhand. Besides placing small
buttons in the middle of a line of larger text, you can also use the
variables to place a large button in the middle of a line of smaller
text. This is often visually more appealing than simply using the
numbered button with a large point size and following it with
smaller text, because the button doesn't seem to tower over the
text so much.

TIP

The examples use Helvetica Bold for the numbers, since that gives a nice, clear number that is easily visible. Because these buttons may be smaller than the regular numbered buttons, it is more important to make your numbers very legible. At almost all point sizes the bold version of a font is more legible than the normal version. In the same way, sans-serif fonts, like Helvetica, are quite a bit more legible inside buttons than serif fonts, like Times.

PLACED OUTLINE NUMBERED BUTTON

placed outline num button

Description

The placed outline numbered button has the same relationship to the placed numbered button that the outline numbered button has to the numbered button: It is the same effect but with the number printed in white and outlined in black on a gray background. For this effect, you must not use bitmapped fonts. Bitmapped fonts cannot print in the outline format used here.

Variables

The placed outline numbered button effect requires three variables. These three variables occur at the front of the effect text, as shown here:

```
(88) /Num 12 /Ps [0 0 1 1] /TRBLSideColor save . . .
```

Note that you must observe the range and format rules for the variables very strictly. If you don't, the effect may not print.

Num   The Num variable is the number that you want displayed inside the bullet. You must place your numbers inside the parentheses; both the left and right parentheses are required for the effect to work correctly. The numbers may range from 0 (or any single digit with a space in front of it) to 99.

Ps   The second variable is the Ps variable, which is the point size of the font that you want to match with the bullet. The Ps variable controls the placement of the bullet in a vertical plane. The bullet is positioned so that the center of the bullet will be at the center of a capital X of the given point size. Acceptable values for the Ps variable range from 1 to 99 points.

TRBLSideColor   The name, TRBLSideColor, is quite long because it is intended to help you remember how the variable is used. As you see, the variable consists of four numbers, 0 or 1, enclosed within brackets. This arrangement is called an *array*. These numbers control whether each side of the button is shaded or clear. Each number controls one side, in this order: Top, Right, Bottom, Left. This corresponds to the initials in the variable's name, which should help you remember how they are set. (Another way to remember this is that the sides are set in clockwise order from the top.) Each side is shaded like this: If the corresponding number is a 0, then the side is clear; if the number is 1, then the side is shaded 50 percent gray. For example, the default settings [0 0 1 1] mean that the top and right sides are clear, while the bottom and left sides are shaded. Conversely, if you want to shade the top and right sides, and not the bottom and left, then you would use [1 1 0 0], and so on. You can only use the values 0 or 1 in this array. Using any other numbers will result in possible errors. Also, you must set four numbers, one number for each of the four sides, and have no more than four numbers.

Size and Position

Like the previous buttons, these buttons are sized as a percentage of the font size used for positioning. Therefore, the numbers inside the button themselves are set somewhat smaller than the font that you select for the positioning character. This allows you to combine numbered and unnumbered buttons in the same text. All of the buttons will be the same size as long as they all have the same size positioning character.

In a similar way, the numbers inside the buttons are the same size as the numbers inside a comparable numbered bullet effect. Obviously, the effects themselves are different, but the numbers inside are the same size and font as long as the same positioning character is used for all of them. This allows you to mix numbered bullets and numbered buttons in the same list, for example.

The examples in Figure 4-7 illustrate how you can mix text and button sizes. The text in each example tells you what the size of the button and the associated text line are for that example. As you can see, the button is positioned with its center in line with the point where the two lines of the X cross.

In the horizontal direction, the button is centered on the point after the positioning character. This allows enough room for most buttons to print without running over the text around them.

Using the Effect

The examples in Figure 4-7 show you some of the uses for placed outline numbered buttons. You should note an important point when using the placed outline numbered button effect. Like the other numbered buttons, the buttons themselves are sized to the numbers that go inside them. Therefore, buttons with two-digit numbers naturally require more room, and hence are larger, than buttons with single-digit numbers. To allow you to use both single- and double-digit numbers in a series of buttons without having

X 24-point text with 14-point button

X 18-point text with 14-point button

X 20-point text with 14-point button

X 22-point text with 14-point button

X 14-point text with 24-point button

Figure 4-7. Examples of the placed outline numbered button effect

the buttons change sizes unexpectedly as you go from 9 to 10, you must insert the single-digit numbers between the parentheses with a space in front of the number. If we use a 'b' to represent the blank space, then a single-digit number would look like this in the effect: (b4). If you are only using numbers from 0 to 9, then you can simply insert the number that you want inside the parentheses, like this: (4). The examples in Figure 4-7 show you how to insert both single- and double-digit numbers into the effect, and what the results look like for each choice.

The last example in Figure 4-7 illustrates a use for these placed buttons that might not occur to you offhand. Besides placing small buttons in the middle of a line of larger text, you can also use the variables to place a large button in the middle of a line of smaller text. This is often visually more appealing than simply using the numbered button with a large point size and following it with smaller text, because the button doesn't seem to tower over the text so much.

TIP

The examples in Figure 4-7 use Helvetica Bold, since that gives a nice, clear number that is easily visible. Even more than regular numbered buttons, it is essential to make your numbers very legible when they are printed in outline. At almost all point sizes, the bold version of a font is more legible than the normal version. In the same way, sans-serif fonts, like Helvetica, are quite a bit more legible inside buttons than serif fonts, like Times. In general, for outline numbered buttons, I recommend using bold, sans-serif fonts in all cases unless you have some special reason for using other types of fonts. Also remember that bitmapped fonts, like Geneva and Monaco, will not print in the outline format required by the button effect.

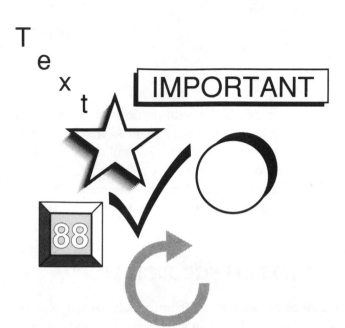

IMPORTANT

88

5

Boxed

Text

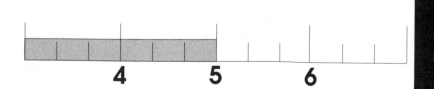

PLACING TEXT INSIDE A BORDER IS SIMILAR TO THE TEXT-box effect introduced in Chapter 1. You can enclose any text from your word processing program in a border or box of some type. The box will enclose any single line of text, but will not generally enclose multiple lines. (For some effects, you can use the procedure explained under "Using the Effect" to enclose multiple lines of text.) The boxes may be single- or multi-ruled with or without drop shadows.

INSERTING BOXED TEXT IN MICROSOFT WORD

1. Open your document. Insert a positioning character where you want to begin the box that will surround your text block.

2. Open the begin effect.w file. If you see only one line of text, click on the Show Hidden Text box in the Preferences . . . selection of the Edit menu. Select and copy the text of this file and place it at the beginning of the page in your document that contains the effect. Notice that the major part of the text in the begin effect.w file is in Word's PostScript style. (If you are unclear about how to use this style, review the instructions in Chapter 1.)

3. Open the xxxx.w file, where xxxx represents the name of the desired effect. Select and copy all the text of the effect and place it at the beginning of your document that will contain the effect. Notice that the major part of the text in this file is also in Word's PostScript style.

4. Cut the text at the end of the begin effect.w file that is *not* in the PostScript style from the end of the effect text. Copy the text into your Word document immediately after (to the right of) the positioning character.

5. Select all of the text, and only the text, that you just pasted from the begin effect file into your document. Change the font to the PostScript Escape font selection. The effect text will disappear.

6. If you have not entered the text that you want to be inside the box, enter it now. The text to appear inside the box must be placed after the begin effect text. You can use any font or style that is available in your word processing program. The text to display inside the box must be no more than one line of text; however, the line may be of any length supported by your word processing application. If you add spaces in front or behind this text, these spaces will also be included inside the box.

7. Cut the text that is *not* in the PostScript style from the end of the effect text. This is the second part of the effect.

8. Paste this text into your Word document immediately after (to the right of) the text that you want to enclose in the box.

9. Select all of the text, and only the text, from the second part of the effect file that you pasted into your document. Change the font to the PostScript Escape font. This part of the effect text will disappear.

10. Be sure that the Print Hidden Text box in the Print dialog box is not checked. Print your document. The effect will print over the positioning character.

INSERTING BOXED TEXT IN OTHER WORD PROCESSING APPLICATIONS

1. Open your document. Insert a positioning character where you want to place the effect.

2. Open the begin effect file and select and copy the effect text.

3. Paste the begin effect text into your document immediately after (to the right of) the positioning character.

4. Select all of the begin effect text, and only the begin effect text, that you inserted into your document and change it to the PostScript Escape font.

5. If you have not entered the text that you want inside the box, enter it now. The text must follow begin effect. You can use any font or style in your word processing program. The text to appear inside the box must fit on one line, but can be of any length supported by your word processing application. Any spaces you insert in front of or behind this text will also be included inside the box.

6. Open the effect file and select and copy the effect text.

7. Paste the effect text into your document immediately after (to the right of) the text block that you want to show in the box.

8. Select all of the effect text, and only the effect text, that you inserted into your document and change it to the PostScript Escape font.

9. Print your document in the ordinary way. The effect will print over the positioning character.

TEXT

TEXTBOX

textbox

Description

This, the simplest form of box text, simply draws a single line around the block of text that you have placed between the beginning of the effect and the end.

Size and Position

Unlike the effects in other chapters, the basic textbox and the other effects in this chapter are sized according to the text that is placed inside the box, *not* according to the positioning character. The positioning character is used only to establish the starting position of the textbox. Even if you set a positioning character at a different size than the text, you will get the size box that is appropriate for your text. The first two lines in Figure 5-1 both use a 14-point Helvetica positioning character. As you see, the second line, which contains 24-point text, produces a 24-point box even though the positioning character is 14 points.

The text is approximately centered both horizontally and vertically in the box. The box begins at the positioning character and extends the equivalent distance beyond the text. Because of this, you need to leave some room after the boxed text to be sure that the box does not overlap adjacent text.

The last three lines in Figure 5-1 show that you can add spaces before and/or after the text if you want more room around the text inside the box. In the third line, five spaces were added both

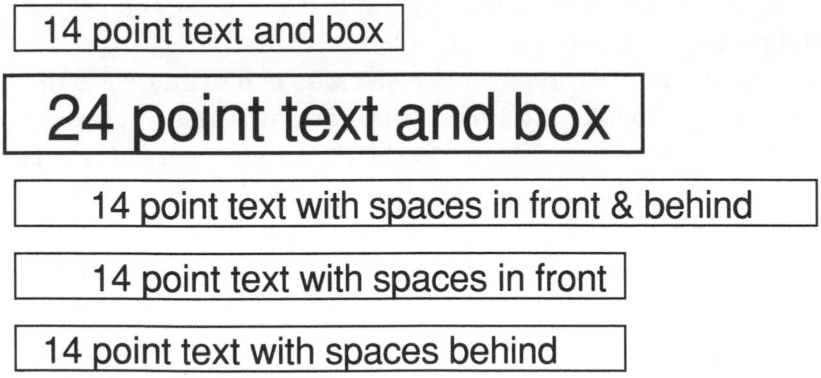

| 14 point text and box |

24 point text and box

| 14 point text with spaces in front & behind |

| 14 point text with spaces in front |

| 14 point text with spaces behind |

Figure 5-1. Sizing the basic textbox effect

before and after the text. In the fourth line five spaces were added before, and in the fifth line five spaces were added behind the text. As you see, adding spaces alters the positioning of the box and the location of the text. The last line also illustrates that you cannot place the beginning of the box any closer to the text than the start of the positioning character. You should keep this in mind if you are adjusting the position of the box around a line of text.

Using the Effect

You can use this effect for marking text or making a line stand out on a page. Boxed text is often used to set off instructions and other special information on a page.

Figure 5-2 shows that textboxes can also be used to provide a box for information that is to be filled out. The two boxes in Figure 5-2 were done in similar ways. For the first box, the caption (Name:) was placed on the line, followed by the positioning character. Then the box was defined by using tabs and spaces to set the size of the box. The size of the box is determined by setting the desired point size for the tabs and spaces. The first box is set to 24 points. Finally, the box effect is placed after the last tab or space on the line to define the end of the box.

In the second example the title text *(Name:)* is placed inside the box. To do so, you begin the box in the normal fashion with the title text at the size that you want. In the example, the title text is 9-point Helvetica Italic. Then you define the box as above, using 24-point tabs and spaces. The box effect text is placed after the last tab or space. The result is a neat textbox for entering a name or other information.

Name: [   ]

Name:

Figure 5-2. Some uses for textboxes

SHADOW TEXTBOX

shadow textbox

Description

This eye-catching effect draws a box around the text, then places a drop shadow behind the box. The added emphasis of the shadow draws the reader's attention because it seems to stand out from the page.

Variables

With the shadow textbox effect, you can control the placement of the shadow in both the horizontal and vertical directions and the darkness of the shadow. The three variables are listed in the front of the effect, as follows:

`−05 /Xoff +05 /Yoff 1.00 /Gray 9 dict...`

Note that you must observe the range and format rules for the variables very strictly. If you don't, the effect may not print.

Xoff/Yoff   You place the shadow behind the box by setting the horizontal distance, called Xoff—an offset in the x, or horizontal, direction. In a similar fashion, the vertical distance for the shadow is called Yoff. Both distances are in points, which are a printer's measure. A point is $1/72$ inch. You can use either positive or negative values for both Xoff and Yoff.

223

Positive values of Xoff move the shadow to the right, while negative values move it to the left. Positive values of Yoff move the shadow down the page, and negative values move it up the page.

You must place plus or minus signs in front of the Xoff and Yoff variables, and you must use two digits, as shown. Acceptable values range from ±00 to ±99. Of course, +00 and − 00 are identical and give you the same result: no offset in that direction.

Gray The darkness of the shadow is set by a control named, reasonably enough, Gray. The values of Gray are percentages, with 1.00 being black and 0.01 being almost white. Although you can use a value of 0.00 (white), this may be somewhat misleading since that value actually means that nothing is printed behind the box. It doesn't cause a white spot on colored paper, for example.

The Gray variable may range from 1.00 to .01. You always need to have a decimal point in the value and two digits after the decimal point, even if you are using exact tenths. For example, use .50 and not .5 as your value. If you don't, the effect may not print.

Size and Position

The size of the textbox depends upon the point size of the text inside the box. The shadow size matches that of the box, as a shadow should. As shown in Figure 5-3, the Xoff and Yoff variables control the position of the shadow and the amount of shadow that shows under the box.

The four examples in Figure 5-3 show you how changes in the offset values move the shadow effect around the textbox. Each line of text is set in 14-point Helvetica, all shadows are .50 Gray, and the position of the shadow for each textbox is set as described in the line of text. As you can see, you can alter the shadowing by changing the signs of the offset values.

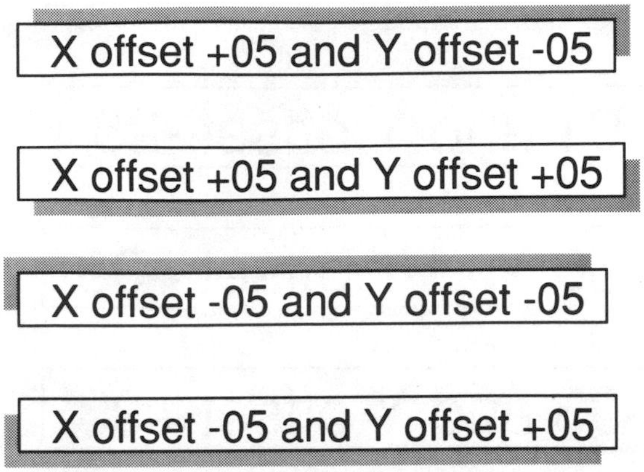

X offset +05 and Y offset -05

X offset +05 and Y offset +05

X offset -05 and Y offset -05

X offset -05 and Y offset +05

Figure 5-3. Examples of the shadow textbox effect

It can be difficult to judge the distance that you want to offset the shadow behind your box. To get it set the way you want, you may have to make some tests using different offsets in your document. For that reason, this effect has two knots: It contains variables, and it may require test prints to set it exactly the way you want it.

Using the Effect

The examples in Figure 5-4 show you some interesting variations on shadow placement. Basically, if you want a realistic shadow, the values for Xoff and Yoff should be equal and neither too large nor too small for the box. On the other hand, if you want a special effect, then setting different values can produce some interesting results. The first two examples illustrate this point. In both cases, using unequal offsets creates a special look. Notice that, since the box is generally longer than it is tall, larger x offset values are required to make a special effect than y values. On the first line, for example, a y offset of 25 points (about the height of the box) positions the shadow above the box. The larger x offset in the second line only moves the shadow part way out from the side of the box.

X offset -01 and Y offset -25

X offset -50 and Y offset +05

X offset -03 and Y offset +03

X offset -15 and Y offset +15

Figure 5-4.   Variations of the shadow textbox effect

Larger boxes will usually require larger offsets, as you might imagine. Notice the examples on lines three and four. These boxes are the same size—24 points—but the shadow is dark and close on one and lighter and further away on the other.

In general, you will find that even the smallest boxes require at least a 2-point offset if you want the shadow to show up clearly. For realistic shadows, offsets of about 20 to 30 percent of the point size of the font seem about right.

FITTED TEXTBOX

fitted textbox

Description

Sometimes you want more white space around a line of text than you can get with the standard textbox effect. With the fitted textbox effect, you can adjust both the height and width of the box to create a textbox that is the exact size that you want.

Variables

The fitted textbox effect lets you control the width and height of the box as a percentage of the font size of the text in the box. The two variables are listed in the front of the effect, as follows:

```
150 /Wid 150 /Hgt 8 dict . . .
```

Note that you must observe the range and format rules for the variables very strictly. If you don't, the effect may not print.

Wid/Hgt   Two variables control the width and height of the box drawn around your text in this effect. The Wid variable controls the width and the Hgt variable controls the height of the box. In each case, the values used represent the percentage of the normal size of the box that you want the actual box to be. For example, a value of 150 for Wid means that you want the box to be one and one-half times the normal width. Since the normal width allows a small amount of white space before and after the text, this provides additional white space at the beginning and end of the box. A value of 150 for Hgt means that you want the box to be one and one-half times the normal height. Since the normal box has a height equal to the point size of the font, this adds additional white space above and below the text. You can use any percentage value between 10 and 999 for Wid and Hgt.

Size and Position

The size of the textbox depends upon the point size of the text inside the box. Once the basic box size is set, then the percentages for the width and the height are applied, and the box is drawn to those percentages of the basic size. As shown in Figure 5-5, the percentages used for width and height determine the final size for the box when it is drawn around the text. Notice that the text is centered inside the resulting box, just as it would be in a standard textbox.

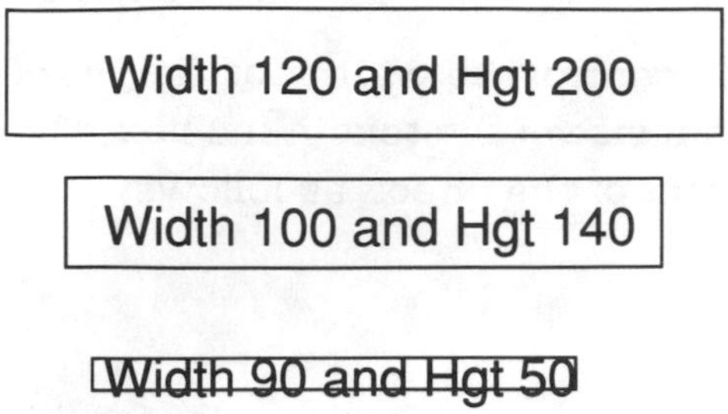

Width 120 and Hgt 200

Width 100 and Hgt 140

Width 90 and Hgt 50

Figure 5-5. Examples of the fitted textbox effect

The three examples in Figure 5-5 show you how changes in the width and height values adjust the size of the box around the line of text. Each line of text is set in 14-point Helvetica, and all the lines of text begin at the same point horizontally. The first two lines are also the same length, which normally would result in identical boxes being drawn around them. As you can see, you can alter the height and width by setting the variables appropriately.

The third example shows what happens when you set values for Wid and Hgt that are less than 100 percent. When you do so, the box is drawn smaller than the text itself. This can be useful to tighten the box around the text and occasionally may be used for special effects. Generally, however, you will want to use percentages greater than 100 to ensure that the box does not obscure the text as in the third example.

It can be difficult to judge precisely the percentages that you need to use to set the size of your box. To set it the way you want, you may have to make some tests using different offsets in your document. For that reason, this effect has two knots: It contains variables, and it may require test prints to set it exactly the way you want it.

Using the Effect

This effect is most useful where you want a box larger than the text. For these circumstances, the box can be fitted to the text block and to the position on the page. You can also create several different box sizes for the same text line. However, since the box is centered on the line of text, this effect is not so useful for boxes to be filled in as the basic textbox, which you saw earlier.

You can use this effect to enclose multiple lines of text. Figure 5-6 shows how you might do this. If you want to box several lines of text, set a large value for the Hgt variable to draw a box that is much higher than the line of text.

The box effect in Figure 5-6 is placed around the center line, "Wid 125 and Hgt 640," which is a separate line in the text. Since the box centers on the given line of text, you must use a line in the center for the effect. The Hgt value, 640, was chosen because the box encloses six lines of text: three above the effect line and two below it. Remember that because the effect does not know about the text above and below the one line of the effect, you must be sure the effect line is long enough for all the text lines to fit. You can use spaces to extend the line if required. As you see, the box is not perfectly centered, but it does set off your text block. If you use this variation on the fitted textbox, you will probably have to make several trials to draw the box that you want.

> Suppose that you have several lines of text.
> You could use this effect with large offsets to make a large box for your text — for example use:
>   Width 125   and   Hgt 640
> Notice that some lines are before the line that has the box effect and some are after the line.

Figure 5-6.   Variation on the fitted textbox effect

SHADOW FITTED TEXTBOX

shadow fitted textbox

Description

This effect draws a fitted textbox and places a drop shadow behind it for added emphasis or visual impact.

Variables

As you might expect, this effect has variables that control the shadow position and darkness and the size of the box. These five variables are listed in the front of the effect text, as follows:

```
150 /Wid 150 /Hgt -05 /Xoff +05 /Yoff 1.00 /Gray 11 dict...
```

Note that you must observe the range and format rules for the variables very strictly. If you don't, the effect may not print.

Wid/Hgt Two variables control the width and height of the box that is drawn around your text in this effect. The Wid variable controls the width and the Hgt variable controls the height of the box. In each case, the values used represent the percentage of the normal size of the box that you want the actual box to be. For example, a value of 150 for Wid means that you want the box to be one and one-half times the normal width. Since the normal width allows a small amount of white space before and after the text, this provides additional white space at the beginning and end of the box. A value of 150 for Hgt means that you want the box to be one and one-half times the normal height. Since the normal box has a height equal to the point size of the font, this adds additional white space above and below the text. You can use any percentage value between 10 and 999 for Wid and Hgt.

Xoff/Yoff   You place the shadow behind the box by setting the horizontal distance, called Xoff—an offset in the x, or horizontal, direction. In a similar fashion, the vertical distance for the shadow is called Yoff. Both distances are in points, which are a printer's measure. A point is $1/72$ inch. You can use either positive or negative values for both Xoff and Yoff.

Positive values of Xoff move the shadow to the right, while negative values move it to the left. Positive values of Yoff move the shadow down the page, and negative values move it up the page.

You must place plus or minus signs in front of the Xoff and Yoff variables, and you must use two digits, as shown. Acceptable values range from ±00 to ±99. Of course, +00 and – 00 are identical and give you the same result: no offset in that direction.

Gray   The darkness of the shadow is set by a control named, reasonably enough, Gray. The values of Gray are percentages, with 1.00 being black and 0.01 being almost white. Although you can use a value of 0.00 (white) this may be somewhat misleading, since that value actually means that nothing is printed behind the box. It doesn't cause a white spot on colored paper, for example.

The Gray variable may range from 1.00 to .01. You always need to have a decimal point in the value and two digits after the decimal point, even if you are using exact tenths. For example, use .50 and not .5 as your value. If you don't, the effect may not print.

Size and Position

The size of the textbox depends upon the point size of the text inside the box. The percentage values that you supply adjust the width and height of the box. The shadow size matches that of the box, as a shadow should. As shown in Figure 5-7, the Xoff and Yoff variables control the position of the shadow and the amount of shadow that shows under the box.

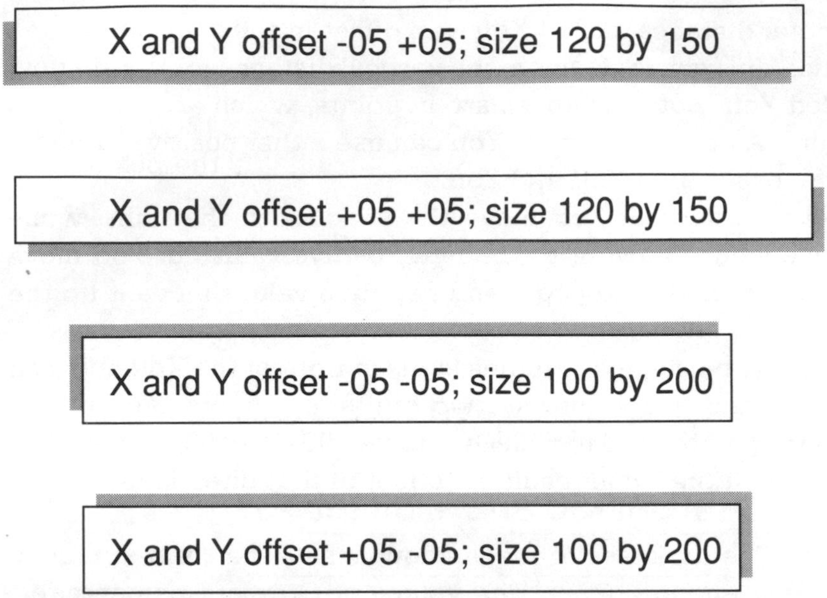

X and Y offset -05 +05; size 120 by 150

X and Y offset +05 +05; size 120 by 150

X and Y offset -05 -05; size 100 by 200

X and Y offset +05 -05; size 100 by 200

Figure 5-7. Examples of the shadow fitted textbox effect

The four examples in Figure 5-7 show you how changes in the offset values move the shadow effect around the textbox. Each line of text is set in 14-point Helvetica, all shadows are .50 Gray, and the position of the shadow and the size of the box for each textbox is set as described in the line of text. As you can see, you can alter the shadowing by changing the signs of the offset values. Notice that the box and shadow sizes change together, as you would expect.

It can be difficult to judge the distance that you want to offset the shadow behind your box, and you may have trouble getting the precise size that you want for the box. To set it the way you want, you may have to make some tests using different offsets and percentages in your document. For that reason, this effect has two knots: It contains variables, and it may require test prints to set it exactly the way you want it.

Using the Effect

The examples in Figure 5-8 show you some interesting variations on shadow placement. To show off the shadow effects, the sizes of the boxes have been made a constant 100 by 120 percent for these examples. If you want, you can also vary the box size as well as the shadow placement to create other effects.

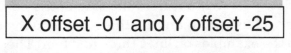

X offset -01 and Y offset -25

X offset -50 and Y offset +05

X offset -03 and Y offset +03

X offset -15 and Y offset +15

ATTENTION

Figure 5-8. Variations of the shadow fitted textbox effect

Basically, if you want a realistic shadow, the values for Xoff and Yoff should be equal and neither too large nor too small for the box. On the other hand, if you want a special effect, then setting different values can produce some interesting results. The first two examples illustrate this point. In both cases, using unequal offsets creates a special look. Notice that, since the box is generally longer than it is tall, larger x offset values are required to make a special effect than y values. On the first line, for example, a y offset of 25 points (about the height of the box) positions the shadow above the box. The larger x offset in the second line only moves the shadow part way out from the side of the box.

Larger boxes will usually require larger offsets, as you might imagine. Notice the examples on lines three and four. These boxes are the same size—24 points—but the shadow is dark and close on one and lighter and further away on the other.

In general, you will find that even the smallest boxes require at least a 2-point offset if you want the shadow to show up clearly. For realistic shadows, offsets of about 20 to 30 percent of the point size of the font seem about right.

The last example in Figure 5-8 shows you another way to use this box to draw the reader's attention. This box uses small type set in the center of a large box with a black drop shadow. The text is set in 9-point Helvetica, the width is 500 percent, and the height is 800 percent of the actual box setting. The black (1.00 Gray) shadow is offset by −15 and +15 points. The result, as you see, is a very noticeable box. The small text attracts the eye and, hopefully, piques the reader's curiosity.

Like the previous fitted box effect, you can use this effect to enclose multiple lines of text. Figure 5-9 shows how you might do this. If you want to box several lines of text, set a large value for the Hgt variable to draw a box that is much higher than the line of text.

The box effect in Figure 5-9 is placed around the center line of the text, "these settings: Wid 120, Hgt 640 and drop shadow,"

Suppose that you have several lines of text.
You could use this effect with large offsets to make a
large box for your text — for example use
these settings: width 120, height 640 and drop shadow
Notice that some lines are before the line that has the
box effect and some are after the line.

Figure 5-9. Another variation for this effect

which is a separate line in the text. Since the box centers on the
given line of text, you must use a line in the center for the effect.
The Hgt value, 640, was chosen because the box encloses six
lines of text: three above the effect line and two below it. Remember
ber that because the effect does not know about the preceding
and following text in the box, you must be sure the effect line is
long enough for all the text lines to fit. You can use spaces to
extend the line if required. As you see, the box is not perfectly
centered, but it does set off your text block. If you use this variation
tion on the fitted textbox, you will probably have to make several
trials to draw the box that you want.

ROUND CORNER TEXTBOX [TEXT]

 round corner textbox

Description

Unlike the basic textbox, which has square corners, this version
has rounded corners. The effect simply draws a single line around
the block of text that you have placed between the beginning of
the effect and the end. The corners of the resulting box are rounded
instead of squared.

Size and Position

Unlike the effects in other chapters, the round corner textbox and the other effects in this chapter are sized according to the text that is placed inside the box, not according to the positioning character. The positioning character is used only to establish the starting position of the textbox. Even if you set a positioning character at a different size than the text, you will get the size box that is appropriate for your text. The first two lines in Figure 5-10 both use a 14-point Helvetica positioning character. As you see, the second line, which contains 24-point text, produces a 24-point box even though the positioning character is 14 points.

The text is approximately centered both horizontally and vertically in the box. The box begins at the positioning character and extends the equivalent distance beyond the text. Because of this, you need to leave some room after the boxed text to be sure that the box does not overlap adjacent text.

The last three lines in Figure 5-10 show that you can add spaces before and/or after the text if you want more room around the text inside the box. In the third line, five spaces were added both before and after the text. In the fourth line, five spaces were added before, and in the fifth line, five spaces were added behind

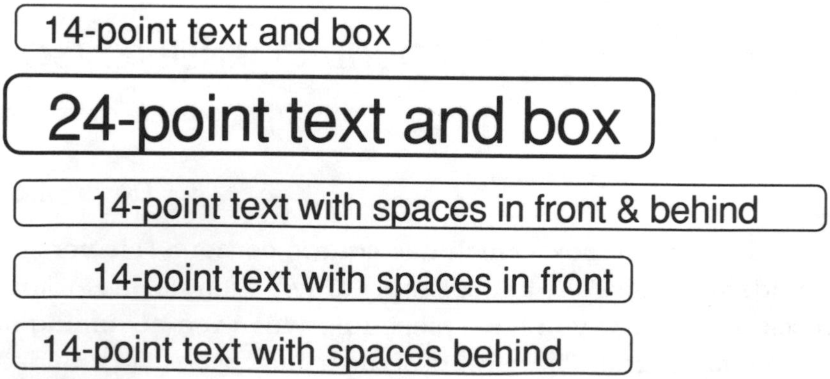

14-point text and box

24-point text and box

14-point text with spaces in front & behind

14-point text with spaces in front

14-point text with spaces behind

Figure 5-10. Sizing the round corner textbox effect

the text. As you see, adding spaces alters the positioning of the box and the location of the text. The last line also illustrates that you cannot place the beginning of the box any closer to the text than the start of the positioning character. You should keep this in mind if you are adjusting the position of the box around a line of text.

Using the Effect

You can use this effect for marking text or making a line stand out on a page. Boxed text is often used for instructions and other special information on a page.

SHADOW ROUND CORNER TEXTBOX

shadow rnd corner textbox

Description

This eye-catching effect draws a round-cornered box around the text, then places a drop shadow behind the box. The added emphasis of the shadow draws the reader's attention because it seems to stand out from the page.

Variables

With the shadow round corner textbox effect, you can control both the darkness and the placement of the shadow in both the horizontal and vertical directions. The three variables are listed in the front of the shadow round corner textbox effect, as follows:

```
-05 /Xoff +05 /Yoff 1.00 /Gray 15 dict...
```

Note that you must observe the range and format rules for the variables very strictly. If you don't, the effect may not print.

237

Xoff/Yoff   You place the shadow behind the box by setting the horizontal distance, called Xoff—an offset in the x, or horizontal, direction. In a similar fashion, the vertical distance for the shadow is called Yoff. Both distances are in points, which is a printer's measure. A point is $1/_{72}$ inch. You can use either positive or negative values for both Xoff and Yoff.

Positive values of Xoff move the shadow to the right, while negative values move it to the left. Positive values of Yoff move the shadow down the page, and negative values move it up the page.

You must place plus or minus signs in front of the Xoff and Yoff variables, and you must use two digits, as shown. Acceptable values range from ±00 to ±99. Of course, +00 and – 00 are identical and give you the same result: no offset in that direction.

Gray   The darkness of the shadow is set by a control named, reasonably enough, Gray. The values of Gray are percentages, with 1.00 being black and 0.01 being almost white. Although you can use a value of 0.00 (white), this may be somewhat misleading, since that value actually means that nothing is printed behind the box. It doesn't cause a white spot on colored paper, for example.

The Gray variable may range from 1.00 to .01. You always need to have a decimal point in the value and two digits after the decimal point, even if you are using exact tenths. For example, use .50 and not .5 as your value. If you don't, the effect may not print.

Size and Position

The size of the textbox depends upon the point size of the text inside the box. The shadow size matches that of the box, as a shadow should. As shown in Figure 5-12, the Xoff and Yoff variables control the position of the shadow and the amount of shadow that shows under the box.

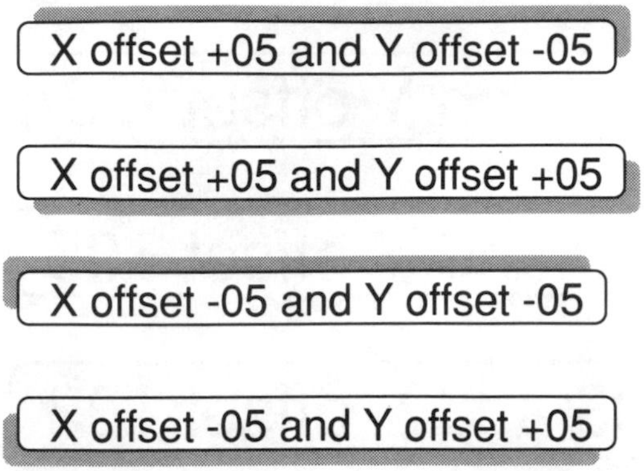

X offset +05 and Y offset -05

X offset +05 and Y offset +05

X offset -05 and Y offset -05

X offset -05 and Y offset +05

Figure 5-11. Examples of the shadow round corner textbox effect

The four examples in Figure 5-11 show you how changes in the offset values move the shadow effect around the textbox. Each line of text is set in 14-point Helvetica, all shadows are .50 Gray, and the position of the shadow for each textbox is set as described in the line of text. As you can see, you can alter the shadowing by changing the signs of the offset values.

It can be difficult to judge the distance that you want to offset the shadow behind your box. To set it the way you want, you may have to make some tests using different offsets in your document. For that reason, this effect has two knots: It contains variables, and it may require test prints to set it exactly the way you want it.

Using the Effect

The examples in Figure 5-12 show you some interesting variations on shadow placement. Basically, if you want a realistic shadow, the values for Xoff and Yoff should be equal and neither too large nor too small for the box. On the other hand, if you want a special effect, then setting different values can produce some interesting results. The first two examples illustrate this point. In

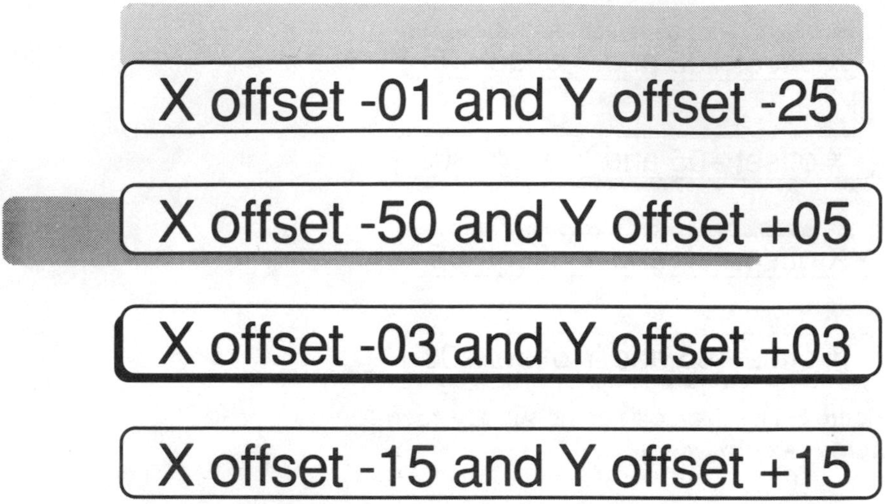

X offset -01 and Y offset -25

X offset -50 and Y offset +05

X offset -03 and Y offset +03

X offset -15 and Y offset +15

Figure 5-12. Variations of the shadow round corner textbox effect

both cases, using unequal offsets creates a special look. Notice that, since the box is generally longer than it is tall, larger x offset values are required to make a special effect than y values. On the first line, for example, a y offset of 25 points (about the height of the box) positions the shadow above the box. The larger x offset in the second line only moves the shadow part way out from the side of the box.

Larger boxes will usually require larger offsets, as you might imagine. Notice the examples on lines three and four. These boxes are the same size—24 points—but the shadow is dark and close on one and lighter and further away on the other.

In general, you will find that even the smallest boxes require at least a 2-point offset if you want the shadow to show up clearly. For realistic shadows, offsets of about 20 to 30 percent of the point size of the font seem about right.

FITTED ROUND CORNER TEXTBOX

fitted rnd corner textbox

Description

Sometimes you want more white space around a line of text than you can get with the standard round corner textbox effect. With the fitted round corner textbox effect, you can adjust both the height and width of the box to create a textbox that is the exact size that you want.

Variables

This effect lets you control the width and height of the box as a percentage of the font size of the text in the box. The two variables are listed in the front of the fitted round corner textbox effect, as follows:

`150 /Wid 120 /Hgt 14 dict...`

Note that you must observe the range and format rules for the variables very strictly. If you don't, the effect may not print.

Wid/Hgt   Two variables control the width and height of the box drawn around your text in this effect. The Wid variable controls the width and the Hgt variable controls the height of the box. In each case, the values used represent the percentage of the normal size of the box that you want the actual box to be. For example, a value of 150 for Wid means that you want the box to be one and one-half times the normal width. Since the normal width allows a small amount of white space before and after the text, this provides additional white space at the beginning and end of the box. A value of 150 for Hgt means that you want the box to be one and one-half times the normal height. Since the

241

normal box has a height equal to the point size of the font, this adds additional white space above and below the text. You can use any percentage value between 10 and 999 for Wid and Hgt.

Size and Position

The fitted textbox initially determines size based on the point size of the text inside the box. Once the basic box size is set, then the percentages for the width and height are applied, and the box is drawn to those percentages of the basic size. As shown in Figure 5-13, the percentages used for width and height determine the final size for the box when it is drawn around the text. Notice that the text is centered inside the resulting box, just as it would be in a standard textbox.

The three examples in Figure 5-13 show you how changes in the width and height values adjust the size of the box around the line of text. Each line of text is set in 14-point Helvetica, and all the lines of text begin at the same point horizontally. The first two lines are also the same length, which normally would result in identical boxes being drawn around them. As you can see, you can alter the height and width by setting the variables appropriately.

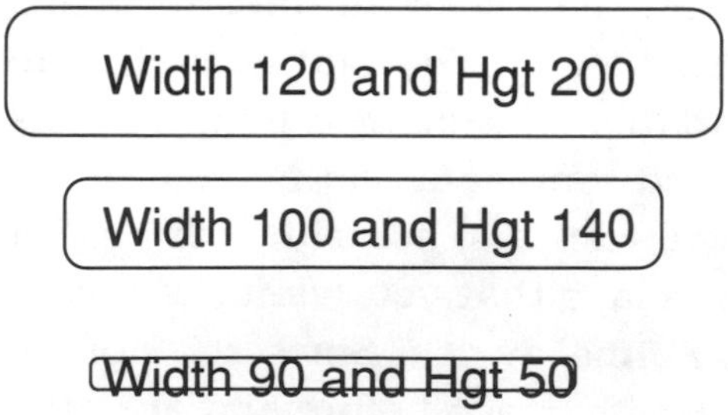

Width 120 and Hgt 200

Width 100 and Hgt 140

Width 90 and Hgt 50

Figure 5-13. Examples of the fitted round corner textbox effect

The third example shows what happens when you set values for Wid and Hgt that are less than 100 percent. When you do so, the box is drawn smaller than the text itself. This can be useful to tighten the box around the text and occasionally may be used for special effects. Generally, however, you will want to use percentages greater than 100 to ensure that the box does not obscure the text as in the third example.

It can be difficult to judge precisely the percentages that you need to use to set the size of your box. To set it the way you want, you may have to make some tests using different offsets in your document. For that reason, this effect has two knots: It contains variables, and it may require test prints to set it exactly the way you want it.

Using the Effect

This effect is most useful where you want a box larger than the text. For these circumstances, the box can be fitted to the text block and to the position on the page. You can also create several different box sizes for the same text line. However, since the box is centered on the line of text, this effect is not so useful for boxes to be filled in as the basic textbox, which you saw earlier.

You can use this effect to enclose multiple lines of text. Figure 5-14 shows how you might do this. If you want to box several lines of text, set a large value for the Hgt variable to draw a box that is much higher than the line of text.

The box effect in Figure 5-14 is placed around the center line, "Wid 125 and Hgt 640," which is a separate line in the text. Since the box centers on the given line of text, you must use a line in the center for the effect. The Hgt value, 640, was chosen because the box encloses six lines of text: three above the effect line and two below it. Remember that because the effect does not know about the preceding and following text in the box, you must be sure the effect line is long enough for all the text lines to fit. You can use

Suppose that you have several lines of text.
You could use this effect with large offsets to make a large
box for your text — for example use:
Width 125   and   Hgt 640
Notice that some lines are before the line that has the box
effect and some are after the line.

Figure 5-14.   Variation on the fitted round corner textbox effect

spaces to extend the line if required. As you see, the box is not perfectly centered, but it does set off your text block. If you use this variation on the fitted textbox, you will probably have to make several trials to draw the box that you want.

TEXT

SHADOW FITTED ROUND CORNER TEXTBOX

shadow fit rnd corner textbox

Description

This effect draws a round corner fitted textbox and places a drop shadow behind it for added emphasis or visual impact.

Variables

As you might expect, this effect has variables that control the shadow position and darkness and the size of the box. These five variables are listed in the front of the effect text, as follows:

150 /Wid **150** /Hgt **-05** /Xoff **+05** /Yoff **1.00** /Gray 17 dict...

Note that you must observe the range and format rules for the variables very strictly. If you don't, the effect may not print.

Wid/Hgt   Two variables control the width and height of the box that is drawn around your text in this effect. The Wid variable controls the width and the Hgt variable controls the height of the box. In each case, the values used represent the percentage of the normal size of the box that you want the actual box to be. For example, a value of 150 for Wid means that you want the box to be one and one-half times the normal width. Since the normal width allows a small amount of white space before and after the text, this provides additional white space at the beginning and end of the box. A value of 150 for Hgt means that you want the box to be one and one-half times the normal height. Since the normal box has a height equal to the point size of the font, this adds additional white space above and below the text. You can use any percentage value between 10 and 999 for Wid and Hgt.

Xoff/Yoff   You place the shadow behind the box by setting the horizontal distance, called Xoff—an offset in the x, or horizontal, direction. In a similar fashion, the vertical distance for the shadow is called Yoff. Both distances are in points, which are a printer's measure. A point is $1/_{72}$ inch. You can use either positive or negative values for both Xoff and Yoff.

Positive values of Xoff move the shadow to the right, while negative values move it to the left. Positive values of Yoff move the shadow down the page, and negative values move it up the page.

You must place plus or minus signs in front of the Xoff and Yoff variables, and you must use two digits, as shown. Acceptable values range from ±00 to ±99. Of course, +00 and – 00 are identical and give you the same result: no offset in that direction.

Gray   The darkness of the shadow is set by a control named, reasonably enough, Gray. The values of Gray are percentages, with 1.00 being black and 0.01 being almost white. Although you can use a value of 0.00 (white), this may be somewhat misleading, since that value actually means that nothing is printed behind the box. It doesn't cause a white spot on colored paper, for example.

245

The Gray variable may range from 1.00 to .01. You always need to have a decimal point in the value and two digits after the decimal point, even if you are using exact tenths. For example, use .50 and not .5 as your value. If you don't, the effect may not print.

Size and Position

The size of the textbox depends upon the point size of the text inside the box. The percentage values that you supply adjust the width and height of the box. The shadow size matches that of the box, as a shadow should. As shown in Figure 5-15, the Xoff and Yoff variables control the position of the shadow and therefore the amount of shadow that shows under the box.

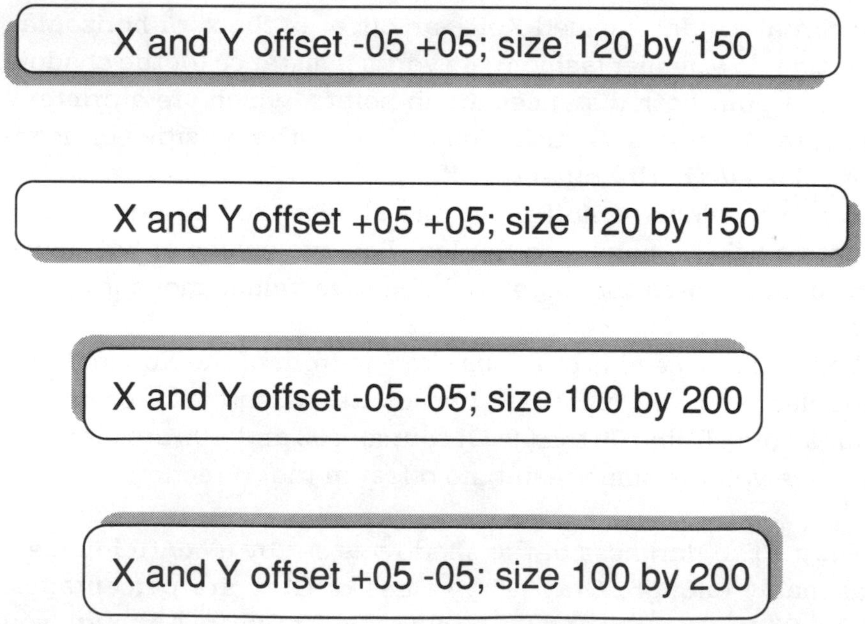

X and Y offset -05 +05; size 120 by 150

X and Y offset +05 +05; size 120 by 150

X and Y offset -05 -05; size 100 by 200

X and Y offset +05 -05; size 100 by 200

Figure 5-15. Examples of the shadow fitted round corner textbox effect

The four examples in Figure 5-15 show you how changes in the offset values move the shadow effect around the textbox. Each line of text is set in 14-point Helvetica, all shadows are .50 Gray and the position of the shadow and the size of the box for each textbox is set as described in the line of text. As you can see, you can alter the shadowing by changing the signs of the offset values. Notice that the box and shadow sizes change together, as you would expect.

It can be difficult to judge the distance that you want to offset the shadow behind your box, and you may have trouble getting the precise size that you want for the box. To set it the way you want, you may have to make some tests using different offsets and percentages in your document. For that reason, this effect has two knots: It contains variables, and it may require test prints to set it exactly the way you want it.

Using the Effect

The examples in Figure 5-16 show you some interesting variations on shadow placement. To show off the shadow effects, the sizes of the boxes have been made a constant 100 by 120 percent for these examples. If you want, you can also vary the box size as well as the shadow placement to create other effects.

Basically, if you want a realistic shadow, the values for Xoff and Yoff should be equal and neither too large nor too small for the box. On the other hand, if you want a special effect, then setting different values can produce some interesting results. The first two examples illustrate this point. In both cases, using unequal offsets creates a special look. Notice that, since the box is generally longer than it is tall, larger x offset values are required to make a special effect than y values. On the first line, for example, a y offset of 25 points (about the height of the box) positions the shadow above the box. The larger x offset in the second line only moves the shadow part way out from the side of the box.

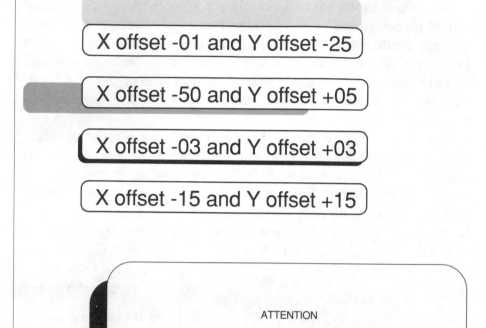

Figure 5-16. Variations of the shadow fitted round corner textbox effect

Larger boxes will usually require larger offsets, as you might imagine. Notice the examples on lines three and four. These boxes are the same size—24 points—but the shadow is dark and close on one and lighter and farther away on the other.

In general, you will find that even the smallest boxes require at least a 2-point offset if you want the shadow to show up clearly. For realistic shadows, offsets of about 20 to 30 percent of the point size of the font seem about right.

The last example in Figure 5-16 shows you another way to use this box to draw the reader's attention. This box uses small type set in the center of a large box with a black drop shadow. The text is set in 9-point Helvetica, the width is 500 percent, and the height is 800 percent of the actual box setting. The black (1.00 Gray) shadow is offset by –15 and +15 points. The result, as you see, is a very noticeable box. The small text attracts the eye and, hopefully, piques the reader's curiosity.

Like the previous fitted box effects, you can use this effect to enclose multiple lines of text. Figure 5-17 shows how you might do this. If you want to box several lines of text, set a large value for the Hgt variable to draw a box that is much higher than the line of text.

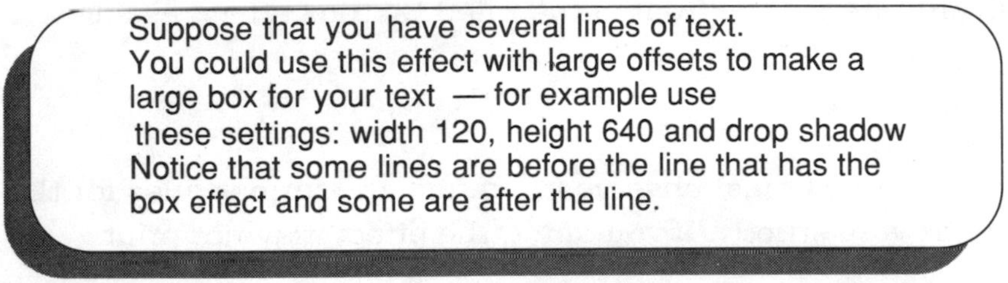

Suppose that you have several lines of text.
You could use this effect with large offsets to make a
large box for your text — for example use
these settings: width 120, height 640 and drop shadow
Notice that some lines are before the line that has the
box effect and some are after the line.

Figure 5-17. Another variation for this effect

The box effect in Figure 5-17 is placed around the center line of the text, "these settings: Wid 120, Hgt 640 and drop shadow," which is a separate line in the text. Since the box centers on the given line of text, you must use a line in the center for the effect. The Hgt value, 640, was chosen because the box encloses six lines of text: three above the effect line and two below it. Remember that because the effect does not know about the preceding and following text in the box, you must be sure the effect line is long enough for all the text lines to fit. You can use spaces to extend the line if required. As you see, the box is not perfectly centered, but it does set off your text block. If you use this variation on the fitted textbox, you will probably have to make several trials to draw the box that you want.

249

$\boxed{\mathcal{TEXT}}$

RULED TEXTBOX

ruled textbox

Description

This effect draws a box with two lines around the text. This is a fancier form of box and makes the box stand out a bit more than the standard textbox.

Variables

This effect is similar to the textbox itself, except that you adjust the lines that make up the box. You can control the width of each of the two lines and the space between the lines. The three variables are listed in the front of the ruled textbox effect, as follows:

1 /Line1 **2** /Line2 **2** /Space 11 dict . . .

Note that you must observe the range and format rules for the variables very strictly. If you don't, the effect may not print.

Line1/Line2   The first two variables control the size of the two lines that go around the box. Line1 sets the size of the inner line, and Line2 sets the size of the outside line. The value for each of these line widths may range from 0 to 9 points. If you use a line width of 0, you will get the thinnest line possible on your device. On a LaserWriter, or other laser printer, this is about $^1/_{300}$ inch wide, which appears as a hairline. However, if you are printing on imagesetting devices, such as a Linotronic, the line produced will be so thin that you cannot see it.

Space   The distance between the two lines, measured in points, is set by the Space variable. The value for the Space variable may range from 0 to 9.

Size and Position

The size of the textbox depends upon the point size of the text inside the box. The sizes of the lines surrounding the text are controlled by the Line1 and Line2 variables. As a result, the box may print closer to the text than a standard textbox.

The five examples in Figure 5-18 show you how changes in the line widths and the spacing between the lines affects the resulting box. Each line of text is set in 14-point Helvetica, while the size and spacing of the lines is set as described in the line of text. As you can see, you can alter the boxes by changing the sizes of the lines and of the spacing value.

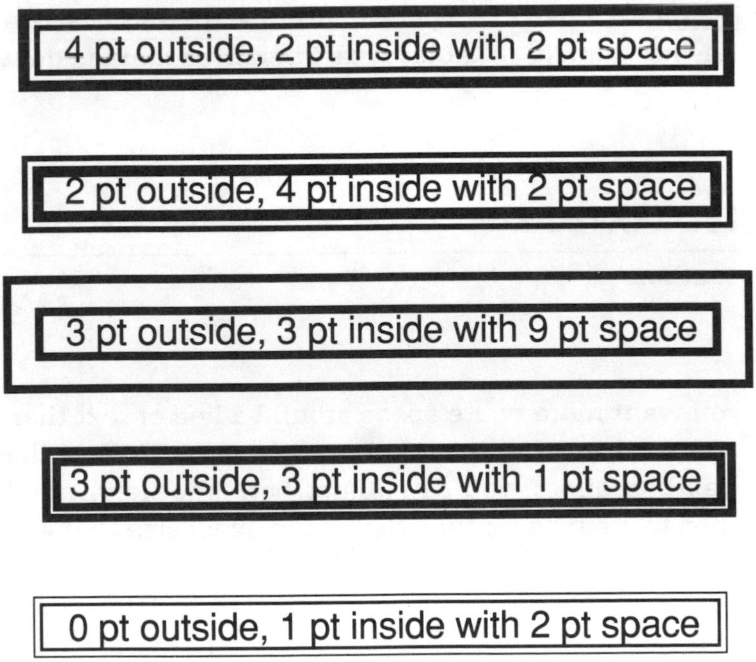

4 pt outside, 2 pt inside with 2 pt space

2 pt outside, 4 pt inside with 2 pt space

3 pt outside, 3 pt inside with 9 pt space

3 pt outside, 3 pt inside with 1 pt space

0 pt outside, 1 pt inside with 2 pt space

Figure 5-18. Examples of the ruled textbox effect

Notice that using large line widths for the inner line results in the box closing in on the text. For this reason, you will generally want to print a test of this effect, particularly if you are using heavy inner lines.

The fifth example shows you a 0 width line, which becomes a hairline on LaserWriter output. If you printed this same effect on a Linotronic or other imagesetter (as in Figure 5-18), the outer line would disappear, since it would be too fine to be seen. If you will be printing your final copy on an imagesetter, you should not use the value of 0 for either of the two lines.

Using the Effect

This effect is primarily used for special output or to emphasize a line of text. It is not usually suitable for tasks such as making data boxes.

FITTED RULED TEXTBOX

fitted ruled textbox

Description

Sometimes you want more white space around a line of text than you can get with the standard ruled textbox effect. With the fitted ruled textbox effect, you can adjust both the height and width of the box to create a textbox that is the exact size that you want.

Variables

The fitted ruled textbox effect lets you control the width and height of the box as a percentage of the font size of the text in the box. You can also control the width of each of the two lines and the space between them. The five variables are listed in the front of the fitted textbox effect, as follows:

```
1 /Line1 2 /Line2 2 /Space 150 /Wid 150 /Hgt 13 dict . . .
```

Note that you must observe the range and format rules for the variables very strictly. If you don't, the effect may not print.

Line1/Line2   The first two variables control the size of the two lines that go around the box. Line1 sets the size of the inner line, and Line2 sets the size of the outside line. The value for each of these line widths may range from 0 to 9 points. If you use a line width of 0, you will get the thinnest line possible on your device. On a LaserWriter, or other laser printer, this is about $1/300$ inch wide, which appears as a hairline. However, if you are printing on imagesetting devices, such as a Linotronic, the line produced will be so thin that you cannot see it.

Space   The distance between the two lines, measured in points, is set by the Space variable. The value for the Space variable may range from 0 to 9.

Wid/Hgt   Two variables control the width and height of the box drawn around your text in this effect. The Wid variable controls the width and the Hgt variable controls the height of the box. In each case, the values used represent the percentage of the normal size of the box that you want the actual box to be. For example, a value of 150 for Wid means that you want the box to be one and one-half times the normal width. Since the normal width allows a small amount of white space before and after the text, this provides additional white space at the beginning and end of the box. A value of 150 for Hgt means that you want the box to be one and one-half times the normal height. Since the normal box has a height equal to the point size of the font, this adds additional white space above and below the text. You can use any percentage value between 10 and 999 for Wid and Hgt.

Size and Position

The size of the textbox depends upon the point size of the text inside the box. Once the basic box size is set, then the percentages for the width and height are applied. As shown in Figure 5-19, the percentages used for width and height determine the final size for the box when it is drawn around the text. Notice that the text is centered inside the resulting box, just as it would be in a standard textbox.

The three examples in Figure 5-19 show you how changes in the width and height values adjust the size of the box around the line of text. Each line of text is set in 14-point Helvetica, and all the lines of text begin at the same point horizontally. The lines are also the same length, which normally would result in identical boxes being drawn around them. As you can see, you can alter height and width by setting the variables appropriately.

These three examples also illustrate how you can change the line and spacing variables to achieve different results, and how

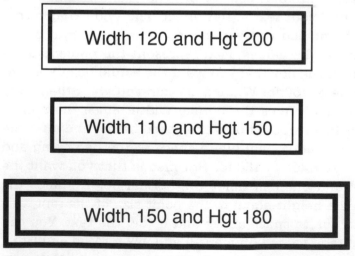

Figure 5-19. Examples of the fitted ruled textbox effect

the percentage settings are affected by differences in line widths and spacing. The first two boxes both use a 3-point and 1-point line, with the thin line outside on the first example and inside on the second. The larger Hgt variable in the first example (200) is necessary to compensate for the thicker line that is near the text. In the second example, the thicker line is outside, so that the Hgt variable can be less and still have sufficient room around the text.

The last example shows you two thick lines (both 4 points, with 4-point spacing) around a line of text. As you can see, the text actually looks smaller than the line above it, even though the text is the same size and the Hgt is larger. This is an excellent illustration of how heavier lines cause the box to move into the text. Using large line widths for the inner line results in the box closing in on the text. For this reason, you generally want to use slightly higher percentages for the height than you would in a standard fitted textbox.

It can be difficult to judge precisely the percentages that you need to set the size of your box, the line weights, and spacing required for your intended effect. You may have to make some tests using different offsets, line widths, and spacing in your document. For that reason, this effect has two knots: It contains variables, and it may require test prints to set it exactly the way you want it.

Using the Effect

This effect is most useful where you want a box larger than the text. For these circumstances, the box can be fitted to the text block and to the position on the page. You can also create several different box sizes for the same text line.

You can use this effect to enclose multiple lines of text. Figure 5-20 shows how you might do this. If you want to draw a box around several lines of text, you can set a large value for the Hgt variable to draw a box that is much higher than the line of text.

Suppose that you have several lines of text.
You could use this effect with large offsets to make a large
box for your text — for example use:
Wid   125   and   Hgt 650
Notice that some lines are before the line that has the box
effect and some are after the line.

Figure 5-20. Variation on the fitted ruled textbox effect

The box effect in Figure 5-20 is placed around the center line, "Wid 125 and Hgt 650," which is a separate line in the text. Since the box centers on the given line of text, you must use a line in the center for the effect. The Hgt value, 650, was chosen because the box encloses six lines of text: three above the effect line and two below it. Remember that because the effect does not know about the preceding and following text in the box, you must be sure the effect line is long enough for all the text lines to fit. You can use spaces to extend the line if required. As you see, the box is not perfectly centered, but it does set off your text block. If you use this variation on the fitted textbox, you will probably have to make several trials to draw the box that you want.

REGULAR STAR

regular star

Description

Sometimes you want more than just a box around your text. If you want to really make the text stand out from the page, a star around the text is very eye-catching. This effect draws a nine-pointed star around your text. The star in this effect has points of equal length, spaced evenly around the star. The result is that you can enter any text that you want into your document and put it inside a star.

Variables

This effect has one variable that controls the diameter of the star. This variable is listed in the front of the effect text, as shown here:

```
100 /Pct 7 dict . . .
```

Note that you must observe the range and format rules for the variables very strictly. If you don't, the effect may not print.

Pct   The Pct variable controls the diameter of the star that is drawn around your text. The value used in Pct represents the percentage of the normal size of the star that you want the actual star to be. For example, a value of 150 for Pct means that you want the star drawn one and one-half times the normal diameter. Since the normal diameter of the star allows a small amount of white space before and after the text inside the star, the normal star is drawn with a diameter slightly greater than the length of the line of text inside the star. This value for Pct provides additional white space all around the text.

Size and Position

The regular star initially determines size in the same way as the standard textbox effect: The text inside the star sets the size of the star. Once the basic star size is set, the percentage Pct is applied to the star, and it is drawn to that percentage of the basic size. Since a star is formed like a circle, the overall size of the star is the diameter of the circle that would fit inside the points of the star. As illustrated in Figure 5-21, the percentage used for the diameter determines the final size for the star when it is drawn around the text. Notice that the text is centered inside the resulting star, just as it would be in a standard textbox.

257

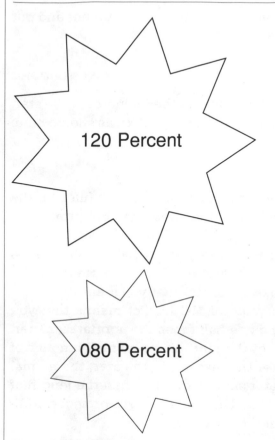

Figure 5-21. Examples of the regular star effect

The two examples in Figure 5-21 show you how changes in the percent values adjust the diameter of the star around the line of text. Each line of text is set in 14-point Helvetica, and the lines of text begin at the same point horizontally. Because of the addition of a 0 in front of the 80, the lines are also the same length, which normally would result in identical stars being drawn around them. However, with the Pct variable set, the results are stars of quite different sizes. As you can see, you can create substantial variation in diameter by setting the percentage variable appropriately.

Notice that the star is much more like a circle than it is like the standard textbox. This means that you have to allow room all around the effect for the star to print. This may require moving or adjusting lines of text both above and below the star effect.

It can be difficult to judge precisely the percentage that you need to use to set the size of the star required for your intended effect. To set it the way you want, you may have to make some tests with different percentage values, different line widths, and spacing settings in your document. For that reason, this effect has three knots: It contains a variable, and it may require several test prints to set it exactly the way you want it.

Using the Effect

This effect is most useful where you want to place text inside a star for emphasis or dramatic value. The star can be fitted very precisely to the text block that you place on the page. The effect also allows you to create several different sizes of star for the same text line, or to make several stars of the same size with different text inside them.

This effect can be used to enclose multiple lines of text with a little extra work on your part. If you want to draw a star around several lines of text, you can set a value for the Pct variable to draw a star that has a diameter suitable for the text block that you want to enclose.

Figure 5-22 shows how you might do this. This star is drawn around the line of text that says "15 to 50 Percent Off." Since the star centers on the given line of text, you must use a line in the center for the effect. Since this is also the longest line of text in the block, the star here is drawn at 100 Pct. If the text block contained more lines, or if one of the other lines were longer than the center line, then you would have to use a larger value for Pct to enclose all of the text block.

Figure 5-22. Variation on the regular star effect

Remember also that because the effect does not know about the text above and below the line of the effect, you must adjust the percentage and the length of the effect line so that the star does not cut off the text lines above or below. You can use spaces to extend the line if required. If you want to use this variation, you will probably have to make several trials to set the percentage to draw the star that you want.

IRREGULAR STARBURST

irregular star

Description

Sometimes you want more than just a box around your text. If you want to really make the text stand out from the page, a star around the text is very eye-catching. This effect draws a nine-pointed star around your text. The star in this effect has points of unequal length, spaced unevenly around the star. The result is that you can enter any text that you want onto your document and put it inside an irregular star.

Variables

This effect has one variable that controls the diameter of the star. This variable is listed in the front of the effect text, as shown here:

```
100 /Pct 7 dict...
```

Note that you must observe the range and format rules for the variables very strictly. If you don't, the effect may not print.

Pct   The Pct variable controls the diameter of the star that is drawn around your text. The value used in Pct represents the percentage of the normal size of the star that you want the actual star to be. For example, a value of 150 for Pct means that you want the star drawn one and one-half times the normal diameter. Since the normal diameter of the star allows a small amount of white space before and after the text inside the star, the normal star is drawn with a diameter slightly greater than the length of the line of text inside the star. This value for Pct provides additional white space all around the text.

Size and Position

The irregular star initially determines size in the same way as the standard textbox effect: The text inside the star sets the size of the star. Once the basic star size is set, the percentage Pct is applied to the star, and it is drawn to that percentage of the basic size. Even though this star is irregular, it still follows the basic principles for drawing a regular star. Since a star is formed like a circle, the overall size of the star is the diameter of the circle that would fit inside the points of the star. As illustrated in Figure 5-23, the percentage used for the diameter determines the final size for the star when it is drawn around the text. Notice that the text is centered inside the resulting star, just as it would be in a standard textbox.

The two examples in Figure 5-23 show you how changes in the percent values adjust the diameter of the star around the line of

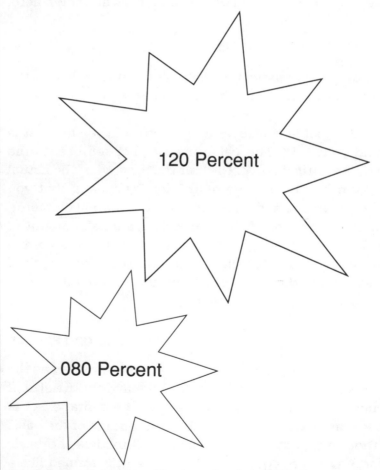

Figure 5-23. Examples of the irregular star effect

text. Each line of text is set in 14-point Helvetica, and the lines of text are offset horizontally, so that the stars do not touch one another. Because of the addition of a 0 in front of the 80, the lines are the same length, which normally would result in identical stars being drawn around them. However, with the Pct variable set, the results are stars of quite different size. As you can see, you can get a substantial variation in diameter by setting the percentage variable appropriately.

Notice that the star is more like a circle than it is like the standard textbox. This means that you have to allow room all around the effect for the star to print. In particular, since the star is irregular and extends out more than you might expect, this may require moving or adjusting lines of text both above and below the star effect.

It can be difficult to judge precisely the percentage that you need to use to set the size of the star required for your intended effect. To set it the way you want, you may have to make some tests with different percentage values, different line widths, and spacing settings in your document. For that reason, this effect has three knots: It contains a variable, and it may require several test prints to set it exactly the way you want it.

Using the Effect

This effect is most useful where you want to place text inside a star for emphasis or dramatic value. The star can be fitted very precisely to the text block that you place on the page. The effect also allows you to create several different sizes of star for the same text line, or to make several stars of the same size with different text inside them.

This effect can be used to enclose multiple lines of text with a little extra work on your part. If you want to draw a star around several lines of text, you can set a value for the Pct variable to draw a star that has a diameter suitable for the text block that you want to enclose.

Figure 5-24 shows how you might do this. This star is drawn around the line of text that says "15 to 50 Percent Off." Since the star centers on the given line of text, you must use a line in the center for the effect. Since this is also the longest line of text in the block, the star here is drawn at 100 Pct. If the text block contained more lines, or if one of the other lines were longer than the center line, then you would have to use a larger value for Pct to enclose all of the text block.

Remember also that because the effect does not know about the text above and below the line of the effect, you must adjust the percentage and the length of the effect line so that the star does not cut off the text lines above or below. You can use spaces to extend the line if required. If you want to use this variation, you will probably have to make several trials to set the percentage to draw the star that you want.

Special!
15 to 50 Percent Off
Today Only!

Figure 5-24. Variation on the irregular star effect

RULER

ruler

Description

One effect that can be very useful in certain circumstances is a ruler. You can use a ruler as an icon and as a measure of progress. This effect draws a ruler over any text that you place on your page and allows you to add a gray progress bar that marks the ruler to any percentage that you want. The result is that you can make a ruler that has a variety of divisions and labels for your text.

Variables

This effect has three variables that control the divisions inside the ruler and the progress bar on the ruler itself. These variables are listed in the front of the effect text, as shown here:

65 /Pct **5** /Maj **1** /Min 12 dict begin...

Note that you must observe the range and format rules for the variables very strictly; if you don't, the effect may not print.

Pct The progress bar in this effect is controlled by the Pct variable. When you create the ruler, the interior of the ruler is filled with a gray progress bar that indicates how far something has gone. The value used in Pct represents the percentage of the ruler that you want the progress bar to fill. For example, a value of 50 for Pct means that you want the progress bar to fill one-half of the ruler. If you don't want a progress bar to show, use the value 00 for the Pct variable; this will eliminate the progress bar. The progress bar Pct can range from 00 to 100. Always use at least two digits in your Pct variable, even if you are using a single-digit value, or the effect may not print. For example, if you want a 5 percent bar, use 05 for Pct.

265

Maj/Min   Every ruler has divisions within it that allow you to tell what is being measured. The divisions in this effect are controlled by the Maj and Min variables. These variables control the major (large) divisions and the minor (small) ones. Each variable defines the number of lines in that division. The Maj variable controls the number of large lines that are drawn on the ruler, and the lines are spaced evenly along the length of the ruler. If the value of Maj is 3, for example, then there is one large line at each end of the ruler and one in the middle; if it is 4, then there would be one line at each end, one one-third of the distance along the ruler, and one two-thirds of the distance. In the same way, the Min variable controls the number of small lines inside each larger division. If the value of Min is 3, for example, then each major division will have three lines, spaced equally, which would divide each large segment into four parts. The Maj and Min variables can range from 0 to 9, but Maj values generally are between 2 and 9 to account for the ends of the ruler. Always use a single digit in your Maj and Min variables, or the effect may not print.

Size and Position

The distance from the beginning of the effect, that is, from the positioning character at the beginning of your effect, to the end of the effect determines the size of the ruler. The ruler is drawn to that length, and positioned so that it is over the top of any text that falls in between these points. You can place any text, or no text at all, between the positioning character and the ruler effect text. Since the ruler is drawn independently of the text, it is your responsibility to make any text, such as labels or numbers for the divisions, match the ruler.

The examples in Figure 5-25 show how changes in the Maj and Min variable values adjust the divisions of the ruler. Each line of text is set in 18-point Helvetica Bold, and the lines of text begin at the same point horizontally. The first example shows five major division lines with two minor division lines between each major division, and the bar is filled to 50 percent. This was done with

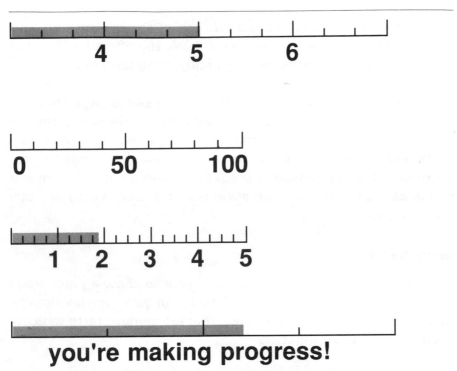

you're making progress!

Figure 5-25. Examples of the ruler effect

these settings: 50 /Pct 5 /Maj 2 /Min. Notice that you must account for the major lines at the beginning and end of the ruler if you want them to print. That means that, normally, you will have a Maj value of at least 2, for the two ends of the ruler. If you use a value of 1 for Maj, only the bar at the end of the ruler will print. If you use a value of 0, nothing prints.

The second example shows numbers at the beginning and end of the ruler bar. In this case, the settings for the ruler were 00 /Pct 3 /Maj 5 /Min. Notice that the 0, which was placed immediately after the begin effect text, is slightly indented. Also, the 100, which is placed just before the ruler effect text, is also slightly under the ruler. The last example shows you that you can use any text, not just numbers, for your ruler.

Notice that the ruler is drawn on top of the line of text. This means that you have to allow room above the effect for the ruler to print. This may require moving or adjusting lines of text above the ruler effect.

It can be difficult to judge precisely the percentage that you need to use to set the size of the ruler required for your intended effect. To set it the way you want, you may have to make several tests with different text positions and spacing settings in your document. For that reason, this effect has three knots: It contains variables, and it may require several test prints to set it exactly the way you want it.

Using the Effect

This effect is most useful where you want to show a percentage of something, such as completed tasks, in your document. The ruler can also be used as a measurement marker, or to indicate specific types of information.

IMPORTANT

Background

Text

6

4   5   6

THIS CHAPTER GIVES YOU A SERIES OF EFFECTS THAT USE text for a background or as a graphic element. These effects include placing text behind your regular document, rotating text, and placing text along an angled line. You met this type of effect in the first chapter, when you worked with rotated text.

For these effects, you must enter the display text into the effect itself, unlike the textboxes in the previous chapter, which are drawn around text in your word processing program. The major issues in using the effects in this chapter are inserting the text and placing the effect correctly. Note: These effects work only with a single line of text of not more than 100 characters.

INSERTING BACKGROUND TEXT IN MICROSOFT WORD

1. Open your document. Insert a positioning character where you want to place the effect. The size of the positioning character determines the basic size of your effect.

2. Open the **xxxx.w** file, where **xxxx** represents the name of the desired effect. If only one line of text appears when you open the file, click on the Show Hidden Text box in the Preferences . . . selection of the Edit menu. Select and copy all the text of the effect and place it at the beginning of the page that will contain the effect. Notice that the major part of the text in this file is in Word's PostScript style. (If you are unclear about how to use this style, review the instructions in Chapter 1.)

3. Cut the text at the end of the .w file that is *not* in the PostScript style from the end of the effect text. This is the second part of the effect.

4. Paste this text into your Word document immediately after (to the right of) the positioning character.

5. Enter the text that you want to use into the Str variable for your effect.

6. Select all of the text, and only the text, from the second part of the effect file that you pasted into your document. Change the font to the PostScript Escape font. This part of the effect text will disappear.

7. Be sure that the Print Hidden Text box in the Print dialog box is not checked. Print your document. The effect will print over the positioning character.

INSERTING BACKGROUND TEXT IN REGULAR WORD PROCESSING APPLICATIONS

1. Open your document. Insert a positioning character where you want to place the effect. The size of the positioning character determines the basic size of your effect.

2. Open the effect file and select and copy the effect text.

3. Paste the effect text into your document immediately after (to the right of) the positioning character.

4. Enter the text that you want to use into the Str variable for your effect.

5. Select the effect text, and only the effect text, up to the % that occurs inside the effect. The portion of the effect that contains the % character will appear as follows:

```
. . . save put } if % cf setfont
```

The % is printed in bold in this line although it is not bold in the file. Be sure that you have selected the text up to, but not including, the % and change it to the PostScript Escape font. This is the first part of the effect.

6. Select the remainder of the effect text, and only the effect text, from the % that occurs inside the effect to the end of the effect.

Be sure that you have selected the text from, but not including, the % and change it to the PostScript Escape font. This is the second part of the effect. When you are done, you should see only the positioning character followed by the % where your effect was.

7. Print your document in the ordinary way. The effect will print over the positioning character and will erase the % as it prints.

ROTATED TEXT

rotated text

Description

You can place a line of text on the page and rotate it to any angle. The text can be displayed in black or any shade of gray that you want. This flexible and useful effect has many applications. One of the most common complaints about the early generations of page layout programs was that they could not rotate text to any angle. As you see here, this procedure isn't very difficult—as long as you don't need to see the result on your screen.

Variables

As with all these text effects, you must enter the string of text to be displayed into the effect itself. You have control over the rotation angle and the color of the text. The three variables are listed in the front of the rotated text effect, as follows:

```
(Text) /Str 45 /Ang 1.00 /Gray save
```

Note that you must observe the range and format rules for the variables very strictly. If you don't, the effect may not print.

272

Str The Str variable contains the string that you want to display in the rotated position. When you change this variable, be sure that both the beginning and ending parentheses remain in the file, as these are essential. The bold characters in the example show you what can be changed in the effect file. Note that the two parentheses are not in bold.

The string variable can contain up to 100 characters. If it exceeds 100 characters, you may find that the effect will not print or will not print correctly.

Ang The text is displayed at an angle set by the Ang variable. The angle is measured counterclockwise from a horizontal line, so that 45 degrees slopes up to the right, for example. The values of Ang are degrees, with 0 being horizontal (the way text normally appears) and proceeding counterclockwise to 360, which is the same as 0.

The Ang variable may range from 0 to 360 degrees. Although you may use larger angles, such values will be transformed into the equivalent angle between 0 and 360. For example, 405 degrees is identical to 45 degrees, since 405 degrees is 360 degrees plus 45 degrees.

Gray The darkness of the text is set by a control named, reasonably enough, Gray. The values of Gray are percentages, with 1.00 being black and 0.01 being almost white. Although you can use a value of 0.00 (white), this may be somewhat misleading, since that value actually means that nothing is printed on the page. It doesn't cause white letters on colored paper, for example.

The Gray variable may range from 1.00 to .01. You always need to have a decimal point in the value and two digits after the decimal point, even if you are using exact tenths. For example, use .50 and not .5 as your value. If you don't, the effect may not print.

Size and Position

The font and size used for displaying the string is determined by the font and size of the positioning character. The text rotates around the positioning character, where the string starts. Think of printing the string on a strip of paper and then rotating the strip of paper by holding the lower left corner of the strip.

As you see in Figure 6-1, in placing the text you must leave extra room for the rotated string to print. It can be quite difficult to judge the distance that you need to allow to have your effect print without obscuring other text on the page. To set it the way you want, you may have to make some tests using different amounts of space in your document. For that reason, this effect has two knots: It contains variables, and it may require test prints to set it exactly the way you want it.

Figure 6-1.   Examples of the rotated text effect

Using the Effect

Figure 6-2 shows you some things that you can do with rotated text. The two lines of headline text, rotated at 45 degrees, is a typical entry that might be placed on an advertising circular. The second example is a company name and address, printed at 90

Special Sale

Cheshire Group
321 S. Main St, Suite 36
Sebastopol, CA 95472

Figure 6-2. Variations of the rotated text effect

degrees. You might use this type of address as part of a flyer or circular, where the body of the text is in normal, portrait mode. Most word processing applications won't let you combine land-scape (rotated) and portrait text on the same page because of display problems or limitations in the application. However, using the rotated text effect, you can easily include landscape text anywhere.

TIP

As mentioned in Chapter 1, there are limitations within applications about length of lines, regardless of the character size and font. Generally you cannot place two or more rotated text effects on the same line. Each line of text in Figure 6-2 is, in fact, on a separate line. Spaces were used to move the lines of text into the correct position, both horizontally and vertically. To produce the second example, each line of the effect was placed on successive separate lines. Then the positioning character on the second line was spaced out past the one on the first line, and the positioning character on the third line was spaced out past the second one. In a similar fashion, the strings in each effect had spaces placed in front of the first character, so that the resulting display lines up properly. This all required about three tries to get it in the form that you see here. It can be done, but you may have to make several test prints to get it right.

ROTATED OUTLINE TEXT

rotated outline text

Description

You can place a line of text on the page and rotate it to any angle. The difference between this effect and the previous rotated text is that this text is displayed as an outline in black or any shade of gray that you want. This type of effect is used quite often in headlines and other display presentations. Using this effect, you can rotate your outline text to any angle.

For this effect, you must not use bitmapped fonts. Bitmapped fonts cannot print in the outline format used here.

Variables

As with all these text effects, you must enter the string of text to be displayed into the effect itself. You have control over the rotation angle and the color of the text outline. The three variables are listed in the front of the rotated text effect, as follows:

```
(Rotated) /Str 45 /Ang 1.00 /Gray save
```

Note that you must observe the range and format rules for the variables very strictly. If you don't, the effect may not print.

Str   The Str variable contains the string that you want to display in the rotated position. When you change this variable, be sure that both the beginning and ending parentheses remain in the file, as these are essential. The bold characters in the example show you what can be changed in the effect file. Note that the two parentheses are not in bold.

The string variable can contain up to 100 characters. If it exceeds 100 characters, you may find that the effect will not print or will not print correctly.

Ang   The text is displayed at an angle set by the Ang variable. The angle is measured counterclockwise from a horizontal line, so that 45 degrees slopes up to the right, for example. The values of Ang are degrees, with 0 being horizontal (the way text normally appears) and proceeding counterclockwise to 360, which is the same as 0.

The Ang variable may range from 0 to 360 degrees. Although you may use larger angles, such values will be transformed into the equivalent angle between 0 and 360. For example, 405 degrees is identical to 45 degrees, since 405 degrees is 360 degrees plus 45 degrees.

Gray   The darkness of the text outline is set by a control named, reasonably enough, Gray. The values of Gray are percentages, with 1.00 being black and 0.01 being almost white. Although you can use a value of 0.00 (white), this may be somewhat misleading. That value actually means that nothing is printed on the page. It doesn't cause white letters on colored paper, for example.

The Gray variable may range from 1.00 to .01. You always need to have a decimal point in the value and two digits after the decimal point, even if you are using exact tenths. For example, use .50 and not .5 as your value. If you don't, the effect may not print.

Size and Position

The font and size used for displaying the string is determined by the font and size of the positioning character. The text rotates around the positioning character, where the string starts. Think of printing the string on a strip of paper and then rotating the strip of paper by holding the lower left corner of the strip.

As you see in Figure 6-3, in placing the text you must leave extra room for the rotated string to print. It can be quite difficult to judge the distance that you need to allow to have your efffect print without obscuring other text on the page. To set it the way you want, you may have to make some tests using different amounts of space in your document. For that reason, this effect has two knots: It contains variables, and it may require test prints to set it exactly the way you want it. In addition, this effect has

Figure 6-3. Examples of the rotated outline text effect

one hourglass to remind you that outlining a string of text takes significantly more time than simply printing it.

Using the Effect

Figure 6-4 shows you one use of rotated text. The two lines of headline text, rotated at 45 degrees, is a typical entry that might be placed on an advertising circular.

Figure 6-4.   Variation of the
rotated outline text effect

TIP

As mentioned in Chapter 1, there are limitations within applications about length of lines, regardless of the character size and font. Generally you cannot place two or more rotated text effects on the same line. Each line of text in Figure 6-4 is, in fact, on a separate line. Spaces were used to move the lines of text into the correct position, both horizontally and vertically. To produce this example, each line of the effect was placed on successive separate lines. Then the positioning character on the second line was spaced out past the one on the first line.

The text in Figure 6-4 is 24-point Helvetica Bold, since that gives nice, clear text that is easily visible. Even more than in regular text effects, it is essential to make your text very legible when you are printing in outline. At almost all point sizes the bold version of a font is more legible than the normal version. In the same way, sans-serif fonts, like Helvetica, are more legible than serif fonts, like Times. In general, for outline text, I recommend using bold, sans-serif fonts in all cases unless you have some special reason for using other fonts. Also remember that bitmapped fonts, like Geneva and Monaco, will not print in the outline format required by this effect.

ANGLED TEXT

angled text

Description

You can place a line of text on the page and print it along a line set at an angle, while each character remains straight. The result is a line of text that looks like it has been set on a hill. You can display the text in black or any shade of gray. This flexible and useful effect has many applications.

Variables

As with all these text effects, you must enter the string of text to be displayed into the effect itself. You have control over the slope (angle) of the line on which the text is printed and over the color of the text. The three variables are listed in the front of the angled text effect, as follows:

(TEXT) /Str **45** /Ang **1.00** /Gray save

Note that you must observe the range and format rules for the variables very strictly. If you don't, the effect may not print.

Str The Str variable contains the string that you want to display in the rotated position. When you change this variable, be sure that both the beginning and ending parentheses remain in the file, as these are essential. The bold characters in the example show you what can be changed in the effect file. Note that the two parentheses are not in bold.

The string variable can contain up to 100 characters. If it exceeds 100 characters, you may find that the effect will not print or will not print correctly.

Ang   The text is displayed at an angle set by the Ang variable. The angle is measured counterclockwise from a horizontal line, so that 45 degrees slopes up to the right, for example. The values of Ang are degrees, with 0 being horizontal (the way text normally appears) and proceeding counterclockwise to 360, which is the same as 0. Straight up is 90; straight down is 270.

The Ang variable may range from 0 to 360 degrees. Although you may use larger angles, such values will be transformed into the equivalent angle between 0 and 360. For example, 405 degrees is identical to 45 degrees, since 405 degrees is 360 degrees plus 45 degrees.

Gray   The darkness of the text is set by a control named, reasonably enough, Gray. The values of Gray are percentages, with 1.00 being black and 0.01 being almost white. Although you can use a value of 0.00 (white), this may be somewhat misleading. That value actually means that nothing is printed on the page. It doesn't cause white letters on colored paper, for example.

The Gray variable may range from 1.00 to .01. You always need to have a decimal point in the value and two digits after the decimal point, even if you are using exact tenths. For example, use .50 and not .5 as your value. If you don't, the effect may not print.

Size and Position

The font and size used for displaying the string is determined by the font and size of the positioning character. The text is set with

the first character of the string on the positioning character. The remainder of the string is set along the line defined from the beginning of the first character at the angle specified in the effect.

As you see in Figure 6-5, in placing the text you must leave extra room for the angled string to print. Straight up and straight down are fairly easy to visualize, but for other angles, it can be quite difficult to judge the distance that you need to allow to have your effect print without obscuring other text on the page. To set it the way you want, you may have to make some tests using different amounts of space in your document. For that reason, this effect has two knots: It contains variables, and it may require test prints to set it exactly the way you want it.

Figure 6-5. Examples of the angled text effect

T
 E
   X
     T

Using the Effect

Figure 6-6 shows you one of the most common uses for angled text—printing straight down a page. This is a typical entry you might use on any advertising circular, a memo, or other document to display some information that is not necessarily part of the text body. The trick here is to put the angled text on the top line and then enter your other text on the lines below it. Remember to allow enough room for the body of your text to print. I usually set the margins for the text block in from the margin of the effect line. You can use the gray effect, as shown, to make the vertical text less overwhelming.

A
P
P
E
A
R
I
N
G

T
O
D
A
Y

Figure 6-6. Variation of the angled text effect

ANGLED OUTLINE TEXT

angled outline text

Description

You can place a line of text on the page and print it along an angled line. The difference between this effect and the previous angled text is that this text is displayed as an outline in black or any shade of gray that you want. This flexible and useful effect has many applications; it is used quite often in headlines and other display presentations.

For this effect, you must not use bitmapped fonts. Bitmapped fonts cannot print in the outline format used here.

Variables

As with all these text effects, you must enter the string of text to be displayed into the effect itself. You have control over the slope (angle) of the line on which the text is printed and over the color of the text outline. The three variables are listed in the front of the angled outline text effect, as follows:

```
(TEXT) /Str 45 /Ang 1.00 /Gray save
```

Note that you must observe the range and format rules for the variables very strictly. If you don't, the effect may not print.

Str   The Str variable contains the string that you want to display in the rotated position. When you change this variable, be sure that both the beginning and ending parentheses remain in the file, as these are essential. The bold characters in the example show you what can be changed in the effect file. Note that the two parentheses are not in bold.

The string variable can contain up to 100 characters. If it exceeds 100 characters, you may find that the effect will not print or will not print correctly.

Ang The text is displayed at an angle set by the Ang variable. The angle is measured counterclockwise from a horizontal line, so that 45 degrees slopes up to the right, for example. The values of Ang are degrees, with 0 being horizontal (the way text normally appears) and proceeding counterclockwise to 360, which is the same as 0. Straight up is 90; straight down is 270.

The Ang variable may range from 0 to 360 degrees. Although you may use larger angles, such values will be transformed into the equivalent angle between 0 and 360. For example, 405 degrees is identical to 45 degrees, since 405 degrees is 360 degrees plus 45 degrees.

Gray The darkness of the text outline is set by a control named, reasonably enough, Gray. The values of Gray are percentages, with 1.00 being black and 0.01 being almost white. Although you can use a value of 0.00 (white), this may be somewhat misleading. That value actually means that nothing is printed on the page. It doesn't cause white letters on colored paper, for example.

The Gray variable may range from 1.00 to .01. You always need to have a decimal point in the value and two digits after the decimal point, even if you are using exact tenths. For example, use .50 and not .5 as your value. If you don't, the effect may not print.

Size and Position

The font and size used for displaying the string is determined by the font and size of the positioning character. The text is set with the first character of the string on the positioning character. The remainder of the string is set along the line defined from the beginning of the first character at the angle specified in the effect.

As you see in Figure 6-7, in placing the text you must leave extra room for the angled string to print. Straight up and straight down are fairly easy to visualize, but for other angles, it can be quite difficult to judge the distance that you need to allow to have your effect print without obscuring other text on the page. To set it the way you want, you may have to make some tests using different amounts of space in your document. For that reason, this effect has two knots: It contains variables, and it may require test prints to set it exactly the way you want it. In addition, this effect has one hourglass to remind you that outlining a string of text takes significantly more time than simply printing it.

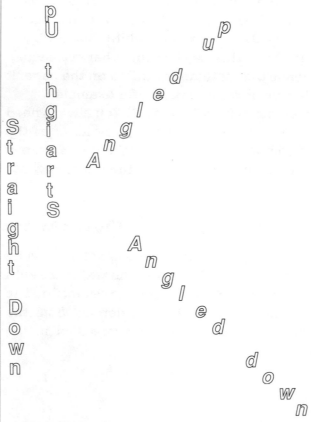

Figure 6-7.   Examples of the angled outline text effect

Using the Effect

Figure 6-8 shows you one of the most common uses for angled text—printing straight down a page. This is a typical entry you might use on an advertising circular, a memo, or other document to display some information that is not necessarily part of the text body. The trick here is to put the angled text on the top line and then enter your other text on the lines below it. Remember to allow enough room for the body of your text to print. I usually set the margins for the text block in from the margin of the effect line. Outline text, as shown, makes the vertical text less overwhelming.

Figure 6-8.   Variation of the angled outline text effect

TIP

The text in Figure 6-8 is 24-point Helvetica Bold, since that gives nice, clear text that is easily visible. Even more than in regular text effects, it is essential to make your text very legible when you are printing in outline. At almost all point sizes the bold version of a font is more legible than the normal version. In the same way, sans-serif fonts, like Helvetica, are more legible than serif fonts, like Times. In general, for outline text, I recommend using bold, sans-serif fonts in all cases unless you have some special reason for using other fonts. Also remember that bitmapped fonts, like Geneva and Monaco, will not print in the outline format required by this effect.

BACKGROUND TEXT

background text

Description

You can place a line of text anywhere on the page and rotate it to any angle. The text can be displayed in black or any shade of gray that you want. The placement of text is determined by variables that you set in the effect, not by where you set the positioning character. This flexible and useful effect has many applications. This effect allows you to place a line of gray text anywhere on the page *beneath* the ordinary text in your document. In this way, you can create background text that appears in addition to your ordinary text without obscuring it. Common examples are printing DRAFT or CONFIDENTIAL underneath a page of output. There are two conditions to placing text as background. First, the effect must print before your ordinary text; if it doesn't, the background text will erase your regular text. Second, you must use a light gray for your background text; if you use a dark gray or a black, the ordinary text will not show clearly enough to be read.

Variables

As with all these text effects, you must enter the string of text to be displayed into the effect itself. You have control over the horizontal and vertical position of the text and the rotation angle and color of the text outline. The five variables are listed in the front of the background text effect, as follows:

```
(TEXT) /Str 4.25 /Xpos 5.50 /Ypos 45 /Ang 1.00 /Gray save
```

Note that you must observe the range and format rules for the variables very strictly. If you don't, the effect may not print.

Str   The Str variable contains the string that you want to display in the rotated position. When you change this variable, be sure that both the beginning and ending parentheses remain in the file, as these are essential. The bold characters in the example show you what can be changed in the effect file. Note that the two parentheses are not in bold.

The string variable can contain up to 100 characters. If it exceeds 100 characters, you may find that the effect will not print or will not print correctly.

Xpos/Ypos   You place the text on the page by setting the horizontal location, called Xpos—a position in the x, or horizontal, direction. In a similar fashion, the vertical location is called Ypos. Both distances are in inches. The location of the point where the text is displayed is measured from the top, left corner of the page. You can use only positive values for Xpos and Ypos.

To give you maximum control in placement of your text, you enter values with two decimal places ($^1/_{100}$ inch). You must use a decimal point followed by two figures, as shown in the example. That means that, if you want to position your text one inch from

289

the left edge of the page and one and one half inches from the top, you enter values of 1.00 and 1.50, respectively, not 1 and 1.5. Acceptable values range from 99.00 to 0.00; however, values that are located off the page will not print and will not generate a message or error indication.

Ang   The text is displayed at an angle set by the Ang variable. The angle is measured counterclockwise from a horizontal line, so that 45 degrees slopes up to the right, for example. The values of Ang are degrees, with 0 being horizontal (the way text normally appears) and proceeding counterclockwise to 360, which is the same as 0.

The Ang variable may range from 0 to 360 degrees. Although you may use larger angles, such values will be transformed into the equivalent angle between 0 and 360. For example, 405 degrees is identical to 45 degrees, since 405 degrees is 360 degrees plus 45 degrees.

Gray   The darkness of the text is set by a control named, reasonably enough, Gray. The values of Gray are percentages, with 1.00 being black and 0.01 being almost white. Although you can use a value of 0.00 (white), this may be somewhat misleading. That value actually means that nothing is printed on the page. It doesn't cause white letters on colored paper, for example.

The Gray variable may range from 1.00 to .01. You always need to have a decimal point in the value and two digits after the decimal point, even if you are using exact tenths. For example, use .50 and not .5 as your value. If you don't, the effect may not print.

Size and Position

In this effect, the positioning character has no influence on the placement of the text. However, the font and size used for displaying the string are determined by the font and size of the positioning character. If you set an angle for the display, the text rotates around the point where the string starts, which is the point determined by the Xpos and Ypos variables.

As you see in Figure 6-9, positioning the text is independent of the placement of the lines on your document. In this case, the three lines are in order on the screen, one beneath the other and all of them flush against the left margin. The printed output, however, is staggered, and the third line prints above the second. If you use the angle variable, you must leave extra room above the text (or below, as the case might be) for the rotated string to print. It can be quite difficult to judge the distance that you need to allow to have your text print where you want it on the page. To set it the way you want, you may have to make some tests using different amounts of space in your document. For that reason, this effect has three knots: It contains variables, and it may require several test prints to set placement and orientation exactly the way you want them.

First line placed at 2,2

Third line placed at 3,3

Second line placed at 4,4

Figure 6-9.   Examples of positioning the background text effect

Using the Effect

The major use for this effect is to print text behind your ordinary output. This is very helpful for draft material, for example, where you want to place the word DRAFT behind the text, as shown in Figure 6-10. Another common use is to label material confidential or proprietary.

In Figure 6-10, the positioning character is 48-point Helvetica Bold, and the Gray variable is set to .50 to make the background light enough so that you can read the text over it.

This is an example of text with a background effect set behind the standard text. This is an example of text with a background effect set behind the standard text. This is an example of text with a background effect set behind the standard text. This is an example of text with a background effect set behind the standard text. This is an example of text with a background effect set behind the standard text. This is an example of text with a background effect set behind the standard text. This is an example of text with a background effect set behind the standard text. This is an example of text with a background effect set behind the standard text. This is an example of text with a background effect set behind the standard text.

Figure 6-10. Variations of the background text effect

OUTLINE BACKGROUND TEXT

outline background text

Description

This effect allows you to place a line of outline text anywhere on the page *beneath* the ordinary text in your document. In this way, you can create background text that appears in addition to your ordinary text without obscuring it. Common examples are printing

DRAFT or CONFIDENTIAL underneath a page of output. There is one condition to placing text as background. The effect must print before your ordinary text; if it doesn't, the background text will erase your regular text. Outline text is ordinarily white inside a black outline, but you may make the outline of your text any darkness that you want. You may want to use a dark gray instead of black for your outline so that the ordinary text will show more clearly.

Variables

As with all these text effects, you must enter the string of text to be displayed into the effect itself. You have control over the horizontal and vertical position of the text and the rotation angle and color of the text. The five variables are listed in the front of the outline background text effect, as follows:

`(`**`TEXT`**`) /Str` **`4.25`** `/Xpos` **`5.50`** `/Ypos` **`45`** `/Ang` **`1.00`** `/Gray save`

Note that you must observe the range and format rules for the variables very strictly. If you don't, the effect may not print.

Str The Str variable contains the string that you want to display in the rotated position. When you change this variable, be sure that both the beginning and ending parentheses remain in the file, as these are essential. The bold characters in the example show you what can be changed in the effect file. Note that the two parentheses are not in bold.

The string variable can contain up to 100 characters. If it exceeds 100 characters, you may find that the effect will not print or will not print correctly.

Xpos/Ypos You place the text on the page by setting the horizontal location, called Xpos—a position in the x, or horizontal, direction. In a similar fashion, the vertical location is called Ypos.

293

Both distances are in inches. The location of the point where the text is displayed is measured from the top left corner of the page. You can use only positive values for both Xpos and Ypos.

To give you maximum control in placement of your text, you enter values with two decimal places ($^1/_{100}$ inch). You must use a decimal point followed by two figures, as shown in the example. That means that if you want to position your text one inch from the left edge of the page and one and one-half inches from the top, you enter values of 1.00 and 1.50, respectively, not 1 and 1.5. Acceptable values range from 99.00 to 0.00. However, values that are located off the page will not print and will not generate a message or error indication.

Ang   The text is displayed at an angle, set by the Ang variable. The angle is measured counterclockwise from a horizontal line, so that 45 degrees slopes up to the right, for example. The values of Ang are degrees, with 0 being horizontal (the way text normally appears) and proceeding counterclockwise to 360, which is the same as 0.

The Ang variable may range from 0 to 360 degrees. Although you may use larger angles, any such values will be transformed into the equivalent angle between 0 and 360. For example, 405 degrees is identical to 45 degrees, since 405 degrees is 360 degrees plus 45 degrees.

Gray   The darkness of the text is set by a control named, reasonably enough, Gray. The values of Gray are percentages, with 1.00 being black and 0.01 being almost white. Although you can use a value of 0.00 (white), this may be somewhat misleading. That value actually means that nothing is printed on the page. It doesn't cause white letters on colored paper, for example.

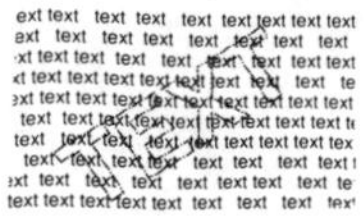

The Gray variable may range from 1.00 to .01. You always need to have a decimal point in the value and two digits after the decimal point, even if you are using exact tenths. For example, use .50 and not .5 as your value. If you don't, the effect may not print.

Size and Position

In this effect, the positioning character has no influence on the placement of the text. However, the font and size used for displaying the string are determined by the font and size of the positioning character. If you set an angle for the display, the text rotates around the point where the string starts, which is the point determined by the Xpos and Ypos variables.

As you see in Figure 6-11, positioning the text is independent of the placement of the lines on your document. In this case, the three lines are in order on the screen, one beneath the other and all of them flush against the left margin. The printed output, however, is staggered, and the third line prints above the second. If you use the angle variable, you must leave extra room for the

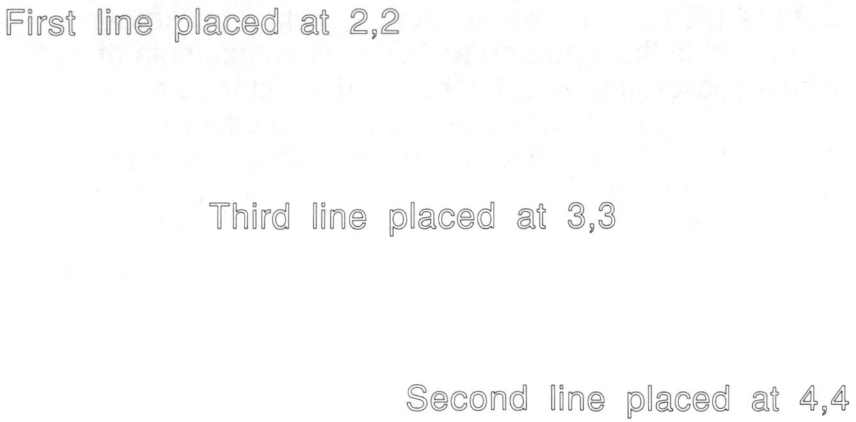

First line placed at 2,2

Third line placed at 3,3

Second line placed at 4,4

Figure 6-11. Examples of the outline background text effect

rotated string to print. It can be quite difficult to judge the distance that you need to allow to have your text print where you want it on the page. To set it the way you want, you may have to make some tests using different amounts of space in your document. For that reason, this effect has three knots: It contains variables, and it may require several test prints to set placement and orientation exactly the way you want them. In addition, this effect has one hourglass to remind you that outlining a string of text takes significantly more time than simply printing it.

Using the Effect

The major use for this effect is to print text behind your ordinary output. This is very helpful for draft material, for example, where you want to place the word DRAFT behind the text, as shown in Figure 6-12. Another common use for this type of effect is to label material confidential or proprietary.

This is an example of text with a background effect set behind the standard text. This is an example of text with a background effect set behind the standard text. This is an example of text with a background effect set behind the standard text. This is an example of text with a background effect set behind the standard text. This is an example of text with a background effect set behind the standard text. This is an example of text with a background effect set behind the standard text. This is an example of text with a background effect set behind the standard text. This is an example of text with a background effect set behind the standard text. This is an example of text with a background effect set behind the standard text.

Figure 6-12. Variations of the outline background text effect

In Figure 6-12, the positioning character is set in 48-point Helvetica Bold, and the Gray variable is set to .50 to make the outline light enough so that you can read the text over it.

TIP

The text in Figure 6-12 is 48-point Helvetica Bold, since that gives nice, clear text that is easily visible, even behind a block of text. Even more than in regular text effects, it is essential to make your text very legible when you are printing in outline. At almost all point sizes the bold version of a font is more legible than the normal version. In the same way, sans-serif fonts, like Helvetica, are more legible than serif fonts, like Times. In general, for outline text, I recommend using bold, sans-serif fonts in all cases unless you have some special reason for using other fonts. Also remember that bitmapped fonts, like Geneva and Monaco, will not print in the outline format required by this effect.

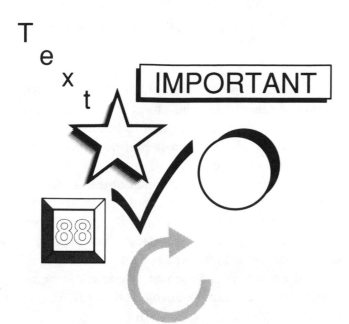

Checkmarks

7

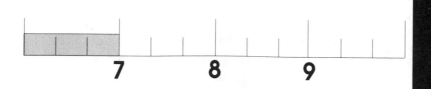

7   8   9

CHECKMARKS CAN BE USED TO ANNOTATE LISTS, MARK TASK status, or add emphasis or clarity. In this chapter you will find three varieties of checkmarks—normal, flared, and pointed—each with some options. Each type of checkmark has one form that allows you to combine it with other effects.

This chapter also shows you how to use these combined forms to achieve the result you want. Of course, it would be best if you could insert the checkmark along with any other effect and have them print one on top of the other. Unfortunately, that isn't possible. The combined form of the effect requires another effect in front of it, while the standard version does not. If you try to combine a standard version of the checkmark with another effect, the standard effect will erase part of the original effect.

INSERTING CHECKMARKS IN MICROSOFT WORD

1. Open your document. Insert a positioning character where you want to place the effect(s). The size of the positioning character determines the basic size of your effect(s).

2. *If you are using the standard checkmark effect (not the combined effect):* Open the **xxxx.w** file, where **xxxx** represents the name of the desired checkmark effect.

   If you are using the combined checkmark effect (one that works with another effect): Follow the standard steps to insert the non-checkmark effect into your document, but do not change the second part of the effect into the PostScript Escape font. Then, open the **xxxx(cmb).w** file, where **xxxx** represents the name of the desired checkmark effect.

   If only one line of text appears when you open the file, click on the Show Hidden Text box in the Preferences... selection of the Edit menu. Select and copy all the text of the checkmark effect and place it at the beginning of the page that will contain the effect. Notice that the major part of the text in this file is in

Word's PostScript style. (If you are unclear about how to use this style, review the instructions in Chapter 1.)

3. Select and cut the text that is *not* in the PostScript style from the end of the checkmark effect text. This is the second part of the effect.

4. *If you are using the standard effect:* Paste the second part of the effect into your Word document immediately after (to the right of) the positioning character.

   If you are using a combined checkmark effect: Paste the second part of the effect (the text that you cut from the end of the checkmark effect) into your Word document immediately after (to the right of) the second part of the first effect, leaving at least one space between the two effects.

5. Select all of the text, and only the text, from the second part of the effect file(s) that you pasted into your document. Change the font to the PostScript Escape font. This part of the effect text will disappear.

6. Be sure that the Print Hidden Text box in the Print dialog box is not checked. Print your document. The effect will print over the positioning character.

INSERTING CHECKMARKS IN OTHER WORD PROCESSING APPLICATIONS

1. Open your document. Insert a positioning character where you want to place the effect. The size of the positioning character determines the size of your checkbox.

2. *If you are using the standard checkmark effect (not the combined effect):* Open the effect file and copy the effect text.

If you are using the combined checkmark effect (one that works with another effect): Follow the standard steps to insert the non-checkmark effect into your document. Then, open the **xxxx**(cmb) file, where **xxxx** represents the name of the desired checkmark effect.

3. *If you are using the standard effect:* Paste the effect text into your document immediately after (to the right of) the positioning character.

   If you are using the combined checkmark effect: Paste the effect text into your document immediately after (to the right of) the text for the first effect. Be sure to leave at least one space between the texts.

4. Select all of the text, and only the text, that you copied into your document for one or both effects, and change it to the PostScript Escape font.

5. Print your document in the ordinary way. The effect will print over the positioning character.

CHECKMARK

checkmark

Description

This effect draws a fairly thick check mark at the point specified. You can use it to mark a line of text or check an item in a list. This is NOT the form to use if you want to combine the checkmark with another effect.

Variables

You can set the darkness of the checkmark to any shade of gray. If you set the value to .00, the checkmark is filled with white and outlined in black. The single variable is listed in the front of the checkmark effect, as follows:

```
1.00 /Gray 6 dict begin . . .
```

You must observe the range and format rules for the variables very strictly. If you don't, the effect may not print.

Gray   The darkness of the checkmark is set by a control named, reasonably enough, Gray. The values of Gray are percentages, with 1.00 being black and 0.00 being white. Using a value of 0.00 (white) may be somewhat misleading since that value actually means that the effect is outlined in black with nothing printed inside the checkmark. It doesn't print a white checkmark on colored paper, for example.

The Gray variable may range from 1.00 to .00. You always need to have a decimal point in the value and two digits after the decimal point, even if you are using exact tenths. For example, use .50 and not .5 as your value. If you don't, the effect may not print.

Size and Position

The examples in Figure 7-1 show you different sizes of the checkmark effect. The first three lines show checkmarks created using 18-, 24-, and 36-point type. Using a different font has no effect on the size or positioning of the checkmark as you can see by comparing lines three and four, which display a 36-point check in Helvetica and Times. The second (24-point) example uses a .50 Gray checkmark, and the last example shows you a white checkmark. The Gray value in the fourth checkmark is set to 0.00, which results in an outlined checkmark. In these examples, the font and size of the positioning character, which governs the size of the checkmark, is identical to the font and size used for the X in the line of text next to the checkmark.

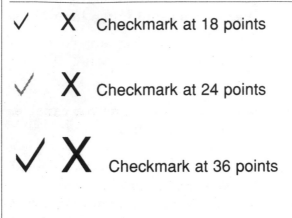

Figure 7-1 also shows you how the checkmark is sized and placed by the positioning character. Like many of the effects, the checkmark is sized to match the height of a capital X. The positioning character and the capital X in the examples are the same font and size to illustrate this. Remember that the size of the effect is set by the font and size of the *positioning character,* not that of the following text. You must ensure that these are the same if you want them to match.

In a similar fashion, the checkmark is positioned so that its tip is at the point where the positioning character ends. This is consistent with other effects and will be important when you are combining effects.

Using the Effect

This effect can be used anywhere that you want to check an item or a line of text. You can also insert it into the middle of some text. Remember that the checkmark extends to the right, along the line of the text. If you use it with other text on the line, be sure to allow enough room after the effect for the checkmark to print.

CHECKMARK (COMBINED)

checkmark (combined)

Description

This effect resembles the basic checkmark, except that this file can be used with other effects in front of it. You can use it to mark a checkbox or a bullet with a checkmark. This is the form to use if you want to combine the checkmark with another effect.

Variables

As in the basic checkmark, you can set the darkness of the checkmark to any shade of gray. If you set the darkness to .00, the checkmark is filled with white and outlined in black.

For combined effects, two variables allow you to position the final effect. This allows you to place the second effect exactly over the first.

The three variables are listed in the front of the checkmark (combined) effect, as follows:

```
-01 /Xoff -01 /Yoff 1.00 /Gray 7 dict begin . . .
```

You must observe the range and format rules for the variables very strictly. If you don't, the effect may not print.

Xoff/Yoff You place the effect where you want it by setting the horizontal distance, called Xoff—an offset in the x, or horizontal, direction. In a similar fashion, the vertical distance for the effect is called Yoff. Both distances are in points, which are a printer's measure. A point is $1/72$ inch. You can use either positive or negative values for both Xoff and Yoff.

Positive values of Xoff move the effect to the right, while negative values move it to the left. Positive values of Yoff move the effect down the page, and negative values move it up the page.

You must place plus or minus signs in front of the Xoff and Yoff variables, and you must use two digits, as shown. Acceptable values range from ±00 to ±99. Of course, +00 and – 00 are identical and give you the same result: no offset in that direction.

Gray   The darkness of the checkmark is set by a control named, reasonably enough, Gray. The values of Gray are percentages, with 1.00 being black and 0.00 being white. Using a value of 0.00 (white) may be somewhat misleading. That value actually means that the effect is outlined in black with nothing printed inside the checkmark. It doesn't print a white checkmark on colored paper, for example.

The Gray variable may range from 1.00 to .00. You always need to have a decimal point in the value and two digits after the decimal point, even if you are using exact tenths. For example, use .50 and not .5 as your value. If you don't, the effect may not print.

Size and Position

The examples in Figure 7-2 show you different combinations of the checkmark and other effects. For each example, the offsets had to be adjusted to place the checkmark where you see it. For the first example, the offsets are set to Xoff – 01 and Yoff – 02. For the second and third examples, the offsets are +00 and – 08. The values that you use for the offsets will depend on the nature of the effect that you are using the checkmark with and the final result you want to achieve. Since the checkmark and the additional effect share the same positioning character, they also share font selection and sizing information.

It can be very difficult to judge the distance that you want to offset the checkmark to match it to the other effect. To set it the way you want, you may have to make some tests using different offsets in your document. This effect has three knots because it

X Checkmark and checkbox

 X Checkmark and round bullet

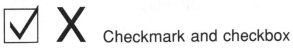 X Checkmark and star

Figure 7-2. Examples of checkmarks combined with other effects

contains variables, and it may require several test prints to set it exactly the way you want it. For the same reasons, all combined effects have three knots.

Using the Effect

This effect can be used with most of the other effects in this book. Obviously, you wouldn't use it with some of the effects, such as placed or rotated text. Remember that the combined checkmark must be used with another effect to work correctly, because it must collect position and size information from the preceding effect. For that reason, all of the combined effects must be placed in your document so that the combined effect text comes after the original effect text.

All combined effects resemble the standard version of the effect and have the same controls and settings, except that they also have Xoff and Yoff variables in front of all other variables. Since that is so, this is the only separate discussion of the combined version of any effect. You simply use the standard effect when you don't want to mix effects and use the combined versions when you do.

SIZED CHECKMARK (& COMBINED)

sized checkmark

sized checkmark (combined)

Description

Sometimes you may want a checkmark that is smaller than the text or the other effect that you are combining it with. Using the sized checkmark effect, you can insert a standard checkmark that is sized as you want. This effect allows you to use various sizes of checkmarks in lists, for example, without multiple font changes (which slow processing) and with complete control over size. You can also use the combined form with other sized effects, like the sized bullet, to create a range of combinations.

Variables

You set the size of the checkmark by setting the Pct variable. You can also set the darkness of the checkmark to any shade of gray. If you set the value to .00, the checkmark is filled with white and outlined in black. The two variables are listed in the front of the checkmark effect, as follows:

```
100 /Pct 1.00 /Gray 7 dict begin...
```

If you are using the combined effect, you will have the following variables :

```
-01 /Xoff -01 /Yoff 100 /Pct 1.00 /Gray 8 dict begin
```

All combined effects resemble the standard version of the effect and have the same controls and settings, except that they also have Xoff and Yoff variables in front of all other variables.

Since that is so, there is no separate discussion of the combined version of the effect. You simply use the standard effect when you don't want to mix effects and use the combined versions when you do.

You must observe the range and format rules for the variables very strictly. If you don't, the effect may not print.

Pct   The Pct variable allows you to set the ratio of the size of the checkmark to the size of the positioning character. This value represents the size of the checkmark, from top to bottom, as a percentage of the font size. You can use any value between 10 and 999 for Pct without trouble. A 100 percent checkmark is the same size as a capital X.

Gray   The darkness of the checkmark is set by a control named, reasonably enough, Gray. The values of Gray are percentages, with 1.00 being black and 0.00 being white. Using a value of 0.00 (white) may be somewhat misleading since that value actually means that the effect is outlined in black with nothing printed inside the checkmark. It doesn't print a white checkmark on colored paper, for example.

The Gray variable may range from 1.00 to .00. You always need to have a decimal point in the value and two digits after the decimal point, even if you are using exact tenths. For example, use .50 and not .5 as your value. If you don't, the effect may not print.

Xoff/Yoff   You place the effect where you want it by setting the horizontal distance, called Xoff—an offset in the x, or horizontal, direction. In a similar fashion, the vertical distance for the effect is called Yoff. Both distances are in points, which are a printer's measure. A point is $1/72$ inch. You can use either positive or negative values for both Xoff and Yoff.

Positive values of Xoff move the effect to the right, while negative values move it to the left. Positive values of Yoff move the effect down the page, and negative values move it up the page.

You must place plus or minus signs in front of the Xoff and Yoff variables, and you must use two digits, as shown. Acceptable values range from ±00 to ±99. Of course, +00 and – 00 are identical and give you the same result: no offset in that direction.

If you have any questions about how to use the other variables, see the discussion under the standard effect.

Size and Position

The examples in Figure 7-3 illustrate how your checkmark is sized. The percentage shown in the text next to the checkmarks is the value placed into each effect for Pct. As you see, the 25 percent checkmark is one quarter the height of the X, the 50 percent checkmark is half the height, and so on, up to the 150 percent checkmark which is one and a half times as high. Obviously, using 100 percent gives you a checkmark that is the same height as the X. Using the Pct variable along with the font size, you can make your checkmark any size you want.

The examples also show you how the Pct variable affects your checkmark. All of the checkmarks in Figure 7-3 are based on a 36-point positioning character. The X next to them on the line of text is also 36 points. As you can see, the checkmark aligns with the point where the two lines of the X cross. The 100 percent checkmark also shows you that the checkmark is sized to match the height of a capital X in your designated font.

In the horizontal direction, the checkmark is centered on the point after the positioning character. This allows enough room for the checkmark to print without running over the text that follows. Remember that the checkmark extends behind the positioning character, however. If you use large checkmarks, you may have to adjust the following text to allow enough room for the checkmark to print.

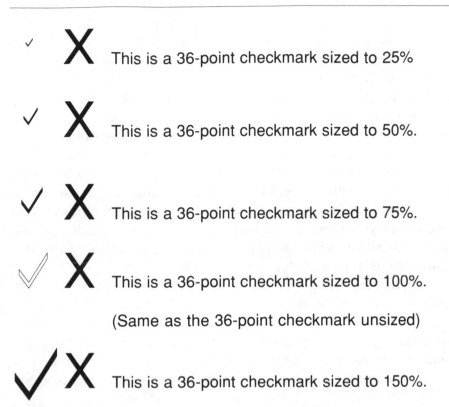

This is a 36-point checkmark sized to 25%

This is a 36-point checkmark sized to 50%.

This is a 36-point checkmark sized to 75%.

This is a 36-point checkmark sized to 100%.

(Same as the 36-point checkmark unsized)

This is a 36-point checkmark sized to 150%.

Figure 7-3. Examples of the sized checkmark effect

Using the Effect

The examples in Figure 7-3 show you some of the uses for sized checkmarks. The most common use for the sized checkmark is to make a smaller check than the size of the text that it accompanies.

The last example illustrates another use for these checkmarks. Besides positioning small checkmarks next to a line of larger text, you can also place a large checkmark by a line of smaller text. This may be visually more appealing than using the checkmark with a large point size and following it with smaller text, because the checkmark doesn't seem to tower over the text so much.

The examples in Figure 7-4 show you different combinations of the sized checkmark with other sized effects. As you see, you can create unique combinations by choosing different percentages and offsets. In all of the examples, the positioning character is set to 36-point Helvetica. For each example, the Pct variables for both effects are as shown in the text and the offsets are adjusted to place the checkmark where you see it. For the first example, the offsets are set to Xoff – 01 and Yoff +03. For the second example, the offsets are +00 and – 10. For the third, they are – 02 and +03. The values that you use for the offsets will depend on the nature of the effect that you are using the checkmark with and the final result that you want to achieve. Since the checkmark and the additional effect share the same positioning character, they also share font selection and sizing information.

It can be very difficult to judge the percentage that you want to use to set a checkmark precisely. This effect has two knots because it contains variables and may require a test print or two to set it exactly the way you want it. In addition, if you are using the combined form of the effect, you may have to adjust the distance that you want to offset the checkmark to match it to the other

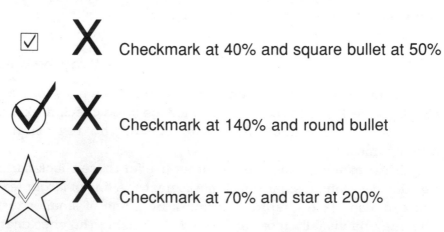

Checkmark at 40% and square bullet at 50%

Checkmark at 140% and round bullet

Checkmark at 70% and star at 200%

Figure 7-4. Examples of the sized checkmark combined with other effects

effect. To set it the way you want, you may have to make some tests using different offsets in your document. All combined effects have three knots, since they will usually require several tests.

FLARED CHECKMARK (& COMBINED)

flared checkmark
flared checkmark (combined)

Description

This variation on the checkmark draws a fairly thick checkmark whose arms are slightly curved. You can use this effect where you want additional emphasis or a stronger graphic element than the ordinary checkmark.

Variables

You can set the darkness of the checkmark to any shade of gray. If you set the value to .00, the checkmark is filled with white and outlined in black. The single variable is listed in the front of the checkmark effect, as follows:

1.00 /Gray 6 dict begin...

If you are using the combined effect, you will have the following variables:

-01 /Xoff **-01** /Yoff **1.00** /Gray 7 dict begin

All combined effects resemble the standard version of the effect and have the same controls and settings, except that they also have Xoff and Yoff variables in front of all other variables. Since that is so, there is no separate discussion of the combined version of the effect. You simply use the standard effect when you don't want to mix effects and use the combined versions when you do.

You must observe the range and format rules for the variables very strictly. If you don't the effect may not print.

Gray   The darkness of the checkmark is set by a control named, reasonably enough, Gray. The values of Gray are percentages, with 1.00 being black and 0.00 being white. Using a value of 0.00 (white) may be somewhat misleading. That value actually means that the effect is outlined in black with nothing printed inside the checkmark. It doesn't print a white checkmark on colored paper, for example.

The Gray variable may range from 1.00 to .00. You always need to have a decimal point in the value and two digits after the decimal point, even if you are using exact tenths. For example, use .50 and not .5 as your value. If you don't, the effect may not print.

Xoff/Yoff   You place the effect where you want it by setting the horizontal distance, called Xoff—an offset in the x, or horizontal, direction. In a similar fashion, the vertical distance for the effect is called Yoff. Both distances are in points, which are a printer's measure. A point is $1/72$ inch. You can use either positive or negative values for both Xoff and Yoff.

Positive values of Xoff move the effect to the right, while negative values move it to the left. Positive values of Yoff move the effect down the page, and negative values move it up the page.

You must place plus or minus signs in front of the Xoff and Yoff variables, and you must use two digits, as shown above. Acceptable values range from ±00 to ±99. Of course, +00 and −00 are identical, and give you the same result: no offset in that direction.

If you have any questions about how to use the other variables, see the discussion under the standard effect.

Size and Position

The examples in Figure 7-5 show you different sizes of the flared checkmark effect. The first three lines show checkmarks created using 18-, 24-, and 36-point type. Using a different font has no effect on the size or positioning of the checkmark as you can see by comparing lines three and four, which display a 36-point checkmark in Helvetica and Times. The second (24-point) example uses a .50 Gray checkmark, and the last example shows you a white checkmark. The Gray value in the last checkmark is set to 0.00, which results in an outlined checkmark. In these examples, the font and size of the positioning character, which governs the size of the checkmark, is identical to the font and size used for the X in the line of text next to the checkmark.

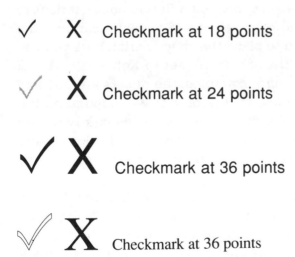

Figure 7-5. Examples of the flared checkmark effect

Figure 7-5 also shows you how the checkmark is sized and placed by the positioning character. Like many of the effects, the checkmark is sized to match the height of a capital X. The positioning character and the capital X in the examples are the same font and size to illustrate this. Remember that the size of the effect is set by the font and size of the *positioning character,* not that of the following text. You must ensure that these are the same if you want them to match.

In a similar fashion, the checkmark is positioned so that its tip is at the point where the positioning character ends. This is consistent with other effects.

Using the Effect

This effect can be used anywhere that you want to check an item or a line of text. You can also insert it into the middle of some text. Remember that the checkmark extends to the right, along the line of the text. If you use it with other text on the line, be sure to allow enough room after the effect for the checkmark to print.

The examples in Figure 7-6 show you different combinations of the flared checkmark and other effects. For each example, the offsets had to be adjusted to place the checkmark where you see it. For the first example, the offsets are set to Xoff − 01 and Yoff − 02. For the second and third examples, the offsets are +00 and − 08. The values that you use for the offsets will depend on the nature of the effect that you are using the checkmark with and the final result that you want to achieve. Since the checkmark and the additional effect share the same positioning character, they also share font selection and sizing information.

It can be very difficult to judge the distance that you want to offset the checkmark to match it to the other effect. To set it the way you want, you may have to make some tests using different offsets in your document. This effect has three knots because it contains variables and may require several test prints to set it the way you want it. For the same reasons, all combined effects have three knots.

 Checkmark and checkbox

 Checkmark and round bullet

Checkmark and star

Figure 7-6. Examples of flared checkmarks combined with other effects

SIZED FLARED CHECKMARK (& COMBINED)

sized flared checkmark
sized flared checkmark (combined)

Description

Sometimes you may want a version that is smaller than the text or the other effect that you are combining it with. Using the sized flared checkmark effect, you can insert a flared checkmark that is sized as you want. This effect allows you to use various sizes of checkmarks in lists, for example, without multiple font changes (which slow processing) and with complete control over size. You can also use the combined form with other sized effects, like the sized bullet, to create a range of combinations.

Variables

You set the size of the checkmark by setting the Pct variable. You can also set the darkness of the checkmark to any shade of gray. If you set the value to .00, the checkmark is filled with white and outlined in black. The two variables are listed in the front of the sized flared checkmark effect, as follows:

```
100 /Pct 1.00 /Gray 7 dict begin...
```

If you are using the combined effect, you will have the following variables:

```
-01 /Xoff -01 /Yoff 100 /Pct 1.00 /Gray 8 dict begin
```

All combined effects resemble the standard version of the effect and have the same controls and settings, except that they also have Xoff and Yoff variables in front of all other variables. Since that is so, there is no separate discussion of the combined version of the effect. You simply use the standard effect when you don't want to mix effects and use the combined versions when you do.

You must observe the range and format rules for the variables very strictly. If you don't the effect may not print.

Pct   The Pct variable allows you to set the ratio of the size of the checkmark to the font size used for the positioning character. This value represents the size of the checkmark, from top to bottom, as a percentage of the font size. You can use any value between 10 and 999 for Pct without trouble. A 100 percent checkmark is the same size as a capital X.

Gray   The darkness of the checkmark is set by a control named, reasonably enough, Gray. The values of Gray are percentages, with 1.00 being black and 0.00 being white. Using a value of 0.00 (white) may be somewhat misleading since that value actually means that the effect is outlined in black with nothing printed inside the checkmark. It doesn't print a white checkmark on colored paper, for example.

The Gray variable may range from 1.00 to .00. You always need to have a decimal point in the value and two digits after the decimal point, even if you are using exact tenths. For example, use .50 and not .5 as your value. If you don't, the effect may not print.

Xoff/Yoff You place the effect where you want it by setting the horizontal distance, called Xoff—an offset in the x, or horizontal, direction. In a similar fashion, the vertical distance for the effect is called Yoff. Both distances are in points, which are a printer's measure. A point is $^1/_{72}$ inch. You can use either positive or negative values for both Xoff and Yoff.

Positive values of Xoff move the effect to the right, while negative values move it to the left. Positive values of Yoff move the effect down the page, and negative values move it up the page.

You must place plus or minus signs in front of the Xoff and Yoff variables, and you must use two digits, as shown. Acceptable values range from ±00 to ±99. Of course, +00 and − 00 are identical and give you the same result: no offset in that direction.

If you have any questions about how to use the other variables, see the discussion under the standard effect.

Size and Position

The examples in Figure 7-7 illustrate how your checkmark is sized. The percentage shown in the text next to the checkmarks is the value placed into each effect for Pct. As you see, the 25 percent checkmark is one quarter of the height of the X, the 50 percent checkmark is half the height, and so on, up to the 150 percent checkmark which is one and a half times as high. Obviously, using 100 percent gives you a checkmark that is the same height as the X. Using the Pct variable along with the font size, you can make your checkmark any size you want.

The examples also show you how the Pct variable affects your checkmark. All of the checkmarks in Figure 7-7 are based on a 36-point positioning character. The X next to them on the line of text is also 36 points. As you can see, the checkmark aligns with the point where the two lines of the X cross. The 100 percent checkmark also shows you that the checkmark is sized to match the height of a capital X in your designated font.

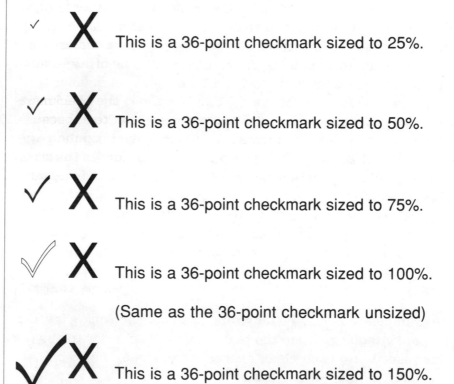

This is a 36-point checkmark sized to 25%.

This is a 36-point checkmark sized to 50%.

This is a 36-point checkmark sized to 75%.

This is a 36-point checkmark sized to 100%.

(Same as the 36-point checkmark unsized)

This is a 36-point checkmark sized to 150%.

Figure 7-7. Examples of the sized flared checkmark effect

In the horizontal direction, the checkmark is centered on the point after the positioning character. This allows enough room for the checkmark to print without running over the text that follows. Remember that the checkmark extends behind the positioning character, however. If you use large checkmarks, you may have to adjust the following text to allow enough room for the checkmark to print.

Using the Effect

The examples in Figure 7-7 show you some of the uses for sized checkmarks. The most common use for the sized checkmark is to make a smaller check than the size of the text that it accompanies.

The last example illustrates another use for these checkmarks. Besides positioning small checkmarks next to a line of larger text, you can also place a large checkmark by a line of smaller text. This may be visually more appealing than using the checkmark with a large point size and following it with smaller text, because the checkmark doesn't seem to tower over the text so much.

The examples in Figure 7-8 show you combinations of the sized checkmark with other sized effects. As you see, you can create unique combinations by choosing different percentages and offsets. In all of the examples, the positioning character is set to 36-point Helvetica. For each example, the Pct variables for both effects are set as shown in the text and the offsets are adjusted to place the checkmark where you see it. For the first example, the offsets are set to Xoff − 01 and Yoff +03. For the second example, the offsets are +00 and − 10. For the third, they are − 02 and +03. The values that you use for the offsets will depend on the nature of the effect that you are using the checkmark with and the final result that you want to achieve. Since the checkmark and the additional effect share the same positioning character, they also share font selection and sizing information.

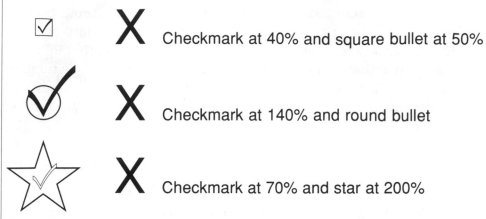

Checkmark at 40% and square bullet at 50%

Checkmark at 140% and round bullet

Checkmark at 70% and star at 200%

Figure 7-8.   Examples of sized flared checkmarks with other effects

It can be very difficult to judge the percentage that you want to use to set a checkmark precisely. This effect has two knots because it contains variables and may require a test print or two to set it exactly the way you want it. In addition, if you are using the combined form of the effect, you may have to adjust the distance that you want to offset the checkmark to match it to the other effect. To set it the way you want, you may have to make some tests using different offsets in your document. All combined effects have three knots, since they will usually require several tests.

POINTED CHECKMARK (& COMBINED)

pointed checkmark
pointed checkmark (combined)

Description

This variation on the checkmark draws a checkmark whose arms both come to a point at the end. You can use this effect where you want additional emphasis or a stronger graphic element than the ordinary checkmark.

Variables

You can set the darkness of the checkmark to any shade of gray. If you set the value to .00, the checkmark is filled with white and outlined in black. The single variable is listed in the front of the checkmark effect, as follows:

```
1.00 /Gray 6 dict begin . . .
```

If you are using the combined effect, you will have the following variables:

```
-01 /Xoff -01 /Yoff 1.00 /Gray 7 dict begin
```

All combined effects resemble the standard version of the effect and have the same controls and settings, except that they also have Xoff and Yoff variables in front of all other variables. Since that is so, there is no separate discussion of the combined version of the effect. You simply use the standard effect when you don't want to mix effects and use the combined versions when you do.

You must observe the range and format rules for the variables very strictly. If you don't, the effect may not print.

Gray   The darkness of the checkmark is set by a control named, reasonably enough, Gray. The values of Gray are percentages, with 1.00 being black and 0.00 being white. Using a value of 0.00 (white) may be somewhat misleading since that value actually means that the effect is outlined in black with nothing printed inside the checkmark. It doesn't print a white checkmark on colored paper, for example.

The Gray variable may range from 1.00 to .00. You always need to have a decimal point in the value and two digits after the decimal point, even if you are using exact tenths. For example, use .50 and not .5 as your value. If you don't, the effect may not print.

Xoff/Yoff   You place the effect where you want it by setting the horizontal distance, called Xoff—an offset in the x, or horizontal, direction. In a similar fashion, the vertical distance for the effect is called Yoff. Both distances are in points, which are a printer's measure. A point is $1/72$ inch. You can use either positive or negative values for both Xoff and Yoff.

Positive values of Xoff move the effect to the right, while negative values move it to the left. Positive values of Yoff move the effect down the page, and negative values move it up the page.

You must place plus or minus signs in front of the Xoff and Yoff variables, and you must use two digits, as shown above. Acceptable values range from ±00 to ±99. Of course, +00 and − 00 are identical and give you the same result: no offset in that direction.

If you have any questions about how to use the other variables, see the discussion under the standard effect.

Size and Position

The examples in Figure 7-9 show you different sizes of the pointed checkmark effect. The first three lines show checkmarks created using 18-, 24-, and 36-point type. Using a different font has no effect on the size or positioning of the checkmark as you can see by comparing lines three and four, which display a 36-point checkmark, in Helvetica and Times. The second (24-point) example uses a .50 Gray checkmark, and the last example shows you a white checkmark. The Gray value in the last checkmark is set to 0.00, which results in an outlined checkmark. In these examples, the font and size of the positioning character, which governs the size of the checkmark, is identical to the font and size used for the X in the line of text next to the checkmark.

Figure 7-9 also shows you how the checkmark is sized and placed by the positioning character. Like many of the effects, the checkmark is sized to match the height of a capital X. The positioning character and the capital X in the examples are the same

 Checkmark at 18 points

 Checkmark at 24 points

 Checkmark at 36 points

 Checkmark at 36 points

Figure 7-9. Examples of the pointed checkmark effect

font and size to illustrate this. Remember that the size of the effect is set by the font and size of the *positioning character,* not that of the following text. You must ensure that these are the same if you want them to match.

In a similar fashion, the checkmark is positioned so that its tip is at the point where the positioning character ends. This is consistent with other effects.

Using the Effect

This effect can be used anywhere that you want to check an item or a line of text. You can also insert it into the middle of some text. Remember that the checkmark extends to the right, along the line of the text. If you use it with other text on the line, be sure to allow enough room after the effect for the checkmark to print.

The examples in Figure 7-10 show you different combinations of the pointed checkmark and other effects. For each example, the offsets had to be adjusted to place the checkmark where you

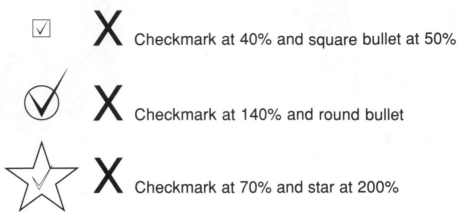

Figure 7-10. Examples of pointed checkmarks
with other effects

see it. For the first example, the offsets are set to Xoff – 01 and Yoff – 02. For the second and third examples, the offsets are +00 and – 08. The values that you use for the offsets will depend on the nature of the effect that you are using the checkmark with and the final result that you want to achieve. Since the checkmark and the additional effect share the same positioning character, they also share font selection and sizing information.

It can be very difficult to judge the distance that you want to offset the checkmark to match it to the other effect. To set it the way you want, you may have to make some tests using different offsets in your document. This effect has three knots because it contains variables and may require several test prints to set it exactly the way you want it. For the same reasons, all combined effects have three knots.

SIZED POINTED CHECKMARK (& COMBINED)

sized pointed checkmark
sized pointed checkmark (combined)

Description

Sometimes you may want a version that is smaller than the text or the other effect that you are using with it. With the sized pointed checkmark effect you can insert a pointed checkmark that is sized as you want. This effect allows you to use various sizes of checkmarks in lists, for example, without multiple font changes (which slow processing) and with complete control over size. You can also use the combined form with other sized effects, like the sized bullet, to create a range of combinations.

Variables

You set the size of the checkmark by setting the Pct variable. You can also set the darkness of the checkmark to any shade of gray. If you set the value to .00, the checkmark is filled with white and outlined in black. The two variables are listed in the front of the sized pointed checkmark effect, as follows:

`100 /Pct 1.00 /Gray 7 dict begin . . .`

If you are using the combined effect, you will have the following variables:

`-01 /Xoff -01 /Yoff 100 /Pct 1.00 /Gray 8 dict begin`

All combined effects resemble the standard version of the effect and have the same controls and settings, except that they also have Xoff and Yoff variables in front of all other variables. Since that is so, there is no separate discussion of the combined version of the effect. You simply use the standard effect when you don't want to mix effects and use the combined versions when you do.

You must observe the range and format rules for the variables very strictly. If you don't, the effect may not print.

Pct   The Pct variable allows you to set the ratio of the size of the checkmark to the font size used for the positioning character. This value represents the size of the checkmark, from top to bottom, as a percentage of the font size. You can use any values between 10 and 999 for Pct without trouble. A 100 percent checkmark is the same size as a capital X.

Gray   The darkness of the checkmark is set by a control named, reasonably enough, Gray. The values of Gray are percentages, with 1.00 being black and 0.00 being white. Using a value of 0.00 (white) this may be somewhat misleading since that value actually means that the effect is outlined in black with nothing printed inside the checkmark. It won't make a white checkmark on colored paper, for example.

The Gray variable may range from 1.00 to .00. You always need to have a decimal point in the value and always have two digits after the decimal point, even if you are using exact tenths. For example, use .50 and not .5 as your value. If you don't, the effect may not print.

Xoff/Yoff   You place the effect where you want it by setting the horizontal distance, called Xoff—an offset in the x, or horizontal, direction. In a similar fashion, the vertical distance for the effect is called Yoff. Both distances are in points, which are a printer's measure. A point is $^1/_{72}$ inch. You can use either positive or negative values for both Xoff and Yoff.

Positive values of Xoff move the effect to the right, while negative values move it to the left. Positive values of Yoff move the effect down the page, and negative values move it up the page.

You must place plus or minus signs in front of the Xoff and Yoff variables, and you must use two digits, as shown. Acceptable values range from ±00 to ±99. Of course, +00 and – 00 are identical and give you the same result: no offset in that direction.

If you have any questions about how to use the other variables, see the discussion under the standard effect.

Size and Position

The examples in Figure 7-11 illustrate how your checkmark is sized. The percentage shown in the text next to the checkmarks is the value placed into each effect for Pct. As you see, the 25 percent checkmark is one quarter of the height of the X, the 50

 This is a 36-point checkmark sized to 25%.

 This is a 36-point checkmark sized to 50%.

This is a 36-point checkmark sized to 75%.

This is a 36-point checkmark sized to 100%.

(same as the 36-point checkmark unsized)

 This is a 36-point checkmark sized to 150%.

Figure 7-11. Examples of the sized pointed checkmark effect

percent checkmark is half the height, and so on, up to the 150 percent checkmark which is one and a half times as high. Obviously, using 100 percent gives you a checkmark that is the same height as the X. Using the Pct variable along with the font size, you can make your checkmark any size you want.

The examples also show you how the Pct variable affects your checkmark. All of the checkmarks in Figure 7-11 are based on a 36-point positioning character. The X next to them on the line of text is also 36 points. As you can see, the checkmark aligns with the point where the two lines of the X cross. The 100 percent checkmark also shows you that the checkmark is sized to match the height of a capital X in your designated font.

In the horizontal direction, the checkmark is centered on the point after the positioning character. This allows enough room for the checkmark to print without running over the text that follows. Remember that the checkmark extends behind the positioning character, however. If you use large checkmarks, you may have to adjust the following text to allow enough room for the checkmark to print.

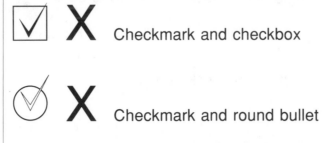

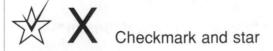

Figure 7-12. Examples of sized pointed checkmarks with other effects

Using the Effect

The examples in Figure 7-11 show you some of the uses for sized checkmarks. The most common use for the sized checkmark is to make a smaller check than the size of the text that it accompanies.

The last example illustrates another use for these checkmarks. Besides positioning small checkmarks next to a line of larger text, you can also use the variables to place a large checkmark by a line of smaller text. This may be visually more appealing than using the checkmark with a large point size and following it with smaller text, because the checkmark doesn't seem to tower over the text so much.

The examples in Figure 7-12 show you combinations of the sized checkmark with other sized effects. As you see, you can create unique combinations by choosing different percentages and offsets. In all of the examples, the positioning character is set to 36-point Helvetica. For each example, the Pct variables for both effects are set as shown in the text and the offsets are adjusted to place the checkmark where you see it. For the first example, the offsets are set to Xoff – 01 and Yoff +03. For the second example, the offsets are +00 and – 10. For the third, they are – 02 and +03. The values that you use for the offsets will depend on the nature of the effect that you are using the checkmark with and the final result that you want to achieve. Since the checkmark and the additional effect share the same positioning character, they also share font selection and sizing information.

It can be very difficult to judge the percentage that you want to use to set a checkmark precisely. This effect has two knots because it contains variables and may require a test print or two to set it exactly the way you want it. In addition, if you are using the combined form of the effect, you may have to adjust the distance that you want to offset the checkmark to match it to the other effect. To set it the way you want, you may have to make some tests using different offsets in your document. All combined effects have three knots, since they will usually require several tests.

331

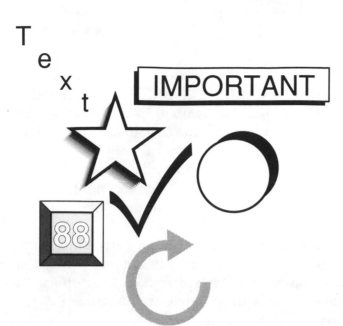

Arrows

8

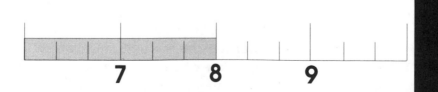

ARROWS, IN ONE FORM OR ANOTHER, ARE PROBABLY USED more often than any other graphic symbol. In this chapter you have a variety of arrows that you can use in your document. The effects include arrowheads (arrows without a body), regular arrows, thick arrows, reverse arrows, and circular arrows. Each of these is presented in several orientations (left and right, up and down). You can use this set of arrows for pointing, for emphasis, and for directional texts.

Only the sized arrow effects are provided in a combined form for use with other effects. You will most often need to vary the size of your arrow when you combine it with another effect. Of course, you can always use a sized effect at 100 percent if you want the regular version of the effect.

INSERTING ARROWS IN MICROSOFT WORD

1. Open your document. Insert a positioning character where you want to place the effect(s). The size of the positioning character determines the basic size of your effect(s).

2. *If you are using the standard arrow effect (not the combined effect):* Open the **xxxx.w** file, where **xxxx** represents the name of the desired arrow effect.

   If you are using the combined arrow effect (one that works with another effect): Follow the standard steps to insert the non-arrow effect into your document, but do not change the second part of the effect into the PostScript Escape font. Then, open the **xxxx(cmb).w** file, where **xxxx** represents the name of the desired arrow effect.

   If only one line of text appears when you open the file, click on the Show Hidden Text box in the Preferences... selection of the Edit menu. Select and copy all the text of the arrow effect and place it at the beginning of the page that will contain the effect. Notice that the major part of the text in this file is in Word's PostScript style. (If you are unclear about how to use this style, review the instructions in Chapter 1.)

3. Select and cut the text that is *not* in the PostScript style from the end of the arrow effect text. This is the second part of the effect.

4. *If you are using the standard effect:* Paste the second part of the effect into your Word document immediately after (to the right of) the positioning character.

   If you are using a combined arrow effect: Paste the second part of the effect (the text that you cut from the end of the arrow effect) into your Word document immediately after (to the right of) the second part of the first effect, leaving at least one space between the two effects.

5. Select all of the text, and only the text, from the second part of the effect file(s) that you pasted into your document. Change the font to the PostScript Escape font. This part of the effect text will disappear.

6. Be sure that the Print Hidden Text box in the Print dialog box is not checked. Print your document. The effect will print over the positioning character.

INSERTING ARROWS IN OTHER WORD PROCESSING APPLICATIONS

1. Open your document. Insert a positioning character where you want to place the effect. The size of the positioning character determines the size of your checkbox.

2. *If you are using the standard arrow effect (not the combined effect):* Open the effect file and copy the effect text.

   If you are using the combined arrow effect (one that works with another effect): Follow the standard steps to insert the non-arrow effect into your document. Then, open the xxxx(cmb) file, where xxxx represents the name of the desired arrow effect.

3. *If you are using the standard arrow effect:* Paste the effect text into your document immediately after (to the right of) the positioning character.

If you are using the combined arrow effect: Paste the effect text into your document immediately after (to the right of) the text for the first effect. Be sure to leave at least one space between the texts.

4. Select all of the text, and only the text, that you copied into your document for one or both effects, and change it to the PostScript Escape font.

5. Print your document in the ordinary way. The effect will print over the positioning character.

ARROW

arrow

Description

You can use the arrow for indicating directions and pointing. The head is as wide as it is high, giving it a sharp point without being exaggerated. You set the size and position of the head of the arrow with the positioning character, while you set the overall length of the arrow with a variable. The arrow effect comes in four variations, pointing in each direction: right, left, up, and down.

Variables

Although the positioning character determines the size of the arrowhead, you can set the overall length of the arrow to any value. You can also set the color of the arrow to any shade of gray. If you set the Gray value to .00, the arrow is filled with white and outlined in black. The two variables are listed in the front of the arrow effect, as follows:

```
30 /Len 1.00 /Gray 7 dict
```

You must observe the range and format rules for the variables very strictly. If you don't, the effect may not print.

Len   The length of the arrow is controlled by a variable named Len that specifies the total length of the arrow in points. A point is a printer's measure and is $1/72$ inch. For example, you measure type sizes in points. The positioning character establishes the size of the head of the arrow. Then the tail of the arrow is drawn out so that the overall length equals the number that you set in this variable. If you specify a value for Len that is less than the point size of the positioning character, the arrow is drawn at a default size equal to the point size. So if you use a 24-point positioning character and set Len to any number less than 24, the actual size of the arrow will be 24 points, not the value that you set.

Len may be any value from 00 to 999. You always need to have at least two digits, even if you are using a single-digit value (for example, 09, not 9). If you don't, the effect may not print.

Gray   The darkness of the arrow is set by a control named, reasonably enough, Gray. The values of Gray are percentages, with 1.00 being black and 0.00 being white. Using a value of 0.00 (white) may be somewhat misleading since that value actually means that the effect is outlined in black with nothing printed inside the arrow. It doesn't print a white arrow on colored paper, for example.

The Gray variable may range from 1.00 to .00. You always need to have a decimal point in the value and two digits after the decimal point, even if you are using exact tenths. For example, use .50 and not .5 as your value. If you don't, the effect may not print.

Size and Position

The examples in Figure 8-1 show you different arrow orientations. The effect comes as four different arrow files on your effects disk: right, left, up, and down. The name of the orientation is set by the direction of the arrowhead. The up arrow points up, and so on. Each orientation is a separate file.

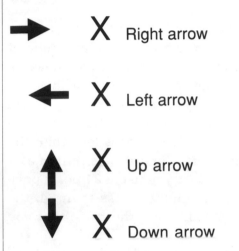

Figure 8-1. Examples of the arrow effect

Figure 8-1 also shows you how the arrow is sized and placed by the positioning character. The head of the arrow is sized to match the height of a capital X. The positioning character and the capital X in the examples are the same font and size to illustrate this.

The overall length of the arrow, from the tip of the arrowhead to the end of the tail, is set by the Len variable. In the examples, the positioning character is 24-point Helvetica, and the length is set to 30. In each orientation the arrowhead is drawn over the positioning character. The tail of the arrow extends out in the given orientation for the length specified. Because the length of the arrow is variable, be sure that you allow enough room for it in the direction that you have selected. For example, if you are using the up arrow, be sure that there is enough room beneath it for the size tail that you have set.

BEHIND THE SCENES

Why do you have four versions of the arrow (and other, similar effects in this chapter), instead of one effect with a rotation control? In addition to rotating, the arrow must be moved and its coordinates changed in each case so that it draws correctly. This means that one effect will not work in all orientations. The arrow itself must move around some common center of rotation, which means that the position of the arrow with relation to the positioning character does not remain constant. This makes it very hard to visualize where the arrow will print if you only have one effect.

Using the Effect

The examples in Figure 8-2 show you several variations for the arrow effect. The top two examples show how you can use the length variable to change the tail of the arrow. In the first example, the Len variable is set to 10, which is less than the 24-point positioning character. The result is the minimum length arrow. In the second example, the Len variable is set to 45 points, making the tail longer. Remember that the length is for the entire arrow, so that the second arrow measures 45 points from its tip to the end of the tail.

The second two examples show you some darkness variations for the arrows. The top arrow is 50 percent gray, while the bottom arrow is 00 percent gray, or white, which produces an outlined arrow.

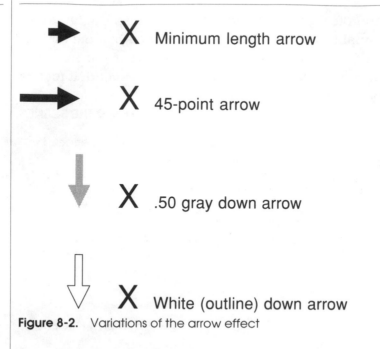

X Minimum length arrow

X 45-point arrow

X .50 gray down arrow

X White (outline) down arrow

Figure 8-2. Variations of the arrow effect

SIZED ARROW

sized arrow
sized arrow (combined)

Description

Sometimes you may want an arrow that is not the size of your font, but rather one that is larger or smaller. With the sized arrow effect, you can add small, centered arrows in a line of text, or you can enlarge an arrow for graphic emphasis, while keeping it centered on the text. You set the basic size and position of the head of the arrow with the positioning character, then modify that by using a percentage. This allows you to use various sizes of arrows in lists, for example, without multiple font changes (which slow processing) and with complete control over size. You can also use the combined form with other effects, like the proportioned button, to create a range of combinations.

The sized arrow effect comes in four variations, pointing in each direction: right, left, up, and down.

Variables

You determine the size of the arrow by setting the Pct variable. You can also set the overall length of the arrow to any value by using the Len variable. You can also set the color of the arrow to any shade of gray. If you set the Gray value to white, the arrow is filled with white and outlined in black. The three variables are listed in the front of the sized arrow effect, as follows:

```
100 /Pct 30 /Len 1.00 /Gray 8 dict...
```

If you are using the combined effect, you will have the following variables:

```
-01 /Xoff -01 /Yoff 100 /Pct 30 /Len 1.00 /Gray 9 dic...
```

All combined effects resemble the standard version of the effect and have the same controls and settings, except that they also have Xoff and Yoff variables in front of all other variables. Since that is so, there is no separate discussion of the combined version of the effect. You simply use the standard effect when you don't want to mix effects and use the combined versions when you do. If you have any questions about how to use this effect combined with other effects, see the discussion under the standard checkmark effect in Chapter 7.

You must observe the range and format rules for the variables very strictly. If you don't, the effect may not print.

Pct   The Pct variable allows you to set the ratio of the size of the arrow to the point size of the positioning character. This value represents the size of the overall arrow, while the length of the arrow is defined by the Len variable. You can use any values between 10 and 999 for Pct without trouble. A 100 percent arrow is the same size as a capital X.

Len The length of the arrow is controlled by a variable named Len that specifies the total length of the arrow in points. A point is a printer's measure and is $^1/_{72}$ inch. For example, you measure type sizes in points. The positioning character establishes the basic size of the head of the arrow, which you can adjust with the Pct variable. Then the tail of the arrow is drawn in the width set by the Pct variable, but with the overall length equal to the number that you set in the Len variable. If you specify a value for Len that is less than the point size of the positioning character adjusted by the Pct variable, the arrow is drawn at a default size equal to the point size times the Pct value. So if you use a 24-point positioning character with a Pct variable of 50 and set Len to any number less than 12, the actual size of the arrow will be 12 points, not the value that you set in Len. However, if you set a Len variable of 20, the resulting arrow will be 20 points long, not 24 points.

The Len may be any value from 00 to 999. You always need to have at least two digits, even if you are using a single-digit value (for example, 09, not 9). If you don't, the effect may not print.

Gray The darkness of the arrow is set by a control named, reasonably enough, Gray. The values of Gray are percentages, with 1.00 being black and 0.00 being white. Using a value of 0.00 (white) may be somewhat misleading since that value actually means that the effect is outlined in black with nothing printed inside the arrow. It doesn't print a white arrow on colored paper, for example.

The Gray variable may range from 1.00 to .00. You always need to have a decimal point in the value and two digits after the decimal point, even if you are using exact tenths. For example, use .50 and not .5 as your value. If you don't, the effect may not print.

Xoff/Yoff You place the effect where you want it by setting the horizontal distance, called Xoff—an offset in the x, or horizontal, direction. In a similar fashion, the vertical distance for the effect is called Yoff. Both distances are in points, which are a printer's measure. A point is $^1/_{72}$ inch. You can use either positive or negative values for both Xoff and Yoff.

Positive values of Xoff move the effect to the right, while negative values move it to the left. Positive values of Yoff move the effect down the page, and negative values move it up the page.

You must place plus or minus signs in front of the Xoff and Yoff variables, and you must use two digits, as shown. Acceptable values range from ±00 to ±99. Of course, +00 and −00 are identical and give you the same result: no offset in that direction.

Size and Position

The examples in Figure 8-3 illustrate how your arrow is sized and positioned. The percentage shown in the text next to the arrows is the value placed into each effect for Pct. As you see, the 25 percent arrow is one quarter of the height of the X, the 50 percent arrow is half the height, and so on, up to the 150 percent arrow which is one and a half times as high. Obviously, using 100 percent gives you an arrow whose head is the same height as the X. Using the Pct variable along with the font size, you can make your arrow any size you want.

The examples also show you how the arrow is positioned. All of the arrows in Figure 8-3 are based on a 36-point positioning character. The X next to them on the line of text is also 36 points. As you can see, the center of the arrowhead aligns with the point where the two lines of the X cross. For the left and right arrows, the tip of the arrow is centered on the line of text, as you see in Figure 8-3. However, for the up and down arrows, the tail extends the length you defined with the Len variable. In those cases, the arrow is not centered on the line of text. The second example shows this with a down arrow sized to 50 percent and a length of 24 points. The 100 percent arrow also shows you that the arrow's head is sized to match the size of a capital X in your designated font.

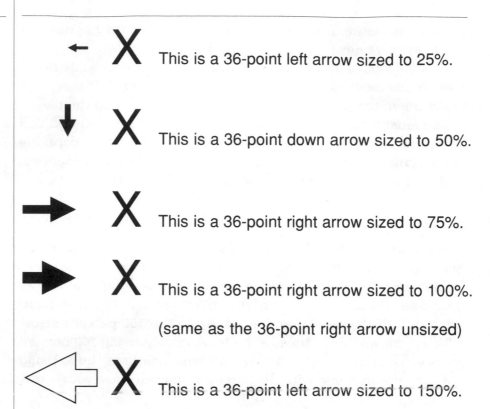

← X   This is a 36-point left arrow sized to 25%.

↓ X   This is a 36-point down arrow sized to 50%.

→ X   This is a 36-point right arrow sized to 75%.

→ X   This is a 36-point right arrow sized to 100%.

(same as the 36-point right arrow unsized)

X   This is a 36-point left arrow sized to 150%.

Figure 8-3.   Examples of the sized arrow effect

In the horizontal direction, the arrow is positioned so that the head prints over the positioning character. Remember that the tail of the arrow extends out opposite the direction selected by the orientation, however. If you use a down arrow, for example, you may have to adjust the lines of text above the effect to allow enough room for the tail to print.

Using the Effect

The examples in Figure 8-3 show you some of the uses for sized arrows. The most common use for the sized arrow is to make a smaller arrow than the size of the text that it accompanies.

The last example illustrates another use for sized arrows. Besides placing small arrows next to a line of larger text, you can also place a large arrow by a line of smaller text. This may be visually more appealing than using the arrow with a large point size and following it with smaller text, because the arrow seems more proportioned to the surrounding text.

The examples in Figure 8-4 show you three combinations of the sized arrow effect with the proportioned button effect. As you see, you can create unique combinations by choosing different percentages and offsets. In the first example, the positioning character is 40-point Helvetica. In both of the following examples, the positioning character is set to 36-point Helvetica. For each example, the Pct variables for both effects are as shown in the

  Up arrow at 40% and button at 60%

  Right arrow at 70% and button at 200%

  Left arrow at 70% and button at 200%

Figure 8-4. Examples of sized arrows with other effects

text and the offsets are adjusted to place the arrow where you see it. For the first example, the offsets are set to Xoff +00 and Yoff – 05. For the second example, the offsets are +15 and +00. For the third, they are +02 and +00. The values that you use for the offsets will depend on the orientation of the arrow that you are using, the nature of the effect that you are using the arrow with, and the final effect that you want to achieve. Since the arrow and the additional effect share the same positioning character, they also share font selection and sizing information.

It can be very difficult to judge the percentage that you want to use to set an arrow precisely. This effect has two knots because it contains variables and may require a test print or two to set it exactly the way you want it. In addition, if you are using the combined form of the effect, you may have to adjust the distance that you want to offset the arrow to match it to the other effect. To set it the way you want, you may have to make some tests using different offsets in your document. All combined effects have three knots, since they will usually require several tests.

DROP SHADOW ARROW

shadow arrow

Description

You may notice that some people make arrows stand out on the page by placing a shadow behind them. The shadow arrow effect allows you to make a shadow behind your arrow. This effect comes in four variations, pointing in each direction: right, left, up, and down.

Variables

This effect resembles the arrow effect, except that you can place a shadow behind the arrow. You have controls in the effect for the placement of the shadow in both the horizontal and vertical directions, or the darkness of the shadow. You can set the overall length of the arrow to any value that you want by using the Len variable. Finally, you can also set the darkness of the arrow to any shade of gray. If you set the value to .00, the arrow is filled with white and outlined in black. The five variables are listed in the front of the shadow arrow effect, as follows:

`-04 /Xoff +05 /Yoff .50 /Shadow 30 /Len 1.00 /Gray 10 dict...`

You must observe the range and format rules for the variables very strictly. If you don't, the effect may not print.

Xoff/Yoff   You place the shadow behind the box by setting the horizontal distance, called Xoff—an offset in the x, or horizontal, direction. In a similar fashion, the vertical distance for the shadow is called Yoff. Both distances are in points, which are a printer's measure. A point is $^1/_{72}$ inch. You can use either positive or negative values for both Xoff and Yoff.

Positive values of Xoff move the shadow to the right, while negative values move it to the left. Positive values of Yoff move the shadow down the page, and negative values move it up the page.

You must place plus or minus signs in front of the Xoff and Yoff variables, and you must use two digits, as shown. Acceptable values range from ±00 to ±99. Of course, +00 and – 00 are identical and give you the same result: no offset in that direction.

Shadow   The darkness of the shadow is set by a control named Shadow. This makes it different from most shadows, since the Gray variable is used to set the darkness of the arrow itself. The values of Shadow are percentages, with 1.00 being black and 0.01 being almost white. Although you can use a value of 0.00 (white), this may be somewhat misleading since that value actually means that nothing is printed behind the arrow. It doesn't print a white shadow on colored paper, for example.

The Shadow variable may range from 1.00 to .01. You always need to have a decimal point in the value and two digits after the decimal point, even if you are using exact tenths. For example, use .50 and not .5 as your value.

Len　The length of the arrow is controlled by a variable named Len that specifies the total length of the arrow in points. A point is a printer's measure and is $^1/_{72}$ inch. For example, you measure type sizes in points. The positioning character establishes the size of the head of the arrow. Then the tail of the arrow is drawn out to make the overall length equal to the number that you set in this variable. If you specify a value for Len that is less than the point size of the positioning character, the arrow is drawn at a default size equal to the point size. So if you use a 24-point positioning character and set Len to any number less than 24, the actual size of the arrow will be 24 points, not the value that you set.

The Len may be any value from 00 to 999. You always need to have at least two digits, even if you are using a single-digit value (for example, 09, not 9). If you don't, the effect may not print.

Gray　The darkness of the arrow is set by a control named, reasonably enough, Gray. The values of Gray are percentages, with 1.00 being black and 0.00 being white. Using a value of 0.00 (white) may be somewhat misleading since that value actually means that the effect is outlined in black with nothing printed inside the arrow. It doesn't print a white arrow on colored paper, for example.

The Gray variable may range from 1.00 to .00. You always need to have a decimal point in the value and two digits after the decimal point, even if you are using exact tenths. For example, use .50 and not .5 as your value. If you don't, the effect may not print.

Size and Position

The shadowed arrow is sized in the same way as the standard arrow effect. The positioning character determines the size of the arrow's head, and the value that you set in the Len variable determines the overall length of the arrow. The shadow size matches that of the arrow, as a shadow should. As illustrated in Figure 8-5, the position of the shadow, and therefore the amount of shadow that shows under the arrow, is determined by the Xoff and Yoff variables.

The four examples in Figure 8-5 show you how changes in the offset values move the shadow effect around the arrow. As you can see, you can create any variation in shadowing by changing the signs of the offset values.

It can be very difficult to judge the distance that you want to offset the shadow behind your arrow. To set it the way you want, you may have to make some tests using different offsets in your document. This effect has two knots because it contains variables and may require test prints to set it exactly the way you want it.

Using the Effect

Both sets of examples in Figures 8-5 and 8-6 illustrate some interesting issues for you to consider as you work with drop shadows and arrows. The examples in Figure 8-5 use the same offset values and different signs to move the shadow around a right arrow. The examples in Figure 8-6 use the same offset values with the same signs for each of the four orientations of the arrow effect. As you see, the results are not what you might expect.

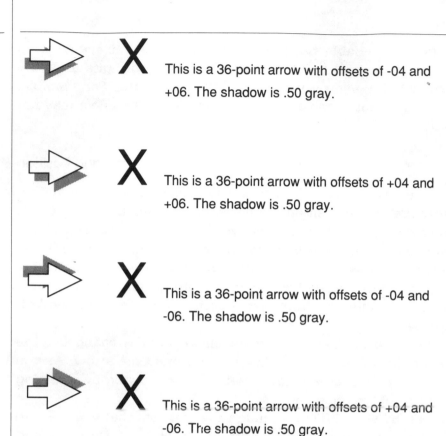

This is a 36-point arrow with offsets of -04 and +06. The shadow is .50 gray.

This is a 36-point arrow with offsets of +04 and +06. The shadow is .50 gray.

This is a 36-point arrow with offsets of -04 and -06. The shadow is .50 gray.

This is a 36-point arrow with offsets of +04 and -06. The shadow is .50 gray.

Figure 8-5. Examples of the shadow arrow effect

One of the most noticeable things in the Figure 8-6 examples is that the shadows appear to be larger or smaller distances from the arrow, even though the offsets are identical. When placing the shadows for your arrows, you need to take into account the orientation of the arrow and the position that you want the shadow to show. As you can see, the shadow is less visible when it is behind the head of the arrow. If the orientation and offsets place the tip of the shadow behind the tip of the arrow, then you should increase the offset in the direction that is at right angles to the orientation. For example, if you are placing a shadow with a negative x offset behind an up arrow, similar to the first line in Figure 8-6, then you should increase the Xoff variable to make the shadow more visible.

350

This is a 36-point up arrow with offsets of -04 and +06. The shadow is .50 gray.

  This is a 36-point right arrow with offsets of -04 and +06. The shadow is .50 gray.

  This is a 36-point left arrow with offsets of -04 and +06. The shadow is .50 gray.

  This is a 36-point down arrow with offsets of -04 and +06. The shadow is .50 gray.

Figure 8-6. Orientation and the shadow arrow effect

TIP

Normally you will use relatively small values for the offsets. Remember that for different orientations you will need different offsets to make the shadow look most natural when it prints. Typically you should have about 4 to 6 points difference in the offsets (depending on the size of the arrow) for the most natural result.

FADED ARROW

faded arrow

Description

The faded arrow effect is essentially a fancy variant of the shadowed arrow. As you can see, the faded arrow has a shadow that changes from white to black over a short distance. Like the other arrow effects, the faded arrow comes in four variations, pointing in each direction: right, left, up, and down.

Variables

While the size of the arrowhead is set by the positioning character, you can set the overall length of the arrow to any value. The variable is listed in the front of the faded arrow effect, as follows:

30 /Len 6 dict

You must observe the range and format rules for the variable very strictly. If you don't, the effect may not print.

Len The length of the arrow is controlled by a variable named Len that specifies the total length of the arrow in points. A point is a printer's measure and is $1/72$ inch. For example, you measure type sizes in points. The positioning character establishes the size of the head of the arrow. Then the tail of the arrow is drawn out so that the overall length equals the number that you set in this variable. If you specify a value for Len that is less than the point size of the positioning character, the arrow is drawn at a default minimum size equal to the point size. So if you use a 24-point positioning character and set Len to any number less than 24, the actual size of the arrow will be 24 points, not the value that you set.

The Len may be any value from 00 to 999. You always need to have at least two digits, even if you are using a single-digit value (for example, 09, not 9). If you don't, the effect may not print.

Size and Position

The faded arrow is sized in the same way as the standard arrow effect. The positioning character determines the size of the arrowhead before the faded effect is in place. The head of the arrow is sized to match the height of a capital X. The overall length of the arrow, from the tip of the arrowhead to the end of the tail, is set by the Len variable. The faded shadow size is a standard size for all the arrows and changes its position to match the orientation of the arrow. For example, it extends to the left and below the right arrow by a fixed amount and matches the arrow in all dimensions. As shown in Figure 8-7, this gives somewhat different results for arrows with different sizes and orientations.

Like the other arrows, the faded arrow has four orientations: right, left, up, and down. The name of the orientation is set by the direction of the arrowhead. The up arrow points up, and so on. Each of these orientations is a separate effect file.

The arrow itself is placed over the positioning character where the standard arrow would appear. If you use the faded arrow effect with small size text, be sure to allow enough room below the effect so that the faded shadow does not touch the text below and to the left of the arrow.

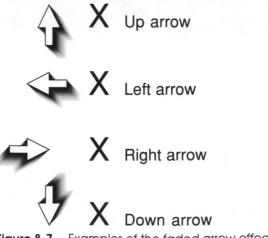

Figure 8-7. Examples of the faded arrow effect

Using the Effect

Although this effect looks something like the shadow arrow effect, it has no variables and no controls for shadow placement. Fading a shadow is quite complex and time-consuming, so you don't have alternatives here for shadow placement or coloring. The examples in Figure 8-8 demonstrate how this affects the resulting output. The size of the positioning character is given in the example, and the length of the arrow is 8 points greater than the size. As you can see, smaller point sizes have a faded effect that extends out a great distance, relative to the size of the arrow. On the other hand, on large arrows the faded background hardly differs from the simple shadow effect. The best results are generally between 18 and 48 points, but you may want larger or smaller arrows for special purposes.

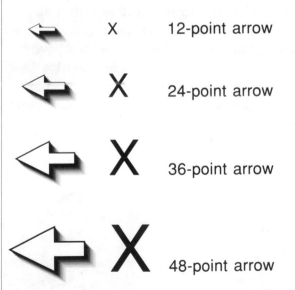

Figure 8-8. Variations of the faded arrow effect

THICK ARROW

thick arrow

Description

This is a variation on the simple arrow, which can be used for indicating directions and pointing. The head is shorter than it is high, and the tail is wider than the ordinary arrow, giving this effect a more solid look. You set the size and position of the head of the arrow with the positioning character, while you set the overall length of the arrow with a variable. The thick arrow effect comes in four variations, pointing in each direction: right, left, up, and down.

Variables

Although the positioning character determines the size of the arrowhead, you can set the overall length of the arrow to any value. You can also set the color of the arrow to any shade of gray. If you set the Gray value to .00, the arrow is filled with white and outlined in black. The two variables are listed in the front of the thick arrow effect, as follows:

```
30 /Len 1.00 /Gray 7 dict
```

You must observe the range and format rules for the variables very strictly. If you don't, the effect may not print.

Len   The length of the arrow is controlled by a variable named Len that specifies the total length of the arrow in points. A point is a printer's measure and is $1/72$ inch. For example, you measure type sizes in points. The positioning character establishes the size of the head of the arrow. Then the tail of the arrow is drawn out so that the overall length equals the number that you set in this variable. If you specify a value for Len that is less than the point size of the positioning character, the arrow is drawn at a default minimum size equal to the point size. So if you use a 24-point positioning character, and set Len to any number less than 24, the actual size of the arrow will be 24 points, not the value that you set.

The Len may be any value from 00 to 999. You always need to have at least two digits, even if you are using a single digit value (for example, 09, not 9). If you don't, the effect may not print.

Gray   The darkness of the arrow is set by a control named, reasonably enough, Gray. The values of Gray are percentages, with 1.00 being black and 0.00 being white. Using a value of 0.00 (white) may be somewhat misleading since that value actually means that the effect is outlined in black with nothing printed inside the arrow. It doesn't print a white arrow on colored paper, for example.

The Gray variable may range from 1.00 to .00. You always need to have a decimal point in the value and two digits after the decimal point, even if you are using exact tenths. For example, use .50 and not .5 as your value. If you don't, the effect may not print.

Size and Position

The examples in Figure 8-9 show you different orientations of the thick arrow effect. The effect comes as four different files on your effects disk: right, left, up, and down. The name of the orientation is set by the direction of the arrowhead. The up arrow points up, and so on. Each orientation is a separate file.

Figure 8-9 also shows you how the arrow is sized and placed by the positioning character. The head of the arrow is sized to match the height of a capital X. The positioning character and the capital X in the examples are the same font and size to illustrate this.

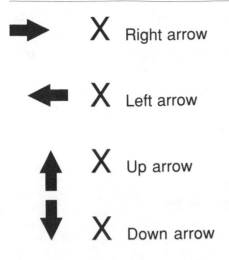

X Right arrow

X Left arrow

X Up arrow

X Down arrow

Figure 8-9. Examples of the thick arrow effect

The overall length of the arrow, from the tip of the arrowhead to the end of the tail, is set by the Len variable. In the examples, the positioning character is 24-point Helvetica, and the length is set to 30. In each orientation the arrowhead is drawn over the positioning character. The tail of the arrow extends out in the given orientation for the length specified. Because the length of the arrow is variable, be sure that you allow enough room for it in the direction that you have selected. For example, if you are using the up arrow, be sure that there is enough room beneath it for the size tail that you have set.

Using the Effect

The examples in Figure 8-10 show you several variations for the thick arrow effect. The top two examples show how you can use the length variable to change the tail of the arrow. In the first example, the Len variable is set to 10, which is less than the 24-point positioning character. The result is the minimum length arrow. In the second example, the Len variable is set to 45 points, making the tail longer. Remember that the length is for the entire arrow, so that the second arrow measures 45 points from its tip to the end of the tail.

The last two examples show you some darkness variations for the arrows. The third arrow is 50 percent gray, while the bottom arrow is 00 percent gray, or white, which produces an outlined arrow.

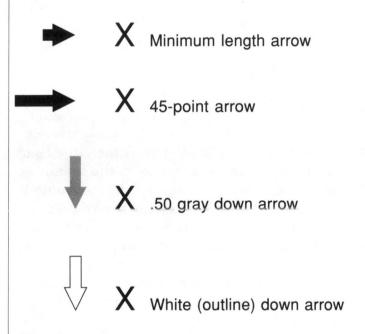

X   Minimum length arrow

X   45-point arrow

X   .50 gray down arrow

X   White (outline) down arrow

Figure 8-10.   Variations of the thick arrow effect

SIZED THICK ARROW

sized thick arrow
sized thick arrow (combined)

Description

Sometimes you may want an arrow that is not the size of your font, but rather one that is larger or smaller. With this effect, you can add small, centered arrows in a line of text, or you can enlarge an arrow for graphic emphasis, while keeping it centered on the text. You set the basic size and position of the head of the arrow with the positioning character, then modify that by using a percentage. This allows you to use various sizes of arrows in lists, for example, without multiple font changes (which slow processing) and with complete control over size. You can also use the combined form with other effects, like the proportioned button, to create a range of combinations.

The sized thick arrow effect comes in four variations, pointing in each direction: right, left, up, and down.

Variables

You determine the size of the arrow by setting the Pct variable. You can set the overall length of the arrow to any value by using the Len variable. You can also set the color of the arrow to any shade of gray. If you set the Gray value to white, the arrow is filled with white and outlined in black. The three variables are listed in the front of the sized thick arrow effect, as follows:

`100 /Pct 30 /Len 1.00 /Gray 8 dict...`

If you are using the combined effect, you will have the following variables:

`-01 /Xoff -01 /Yoff 100 /Pct 30 /Len 1.00 /Gray 9 dic...`

All combined effects resemble the standard version of the effect and have the same controls and settings, except that they also have Xoff and Yoff variables in front of all other variables. Since that is so, there is no separate discussion of the combined version of the effect. You simply use the standard effect when you don't want to mix effects and use the combined versions when you do. If you have any questions about how to use this effect combined with other effects see the discussion under the standard checkmark effect in Chapter 7.

You must observe the range and format rules for the variables very strictly. If you don't, the effect may not print.

Pct   The Pct variable allows you to set the ratio of the size of the arrow to the point size of the positioning character. This value represents the size of the overall arrow, while the length of the arrow is defined by the Len variable. You can use any values between 10 and 999 for Pct without trouble. A 100 percent arrow is the same size as a capital X.

Len   The length of the arrow is controlled by a variable named Len that specifies the total length of the arrow in points. A point is a printer's measure and is $1/72$ inch. For example, you measure type sizes in points. The positioning character establishes the basic size of the head of the arrow, which you can adjust with the Pct variable. Then the tail of the arrow is drawn in the width set by the Pct variable, but with the overall length equal to the number that you set in the Len variable. If you specify a value for Len that is less than the point size of the positioning character adjusted by the Pct variable, the arrow is drawn at a default size equal to the point size times the Pct value. So if you use a 24-point positioning character with a Pct variable of 50 and set Len to any number less than 12, the actual size of the arrow will be 12 points, not the value that you set in Len. However, if you set a Len variable of 20, the resulting arrow will be 20 points long, not 24 points.

The Len may be any value from 00 to 999. You always need to have at least two digits, even if you are using a single digit value (for example, 09, not 9). If you don't, the effect may not print.

Gray The darkness of the arrow is set by a control named, reasonably enough, Gray. The values of Gray are percentages, with 1.00 being black and 0.00 being white. Using a value of 0.00 (white) may be somewhat misleading since that value actually means that the effect is outlined in black with nothing printed inside the arrow. It doesn't print a white arrow on colored paper, for example.

The Gray variable may range from 1.00 to .00. You always need to have a decimal point in the value and two digits after the decimal point, even if you are using exact tenths. For example, use .50 and not .5 as your value. If you don't, the effect may not print.

Xoff/Yoff You place the effect where you want it by setting the horizontal distance, called Xoff—an offset in the x, or horizontal, direction. In a similar fashion, the vertical distance for the effect is called Yoff. Both distances are in points, which are a printer's measure. A point is $1/72$ inch. You can use either positive or negative values for both Xoff and Yoff.

Positive values of Xoff move the effect to the right, while negative values move it to the left. Positive values of Yoff move the effect down the page, and negative values move it up the page.

You must place plus or minus signs in front of the Xoff and Yoff variables, and you must use two digits, as shown. Acceptable values range from ±00 to ±99. Of course, +00 and – 00 are identical and give you the same result: no offset in that direction.

Size and Position

The examples in Figure 8-11 illustrate how your arrow is sized and positioned. The percentage shown in the text next to the arrows is the value placed into each effect for Pct. As you see, the 25 percent arrow is one quarter of the height of the X, the 50 percent arrow is half the height, and so on, up to the 150 percent arrow which is one and a half times as high. Obviously, using 100 percent gives you an arrow whose head is the same height as the X. Using the Pct variable along with the font size, you can make your arrow any size you want.

This is a 36-point left arrow sized to 25%.

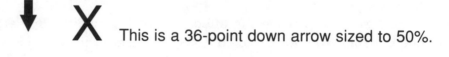
This is a 36-point down arrow sized to 50%.

This is a 36-point right arrow sized to 75%.

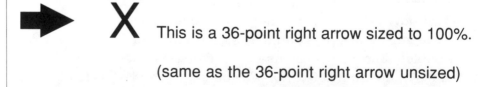
This is a 36-point right arrow sized to 100%.

(same as the 36-point right arrow unsized)

This is a 36-point left arrow sized to 150%.

Figure 8-11. Examples of the sized thick arrow effect

The examples also show you how the arrow is positioned. All of the arrows in Figure 8-11 are based on a 36-point positioning character. The X next to them on the line of text is also 36 points. As you can see, the center of the arrowhead aligns with the point where the two lines of the X cross. For the left and right arrows, the tip of the arrow is centered on the line of text, as you see in Figure 8-11. However, for the up and down arrows, the tail extends the length you defined with the Len variable. In those cases, the arrow is not centered on the line of text. The second example shows this with a down arrow sized to 50 percent and a length of 24 points. The 100 percent arrow also shows you that the arrow's head is sized to match the size of a capital X in your designated font.

In the horizontal direction, the arrow is positioned so that the head prints over the positioning character. Remember that the tail of the arrow extends out opposite the direction selected by the orientation, however. If you use a down arrow, for example, then you may have to adjust the lines of text above the effect to allow enough room for the tail to print.

Using the Effect

The examples in Figure 8-11 show you some of the uses for sized thick arrows. The most common use for the sized arrow is to make a smaller arrow than the size of the text that it accompanies.

The last example illustrates another use for these arrows. Besides placing small arrows next to a line of larger text, you can also place a large arrow by a line of smaller text. This may be visually more appealing than using the arrow with a large point size and following it with smaller text, because the arrow seems more proportioned to the surrounding text.

The examples in Figure 8-12 show you three combinations of the sized arrow effect with the proportioned button effect. As you see, you can create unique combinations by choosing different

Up arrow at 40% and button at 60%

  Right arrow at 70% and button at 200%

  Left arrow at 70% and button at 200%

Figure 8-12. Examples of the sized thick arrow combined with other effects

percentages and offsets. In the first example, the positioning character is 40-point Helvetica. In both of the following examples, the positioning character is set to 36-point Helvetica. For each example, the Pct variables for both effects are set as shown in the text and the offsets are adjusted to place the arrow where you see it. For the first example, the offsets are set to Xoff +00 and Yoff – 05. For the second example, the offsets are +15 and +00. For the third, they are +02 and +00. The values that you use for the offsets will depend on the orientation of the arrow that you are using, the nature of the effect that you are using the arrow with, and the final effect that you want to achieve. Since the arrow and the additional effect share the same positioning character, they also share font selection and sizing information.

It can be very difficult to judge the percentage that you want to use to set an arrow precisely. This effect has two knots because it contains variables and may require a test print or two to set it exactly the way you want it. In addition, if you are using the combined form of the effect, you may have to adjust the distance that you want to offset the arrow to match it to the other effect. To set it the way you want, you may have to make some tests using different offsets in your document. All combined effects have three knots, since they will usually require several tests.

DROP SHADOW THICK ARROW

shadow thick arrow

Description

You may notice that some people make arrows stand out on the page by placing a shadow behind them. The shadow arrow effect allows you to make a shadow behind your arrow. This effect comes in four variations, pointing in each direction: right, left, up, and down.

Variables

This effect resembles the arrow effect, except that you can place a shadow behind the arrow. You have controls in the effect for the placement of the shadow in both the horizontal and vertical directions, or the darkness of the shadow. You can set the overall length of the arrow to any value by using the Len variable. Finally, you can also set the darkness of the arrow to any shade of gray. If you set the value to .00, the arrow is filled with white and outlined in black. The five variables are listed in the front of the drop shadow arrow effect, as follows:

-04 /Xoff +05 /Yoff .50 /Shadow 30 /Len 1.00 /Gray 10 dict...

You must observe the range and format rules for the variables very strictly. If you don't, the effect may not print.

Xoff/Yoff   You place the shadow behind the box by setting the horizontal distance, called Xoff—an offset in the x, or horizontal, direction. In a similar fashion, the vertical distance for the shadow is called Yoff. Both distances are in points, which are a printer's measure. A point is $^1/_{72}$ inch. You can use either positive or negative values for both Xoff and Yoff.

Positive values of Xoff move the shadow to the right, while negative values move it to the left. Positive values of Yoff move the shadow down the page, and negative values move it up the page.

You must place plus or minus signs in front of the Xoff and Yoff variables, and you must use two digits, as shown above. Acceptable values range from ±00 to ±99. Of course, +00 and −00 are identical and give you the same result: no offset in that direction.

Shadow   The darkness of the shadow is set by a control named Shadow. This makes it different from most shadows, since the Gray variable is used to set the darkness of the arrow itself. The values of Shadow are percentages, with 1.00 being black and 0.01 being almost white. Although you can use a value of 0.00 (white), this may be somewhat misleading since that value actually means that nothing is printed behind the arrow. It doesn't print a white shadow on colored paper, for example.

The Shadow variable may range from 1.00 to .01. You always need to have a decimal point in the value and two digits after the decimal point, even if you are using exact tenths. For example, use .50 and not .5 as your value.

Len   The length of the arrow is controlled by a variable named Len that specifies the total length of the arrow in points. A point is a printer's measure and is $^1/_{72}$ inch. For example, you measure type sizes in points. The positioning character establishes the size of the head of the arrow. Then the tail of the arrow is drawn out to make the overall length equal to the number that you set in this variable. If you specify a value for Len that is less than the point size of the positioning character, the arrow is drawn at a default size equal to the point size. So if you use a 24-point positioning character and set Len to any number less than 24, the actual size of the arrow will be 24 points, not the value that you set.

The Len may be any value from 00 to 999. You always need to have at least two digits, even if you are using a single-digit value (for example, 09, not 9). If you don't, the effect may not print.

Gray   The darkness of the arrow is set by a control named, reasonably enough, Gray. The values of Gray are percentages, with 1.00 being black and 0.00 being white. Using a value of 0.00 (white) may be somewhat misleading since that value actually means that the effect is outlined in black with nothing printed inside the arrow. It doesn't print a white arrow on colored paper, for example.

The Gray variable may range from 1.00 to .00. You always need to have a decimal point in the value and two digits after the decimal point, even if you are using exact tenths. For example, use .50 and not .5 as your value. If you don't, the effect may not print.

Size and Position

The shadowed arrow is sized in the same way as the standard arrow effect. The positioning character determines the size of the arrow's head, and the value that you set in the Len variable determines the overall length of the arrow. The shadow size matches that of the arrow, as a shadow should. As illustrated in Figure 8-13, the position of the shadow, and therefore the amount of shadow that shows under the arrow, is determined by the Xoff and Yoff variables.

The four examples in Figure 8-13 show you how changes in the offset values move the shadow effect around the arrow. As you can see, you can create any variation in shadowing by changing the signs of the offset values.

   This is a 36-point arrow with offsets of -04 and +06. The shadow is .50 gray.

   This is a 36-point arrow with offsets of +04 and +06. The shadow is .50 gray.

   This is a 36-point arrow with offsets of -04 and -06. The shadow is .50 gray.

   This is a 36-point arrow with offsets of +04 and -06. The shadow is .50 gray.

Figure 8-13. Examples of the drop shadow thick arrow effect

It can be very difficult to judge the distance that you want to offset the shadow behind your arrow. To set it the way you want, you may have to make some tests using different offsets in your document. This effect has two knots because it contains variables and may require test prints to set it exactly the way you want it.

Using the Effect

Both sets of examples in Figures 8-13 and 8-14 illustrate some interesting issues for you to consider as you work with drop shadows and arrows. The examples in Figure 8-13 use the same offset

This is a 36-point up arrow with offsets of -04 and +06. The shadow is .50 gray.

This is a 36-point right arrow with offsets of -04 and +06. The shadow is .50 gray.

This is a 36-point left arrow with offsets of -04 and +06. The shadow is .50 gray.

This is a 36-point down arrow with offsets of -04 and +06. The shadow is .50 gray .

Figure 8-14. Orientation and the drop shadow thick arrow effect

values and different signs to move the shadow around a right arrow. The examples in Figure 8-14 use the same offset values with the same signs for each of the four orientations of the arrow effect. As you see, the results are not what you might expect.

One of the most noticeable things in Figure 8-14 is that the shadows appear to be larger or smaller distances from the arrow, even though the offsets are identical. When placing the shadows for your arrows, you need to take into account the orientation of the arrow and the position that you want the shadow to show. As you can see, the shadow is less visible when it is behind the head of the arrow. If the orientation and offsets place the tip of the shadow behind the tip of the arrow, then you should increase the offset in the direction that is at right angles to the orientation. For example, if you are placing a shadow with a negative x offset behind an up arrow, similar to the first line in Figure 8-14, then you should increase the Xoff variable to make the shadow more visible.

TIP

Normally you will use relatively small values for the offsets. Remember that for different orientations you will need different offsets to make the shadow look most natural when it prints. Typically you should have about 4 to 6 points difference in the offsets (depending on the size of the arrow) for the most natural result.

FADED THICK ARROW

faded thick arrow

Description

The faded thick arrow effect is essentially a fancy variant of the shadowed thick arrow. As you can see, the faded thick arrow has a shadow that changes from white to black over a short distance.

Like the other arrow effects, the faded thick arrow comes in four variations, pointing in each direction: right, left, up, and down.

Variables

While the size of the arrowhead is set by the positioning character, you can set the overall length of the arrow to any value. The variable is listed in the front of the arrow effect, as follows:

30 `/Len 6 dict`

You must observe the range and format rules for the variable very strictly. If you don't, the effect may not print.

Len   The length of the arrow is controlled by a variable named Len that specifies the total length of the arrow in points. A point is a printer's measure and is $1/72$ inch. For example, you measure type sizes in points. The positioning character establishes the size of the head of the arrow. Then the tail of the arrow is drawn out so that the overall length equals the number that you set in this variable. If you specify a value for Len that is less than the point size of the positioning character, the arrow is drawn at a default minimum size equal to the point size. So if you use a 24-point positioning character and set Len to any number less than 24, the actual size of the arrow will be 24 points, not the value that you set.

Len may be any value from 00 to 999. You always need to have at least two digits, even if you are using a single-digit value (for example, 09, not 9). If you don't, the effect may not print.

Size and Position

The faded thick arrow is sized in the same way as the standard arrow effect. The positioning character determines the size of the arrowhead before the faded effect is in place. The head of the arrow is sized to match the height of a capital X. The overall length of the arrow, from the tip of the arrowhead to the end of the tail, is set by the Len variable. The faded shadow size is a standard size for all the arrows and changes its position to match the orientation of the arrow. For example, it extends to the left and below the right arrow by a fixed amount, and matches the arrow in all dimensions. As shown in Figure 8-15, this gives somewhat different results for arrows with different sizes and orien-

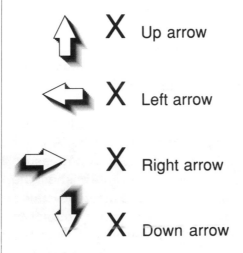

Figure 8-15. Examples of the faded thick arrow effect

tations.

Like the other arrows, the faded thick arrow has four orientations: right, left, up, and down. The name of the orientation is set by the direction of the arrowhead. The up arrow points up, and so on. Each of these orientations is a separate effect file.

The arrow itself is placed over the positioning character where the standard arrow would appear. If you use the faded thick arrow effect with small size text, be sure to allow enough room below the effect so that the faded shadow does not touch the text below and to the left of the arrow.

372

Using the Effect

Although this effect looks something like the shadow arrow effect, it has no variables and no controls for shadow placement. Fading a shadow is quite complex and time-consuming, so you don't have alternatives here for shadow placement or coloring. The examples in Figure 8-16 demonstrate how this affects the resulting output. The size of the positioning character is given in the example, and the length of the arrow is 8 points greater than the size. As you can see, smaller point sizes have a faded effect that extends out a great distance relative to the size of the arrow. On the other hand, on large arrows the faded background hardly differs from the simple shadow effect. The best results are generally between 18 and 48 points, but you may want larger or smaller arrows for special purposes.

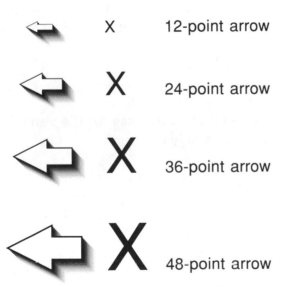

Figure 8-16. Variations of the faded thick arrow effect

ARROWHEAD

arrowhead

Description

This is a simple arrowhead that can be used for indicating directions and as a graphic element. The head is exactly as wide as it is high, giving it a fairly sharp point without being exaggerated. You may find it useful in mimicking various real-life indicators, such as elevator directions, record and playback buttons, and so on.

Variables

The size of the arrowhead is set by the positioning character. You can use the single variable to set the color to any shade of gray. If you set the Gray value to .00, the arrowhead is filled with white and outlined in black. The single variable is listed in the front of the arrowhead effect, as follows:

1.00 /Gray 6 dict

You must observe the range and format rules for the variable very strictly. If you don't, the effect may not print.

Gray   The darkness of the arrowhead is set by a control named, reasonably enough, Gray. The values of Gray are percentages, with 1.00 being black and 0.00 being white. Using a value of 0.00 (white) may be somewhat misleading since that value actually means that the effect is outlined in black with nothing printed inside the arrow. It doesn't print a white arrowhead on colored paper, for example.

The Gray variable may range from 1.00 to .00. You always need to have a decimal point in the value and two digits after the

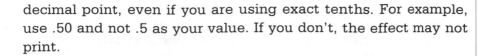

decimal point, even if you are using exact tenths. For example, use .50 and not .5 as your value. If you don't, the effect may not print.

Size and Position

The examples in Figure 8-17 show you different orientations of the arrowhead effect. The effect comes as four different files on your effects disk: right, left, up, and down. The name of the orientation is set by the direction of the arrowhead. The up arrowhead points up, and so on. Each orientation is a separate file.

Figure 8-17 also shows you how the arrowhead is sized and placed by the positioning character. The arrowhead is sized to match the height of a capital X. The positioning character and the capital X in the examples are the same font and size to illustrate this. The arrowhead is positioned in each orientation so that it is drawn over the positioning character.

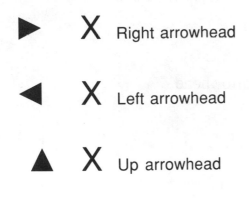

Figure 8-17. Examples of the arrowhead effect

Using the Effect

The examples in Figure 8-18 show you several variations for the arrowhead effect. The top two examples show you some color variations for the arrowheads. The top arrowhead is 50 percent gray, while the next arrowhead is 00 percent gray, or white, which produces an outlined arrow.

TIP

The last example in Figure 8-18 shows you an interesting use for multiple effects on one line. This uses the filled square bullet at full size and the right arrowhead, with the word 'EXIT' placed between them in capital letters. Since both effects are sized to the height of a capital X, the result is a sort of abstract arrow with the word imprinted on it.

Since the effects erase a portion of the space in front of themselves (to remove the positioning character, if it is printable), I used tabs to place the effects and the word in between so that all of the text printed correctly. Needless to say, this type of combination requires several tries to get the spacing and placement correct. But, as you see, the result can be very interesting.

 50% gray Down arrowhead

 White (outline) Down arrowhead

Figure 8-18. Variations of the arrowhead effect

SIZED ARROWHEAD

sized arrowhead
sized arrowhead (combined)

Description

Sometimes you may want an arrowhead that is not the size of your font, but rather one that is larger or smaller. With this effect, you can add small, centered arrowheads in a line of text, or you can enlarge an arrowhead for graphic emphasis, while keeping it centered on the text. You set the basic size and position of the head of the arrow with the positioning character, then modify that by using a percentage. This allows you to use various sizes of arrowheads in lists, for example, without multiple font changes (which slow processing) and with complete control over size. You can also use the combined form with other effects, like the proportioned button, to create a range of combinations.

The sized arrowhead effect comes in four variations, pointing in each direction: right, left, up, and down.

Variables

You determine the size of the arrowhead by setting the Pct variable. You can also set the darkness to any shade of gray. If you set the Gray value to .00, the arrowhead is filled with white and outlined in black. The two variables are listed in the front of the sized arrowhead effect, as follows:

`100` /Pct `1.00` /Gray 7 dict...

If you are using the combined effect, you will have the following variables:

`-01` /Xoff `-01` /Yoff `100` /Pct `1.00` /Gray 8 dict...

377

All combined effects resemble the standard version of the effect and have the same controls and settings, except that they also have Xoff and Yoff variables in front of all other variables. Since that is so, there is no separate discussion of the combined version of the effect. You simply use the standard effect when you don't want to mix effects and use the combined versions when you do. If you have any questions about how to use this effect combined with other effects, see the discussion under the standard checkmark effect in Chapter 7.

You must observe the range and format rules for the variables very strictly. If you don't, the effect may not print.

Pct   The Pct variable allows you to set the ratio of the size of the arrow to the point size of the positioning character. This value represents the size of the overall arrow while the length of the arrow is defined by the Len variable. You can use any values between 10 and 999 for Pct without trouble. A 100 percent arrowhead is the same size as a capital X.

Gray   The darkness of the arrow is set by a control named, reasonably enough, Gray. The values of Gray are percentages, with 1.00 being black and 0.00 being white. Using a value of 0.00 (white) may be somewhat misleading since that value actually means that the effect is outlined in black with nothing printed inside the arrow. It doesn't print a white arrow on colored paper, for example.

The Gray variable may range from 1.00 to .00. You always need to have a decimal point in the value and two digits after the decimal point, even if you are using exact tenths. For example, use .50 and not .5 as your value. If you don't, the effect may not print.

Xoff/Yoff   You place the effect where you want it by setting the horizontal distance, called Xoff—an offset in the x, or horizontal, direction. In a similar fashion, the vertical distance for the effect is called Yoff. Both distances are in points, which are a printer's measure. A point is $1/72$ inch. You can use either positive or negative values for both Xoff and Yoff.

Positive values of Xoff move the effect to the right, while negative values move it to the left. Positive values of Yoff move the effect down the page, and negative values move it up the page.

You must place a plus or minus sign in front of the Xoff and Yoff variables, and you must use two digits, as shown. Acceptable values range from ±00 to ±99. Of course, $+00$ and -00 are identical, and give you the same result: no offset in that direction.

Size and Position

The examples in Figure 8-19 illustrate how your arrowhead is sized and positioned. The percentage shown in the text next to the arrowheads is the value placed into each effect for Pct. As you see, the 25 percent arrowhead is one quarter of the height of the X, the 50 percent arrowhead is half the height, and so on, up to the 150 percent arrowhead which is one and a half times as high. Obviously, using 100 percent gives you an arrowhead that is the same height as the X. Using the Pct variable along with the font size, you can make your arrowhead effect any size you want.

The examples also show you how the arrowhead is positioned. All of the arrowheads in Figure 8-19 are based on a 36-point positioning character. The X next to them on the line of text is also 36 points. As you can see, the arrowhead aligns with the point where the two lines of the X cross. For the left and right arrowheads, the tip of the arrowhead is centered on the line of text, as you see in Figure 8-19. The 100 percent arrowhead also shows you that the arrowhead is sized to match the size of a capital X in your designated font.

In the horizontal direction, the arrowhead is positioned so that it prints over the positioning character.

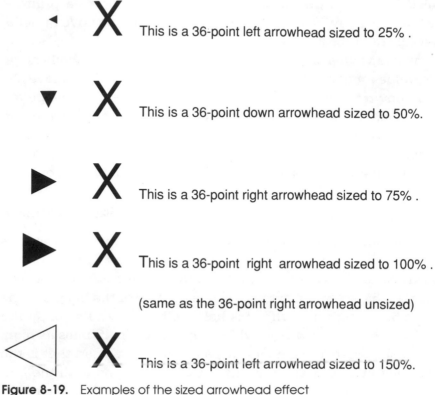

This is a 36-point left arrowhead sized to 25% .

This is a 36-point down arrowhead sized to 50%.

This is a 36-point right arrowhead sized to 75% .

This is a 36-point right arrowhead sized to 100% .

(same as the 36-point right arrowhead unsized)

This is a 36-point left arrowhead sized to 150%.

Figure 8-19.   Examples of the sized arrowhead effect

Using the Effect

The examples in Figure 8-19 show you some of the uses for sized arrowheads. The most common use for the sized arrowhead is to make a smaller arrow than the size of the text that it accompanies.

The last example illustrates another use for these arrowheads. Besides placing small arrowheads next to a line of larger text, you can also place a large arrowhead by a line of smaller text. This may be visually more appealing than simply using the arrowhead with a large point size and following it with smaller text, because the arrowhead seems more proportioned to the surrounding text.

The examples in Figure 8-20 show you three combinations of the sized arrowhead effect with the proportioned button effect. As you see, you can create unique combinations by choosing different percentages and offsets. In all of the examples, the positioning character is set to 36-point Helvetica. For each example, the Pct variables for both effects are set as shown in the text and the offsets are adjusted to place the arrowhead where you see it. For the first example, the offsets are set to Xoff +13 and Yoff +00. For the second example, the offsets are +09 and +00. The third example uses two left arrowheads with the button to make the conventional button for Fast Forward on tape recorders. The offsets used here are +00 and +00 for the first arrowhead and +17 and +00 for the second. These settings allow the two arrowheads to print with the second just touching the first.

  Right arrowhead at 70% and button at 200%

  Left arrowhead at 70% and button at 200%

  Two left arrowheads at 70% and button at 200%

Figure 8-20.   Examples of the sized arrowhead combined with other effects

Of course, the values that you use for the offsets will depend on the orientation of the arrowhead that you are using, the nature of the effect that you are using the arrowhead with, and the final effect that you want to achieve. Since the arrowhead and the additional effect share the same positioning character, they also share font selection and sizing information.

It can be very difficult to judge the percentage that you want to use to set an arrowhead precisely. This effect has two knots because it contains variables and may require a test print or two to set it exactly the way you want it. In addition, if you are using the combined form of the effect, you may have to adjust the distance that you want to offset the arrowhead to match it to the other effect. To set it the way you want, you may have to make some tests using different offsets in your document. All combined effects have 3 knots, since they will usually require several tests.

DROP SHADOW ARROWHEAD

shadow arrowhead

Description

You may notice that some people make arrowheads stand out on the page by placing a shadow behind them. The shadow arrowhead effect allows you to make a shadow behind your arrowhead. This effect comes in four variations, pointing in each directions: right, left, up, and down.

Variables

This effect resembles the arrowhead effect, except that you can place a shadow behind the arrowhead. You have controls in the effect for the placement of the shadow in both the horizontal and vertical directions, and the darkness of the shadow. You can also set the darkness of the arrowhead to any shade of gray. If you set the value to .00, the arrowhead is filled with white and outlined in black. The four variables are listed in the front of the shadow arrowhead effect, as follows:

`-04 /Xoff +05 /Yoff .50 /Shadow 1.00 /Gray 9 dict...`

You must observe the range and format rules for the variables very strictly. If you don't, the effect may not print.

Xoff/Yoff   You place the shadow behind the box by setting the horizontal distance, called Xoff—an offset in the x, or horizontal, direction. In a similar fashion, the vertical distance for the shadow is called Yoff. Both distances are in points, which are a printer's measure. A point is $1/72$ inch. You can use either positive or negative values for both Xoff and Yoff.

Positive values of Xoff move the shadow to the right, while negative values move it to the left. Positive values of Yoff move the shadow down the page, and negative values move it up the page.

You must place plus or minus signs in front of the Xoff and Yoff variables, and you must use two digits, as shown. Acceptable values range from ±00 to ±99. Of course, +00 and – 00 are identical, and give you the same result: no offset in that direction.

Shadow   The darkness of the shadow is set by a control named Shadow. This makes it different from most shadows, since the Gray variable is used to set the darkness of the arrowhead itself. The values of Shadow are percentages, with 1.00 being black and 0.01 being almost white. Although you can use a value of 0.00 (white), this may be somewhat misleading since that value actually means that nothing is printed behind the arrowhead. It doesn't print a white shadow on colored paper, for example.

The Shadow variable may range from 1.00 to .01. You always need to have a decimal point in the value and two digits after the decimal point, even if you are using exact tenths. For example, use .50 and not .5 as your value.

Gray   The darkness of the arrowhead is set by a control named, reasonably enough, Gray. The values of Gray are percentages, with 1.00 being black and 0.00 being white. Using a value of 0.00 (white) may be somewhat misleading since that value actually means that the effect is outlined in black with nothing printed inside the arrowhead. It doesn't print a white arrowhead on colored paper, for example.

The Gray variable may range from 1.00 to .00. You always need to have a decimal point in the value and two digits after the decimal point, even if you are using exact tenths. For example, use .50 and not .5 as your value. If you don't, the effect may not print.

Size and Position

The shadowed arrowhead is sized in the same way as the standard arrowhead effect. The positioning character determines the size of the arrowhead. The shadow size matches that of the arrow, as a shadow should. As illustrated in Figure 8-21, the position of the shadow, and therefore the amount of shadow that shows under the arrow, is determined by the Xoff and Yoff variables.

The four examples in Figure 8-21 show you how changes in the offset values move the shadow effect around the arrow. As you can see, you can create any variation in shadowing by changing the signs of the offset values.

It can be very difficult to judge the distance that you want to offset the shadow behind your arrowhead. To set it the way you want, you may have to make some tests using different offsets in

 This is a 36-point arrowhead with offsets of -04 and +06. The shadow is .50 gray.

 This is a 36-point arrowhead with offsets of +04 and +06. The shadow is .50 gray.

 This is a 36-point arrowhead with offsets of -04 and -06. The shadow is .50 gray.

 This is a 36-point arrowhead with offsets of +04 and -06. The shadow is .50 gray .

Figure 8-21. Examples of the drop shadow arrowhead effect

your document. This effect has two knots because it contains variables and may require test prints to set it exactly the way you want it.

Using the Effect

Both sets of examples in Figures 8-21 and 8-22 illustrate some interesting issues for you to consider as you work with drop shadows and arrowheads. The examples in Figure 8-21 use the same offset values and different signs to move the shadow around a

This is a 36-point up arrowhead with offsets of -04 and +06. The shadow is .50 gray.

 This is a 36-point right arrowhead with offsets of -04 and +06. The shadow is .50 gray.

 This is a 36-point left arrowhead with offsets of -04 and +06. The shadow is .50 gray .

 This is a 36-point down arrowhead with offsets of -04 and +06. The shadow is .50 gray .

Figure 8-22. Orientation and the drop shadow arrowhead effect

right arrowhead. The examples in Figure 8-22 use the same offset values with the same signs for each of the four orientations of the arrowhead effect. As you see, the results are not what you might expect.

One of the most noticeable things in Figure 8-22 is that the shadows appear to be larger or smaller distances from the arrowhead, even though the offsets are identical. When placing the shadows for your arrowheads, you need to take into account the orientation of the arrowhead and the position that you want the shadow to show. As you can see, the shadow is less visible when it is behind the tip of the arrowhead. If the orientation and offsets place the tip of the shadow behind the tip of the arrowhead, then you should increase the offset in a direction that is at right angles to the orientation. For example, if you are placing a shadow with a negative x offset behind an up arrowhead, similar to the first line in Figure 8-22, then you should increase the Xoff variable to make the shadow more visible.

TIP

Normally you will use relatively small values for the offsets. Remember that for different orientations you will need different offsets to make the shadow look most natural when it prints. Typically you should have about 4 to 6 points difference in the offsets (depending on the size of the arrowhead) for the most natural result.

FADED ARROWHEAD

faded arrowhead

Description

The faded arrowhead effect is essentially a fancy variant of the shadowed arrowhead. As you can see, the faded arrowhead has a shadow that changes from white to black over a short distance. Like the other arrow effects, the faded arrowhead comes in four variations, pointing in each direction: right, left, up, and down.

Size and Position

The faded arrowhead is sized in the same way as the standard arrowhead effect. The positioning character determines the size of the arrowhead before the faded effect is in place. The head of the arrow is sized to match the height of a capital X. The faded shadow size is a standard size for all the arrowheads and changes its position to match the orientation of the arrowhead. For example, it extends to the left and below the right arrowhead by a fixed amount and matches it in all dimensions. As shown in Figure 8-23, this gives somewhat different results for arrowheads with different sizes and orientations.

Like the other arrowheads, the faded arrowhead has four different orientations: right, left, up, and down. The name of the orientation is set by the direction of the arrowhead. The up arrowhead points up, and so on. Each of these orientations is a separate effect file.

The arrowhead itself is placed over the positioning character where the standard arrowhead would appear. If you use the faded arrowhead effect with small size text, be sure to allow enough room below the effect so that the faded shadow does not touch the text below and to the left of the arrowhead.

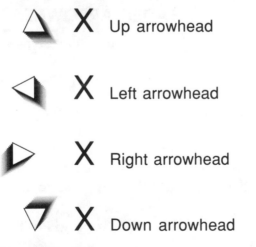

Figure 8-23. Examples of the faded arrowhead effect

Using the Effect

Although this effect looks something like the shadow arrowhead effect, it has no variables and no controls for shadow placement. Fading a shadow is quite complex and time-consuming, so you don't have alternatives here for shadow placement or coloring. The examples in Figure 8-24 demonstrate how this affects the resulting output. The size of the positioning character is given in the example. As you can see, smaller point sizes have a faded effect that extends out a great distance, relative to the size of the arrowhead. On the other hand, on large size arrowheads the faded background hardly differs from the simple shadow effect. The best results are generally between 18 and 48 points, but you may want larger or smaller arrowheads for special purposes.

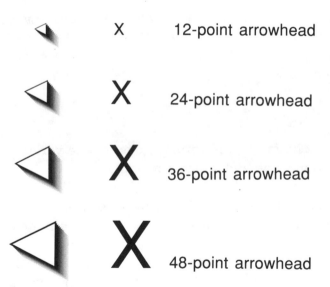

Figure 8-24. Variations of the faded arrowhead effect

REVERSE ARROW

reverse arrow

Description

Sometimes you may want an arrow to indicate that things have to turn around. The reverse arrow effect is an arrow that turns on itself, to point in the reverse direction that it starts from. The arrow begins pointing in one direction, and then turns through half a circle to end with the head pointing in the opposite direction. For this arrow effect, you set the size and position of the entire arrow with the positioning character. The reverse arrow effect comes in two variations, pointing to the right and left.

Variables

You can set the darkness of the arrow to any shade of gray. If you set the Gray value to .00, the arrow is filled with white and outlined in black. The single variable is listed in the front of the reverse arrow effect, as follows:

`1.00` /Gray 6 dict

You must observe the range and format rules for the variable very strictly. If you don't, the effect may not print.

Gray The darkness of the arrow is set by a control named, reasonably enough, Gray. The values of Gray are percentages, with 1.00 being black and 0.00 being white. Using a value of 0.00 (white) may be somewhat misleading since that value actually means that the effect is outlined in black with nothing printed inside the arrow. It doesn't print a white arrow on colored paper, for example.

The Gray variable may range from 1.00 to .00. You always need to have a decimal point in the value and two digits after the

decimal point, even if you are using exact tenths. For example, use .50 and not .5 as your value. If you don't, the effect may not print.

Size and Position

The examples in Figure 8-25 show you different orientations of the reverse arrow effect. The reverse arrow effect comes as two different files on your effects disk: right and left. The name of the orientation is set by the direction of the arrowhead itself. The right arrow starts out pointing left and ends up pointing right.

Figure 8-25 also shows you how the arrow is sized and placed by the positioning character. The diameter of the arrow is sized to match the height of a capital X. The positioning character and the capital X in the examples are the same font and size to illustrate this. The arrow is positioned in each orientation so that it is drawn over the positioning character.

Using the Effect

The examples in Figure 8-26 show you two color variations for the reverse arrow effect. The top arrow is 50 percent gray, while the bottom arrow is 00 percent gray, or white, which produces an outlined arrow.

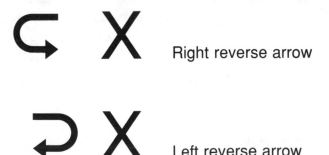

Right reverse arrow

Left reverse arrow

Figure 8-25. Examples of the reverse arrow effect

.50 gray right reverse arrow

 X

White (outline) right reverse arrow

Figure 8-26. Variations of the reverse arrow effect

CIRCULAR ARROW

circular arrow

Description

Almost by definition, most arrows point in a straight line: "straight as an arrow" and so on. However, in spite of that old saying, you may want an arrow that indicates circular motion. The circular arrow effect is a curved arrow that turns three-quarters of a circle. This allows you to show the direction that a dial or button should turn, for example. For this effect, you set the size and position of the entire arrow with the positioning character. The circular arrow effect comes in two variations, rotating clockwise and counter-clockwise.

Variables

While the direction of rotation for the circular arrow is set by the file that you choose, you can set starting and ending positions of the arrow to any value that you want by using the Ang variable.

You can also set the color of the arrow to any shade of gray. If you set the Gray value to .00, the arrow is filled with white and outlined in black. The two variables are listed in the front of the circular arrow effect, as follows:

```
000 /Ang 1.00 /Gray 7 dict
```

You must observe the range and format rules for the variables very strictly. If you don't, the effect may not print.

Ang   The circular arrow rotates in the direction specified by the effect name: clockwise or counterclockwise. The Ang variable specifies where the arrow begins and ends by setting the angle of rotation for the arrow. An angle of 0 means that the arrow begins at the base of the positioning character and turns three-quarters of a circle to point right (if it's a clockwise arrow) or left (if it's a counterclockwise arrow). The angle turns the arrow through the number of degrees specified. Then the tail of the arrow is drawn out to make the overall length.

Ang may be any value from 000 to 359. You may use values greater than 359 degrees, but they are equivalent to, and are treated like, an angle between 0 and 359 degrees. For example, an angle of 360 is equivalent to 0 degrees, and an angle of 405 is equivalent to 45 degrees, and so on. You always need to have three digits, even if you are using a single- or double-digit value. For example, use 045 and not 45 as your value. If you don't, the effect may not print.

Gray   The darkness of the arrow is set by a control named, reasonably enough, Gray. The values of Gray are percentages, with 1.00 being black and 0.00 being white. Using a value of 0.00 (white) may be somewhat misleading since that value actually means that the effect is outlined in black with nothing printed inside the arrow. It doesn't print a white arrow on colored paper, for example.

393

The Gray variable may range from 1.00 to .00. You always need to have a decimal point in the value and two digits after the decimal point, even if you are using exact tenths. For example, use .50 and not .5 as your value. If you don't, the effect may not print.

Size and Position

The examples in Figure 8-27 show you the two different orientations of the circular arrow effect. The effect comes as two different files on your effects disk: clockwise and counterclockwise. The name of the orientation is set by the direction of rotation.

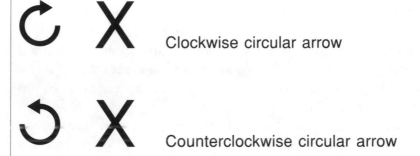

Clockwise circular arrow

Counterclockwise circular arrow

Figure 8-27. Examples of the circular arrow effect

Figure 8-27 also shows you how the arrow is sized and placed by the positioning character. The diameter of the arrow is sized to match the height of a capital X. The positioning character and the capital X in the examples are the same font and size to illustrate this. The arrow is positioned in each orientation so that the arrow is drawn over the positioning character.

Using the Effect

The examples in Figure 8-28 show you several variations for the circular arrow effect. The first four examples show you 90-degree and 180-degree rotations for the clockwise and counterclockwise effect. The last two examples show you a 245-degree rotation with some color variations for the counterclockwise arrow. The fifth arrow is 50 percent gray, while the bottom arrow is 00 percent gray, or white, which produces an outlined arrow.

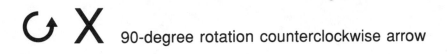

90-degree rotation clockwise arrow

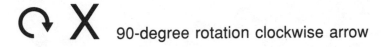

90-degree rotation counterclockwise arrow

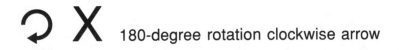

180-degree rotation clockwise arrow

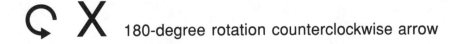

180-degree rotation counterclockwise arrow

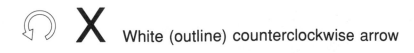

.50 gray counterclockwise arrow

White (outline) counterclockwise arrow

Figure 8-28. Variations of the circular arrow effect

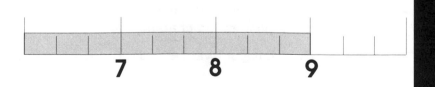

9

Text and

Shapes

THIS CHAPTER PRESENTS SPECIAL TEXT EFFECTS THAT YOU can print on a variety of shapes—a button, an arrow, and two types of starbursts. The starburst effects differ from the previous stars with text because these starbursts (and their associated text) can be rotated to any angle. All the effects in this chapter require you to enter the text into the effect itself. To use these effects, you must know how to insert the text in the effect and how to place the effect correctly. The text used in these effects is restricted to a single line of text containing no more than 100 characters.

INSERTING TEXT AND SHAPE EFFECTS IN MICROSOFT WORD

1. Open your document. Insert a positioning character where you want to place the effect. The size of the positioning character determines the basic size of your shape.

2. Open the **xxxx**.w file, where **xxxx** represents the name of the desired effect. If only one line of text appears when you open the file, click on the Show Hidden Text box in the Preferences . . . selection of the Edit menu. Select and copy all the text of the effect and paste it at the beginning of the page that will contain the effect. Notice that the major part of the text in this file is in Word's PostScript style. (If you are unclear about how to use this style, review the instructions in Chapter 1.)

3. Cut the text at the end of the .w file that is *not* in the PostScript style. This is the second part of the effect.

4. Paste this text into your Word document immediately after (to the right of) the positioning character.

5. Enter the text that you want to use into the Str variable for your effect.

6. Select all of the text, and only the text, from the second part of the effect file that you pasted into your document. Change the font to the PostScript Escape font. This part of the effect text will disappear.

7. Be sure that the Print Hidden Text box in the Print dialog box is not checked. Print your document. The effect will print over the positioning character.

INSERTING TEXT AND SHAPE EFFECTS IN OTHER WORD PROCESSING APPLICATIONS

1. Open your document. Insert a positioning character where you want to place the effect. The size and font of the positioning character determine the size and font used in your effect.

2. Open the effect file, and select and copy the effect text.

3. Paste the effect text into your document immediately after (to the right of) the positioning character.

4. Enter the text that you want to use in the Str variable for your effect.

5. Select the effect text, and only the effect text, up to the % that occurs inside the effect. The portion of the effect that contains the % character will look like this:

```
. . . save put } if % cf setfont . . .
```

The % is printed in bold in this line although it is not bold in the file. Be sure that you have selected the text up to, but not including, the % and change it to the PostScript Escape font. This is the first part of the effect.

6. Select the remainder of the effect text, and only the effect text, after the %. Be sure that you have selected the text after, but not including, the %, and change it to the PostScript Escape font. This is the second part of the effect. When you are done, you should see only the positioning character followed by the % where your effect was.

7. Print your document in the ordinary way. The effect will print over the positioning character and will erase the % as it prints.

BUTTON TEXT

button text

Description

This effect allows you to place a single line of text onto a button that resembles the buttons presented in Chapter 4. The height of the button is determined by the font and point size of the text that is placed on it, and the length is determined by the length of the line of text. You can use this effect wherever you need a labeled button.

Variables

As with all these effects, you must enter the text to be displayed into the effect itself. Your positioning character determines the font and size that will be used for the text in your effect. You can also control the shading of the sides of the button. The two variables are listed in the front of the text effect, as follows:

(TEXT) /Str [**0 0 1 1**] /TRBLSideColor save

You must observe the range and format rules for the variables strictly. If you don't, the effect may not print.

Str The Str variable contains the string that you want to display. When you change this variable, be sure that both the beginning and ending parentheses remain in the file. They are both essential. The bold characters in the previous example show you what can be changed in the effect file. Note that the two parentheses are not in bold.

The string variable can contain up to 100 characters. If you exceed 100 characters, you might find that the effect will not print, or will not print correctly.

TRBLSideColor   I know that the name TRBLSideColor is quite long, but it is intended to help you remember how the variable is used. As you see, the variable consists of four numbers, 0 or 1, enclosed within brackets. This arrangement is called an *array*. These numbers control whether each side of the button is shaded or clear. Each number controls one side, in this order: Top, Right, Bottom, Left. This order corresponds to the initials in the variable's name, which should help you remember how they are set. (Another way to remember is that the sides are set in clockwise order from the top.) If the corresponding number is a 0, then the side is clear. If the number is 1, then the side is shaded 50 percent gray. For example, the default settings [0 0 1 1] mean that the top and right sides are clear, while the bottom and left sides are shaded. Conversely, if you want to shade the top and right sides, and not the bottom and left, then you would use [1 1 0 0].

You can only use the values 0 or 1 in this array. Using any other numbers will result in possible errors. Also, you must set only four numbers—one for each of the sides.

Size and Position

Button text is sized the same as any other standard text effect— the positioning character determines the size of the effect and the font used for the text. The button height is set by the positioning character, so that the interior surface of the button is approximately as high as a capital X. (This is the same size as a standard button effect would be with the same positioning character.) The text inside the button is in the same font as the positioning character and is set slightly smaller than the positioning character so that the text fits correctly onto the button. The button is wide enough to enclose the string of text. As you can see in Figure 9-1, the position of the shadow around the button is determined by the TRBLSideColor array variable.

The text is centered on the point after the positioning character in the same manner as the button effect and the numbered button effect. You can easily combine these effects. Because the text string stretches to both the right and left, you must leave enough room around the effect for the text to print correctly.

It can be difficult to judge the distance to allow around your text. To set it the way you want, you may have to make some tests using different spacing in your document. This effect has two knots because it contains variables, and it may require test prints to set it exactly the way you want it.

Using the Effect

The examples in Figure 9-1 illustrate how the button is sized by the positioning character and the text string that you enter. The first two examples use the same text string with different-sized

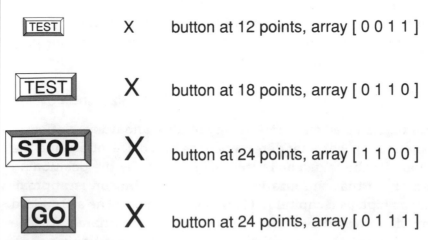

Figure 9-1. Examples of the button text effect

positioning characters. The second two examples use the same positioning character with two different strings.

These examples also show you some variations in shading around the edge of the button. The shading on each side is controlled independently by the TRBLSideColor array. The text next to each example shows you how the array was set for that effect.

ARROW TEXT

arrow text

Description

This effect allows you to place a single line of text onto an arrow that resembles the thick arrows presented in Chapter 8. The height of the arrow is determined by the font and point size of the text that is placed on it and the length is determined by the length of the line of text. You can use this effect wherever you need a labeled arrow. The arrow text effect comes in two variations, pointing right and left.

Variables

As with all these effects, you must enter the text to be displayed into the effect itself. Your positioning character determines the font and size that will be used for the text in your effect. The variable is listed in the front of the text effect, as follows:

(**TEXT**) /Str save . . .

You must observe the range and format rules for the variable strictly. If you don't, the effect may not print.

Str   The Str variable contains the string that you want to display. The bold characters in the example show you what can be changed in the effect file. When you change this variable, be sure that both the beginning and ending parentheses remain in the file. They are both essential. Note that the parentheses are not in bold.

The string variable can contain up to 100 characters. If you exceed 100 characters, you might find that the effect will not print, or will not print correctly.

Size and Position

The examples in Figure 9-2 show you different orientations of the arrow effect. This effect comes as two different files on your effects disk: right and left. The name of the orientation is set by the direction of the arrowhead.

Figure 9-2 also shows you how the arrow is sized and placed by the positioning character. The head of the arrow is sized to match the height of a capital X. (This is the same size as a standard thick arrow effect with the same positioning character.) The text inside the arrow is in the same font as the positioning character and is set slightly smaller than the point size of the positioning character so that the text fits correctly onto the arrow.

The overall length of the arrow, from the tip of the arrowhead to the end of the tail, is the length of the string that you insert in

Figure 9-2.   Examples of the arrow text effect

the effect plus the size of the arrowhead. You can see that the arrow is positioned in each orientation so that the arrowhead is drawn over the positioning character, while the tail extends out for the length required. Because the length of the arrow varies with the text that you insert, you must leave enough room around it for the text to print correctly. For example, if you are using the right arrow, be sure that there is enough room before it for the size tail required by the text that you have set.

It can be difficult to judge the distance to allow around your text. To set it the way you want, you may have to make some tests using different spacing. This effect has two knots because it contains variables, and it may require test prints to set it exactly the way you want it.

REGULAR STARBURST TEXT

regular starburst text

Description

If you look at advertising circulars and other types of displays, you will notice how eye-catching it is to place text inside a multi-pointed star and rotate the entire effect. The overall impression is that last-minute text was added to the page. The star in this effect has nine points of equal length, spaced evenly around the star.

You have already seen stars used as an outline for text. The regular and irregular stars discussed in Chapter 5 use text that is already on the page, so you can't rotate them. The star effects in this chapter include one line of text as a variable, so that you can rotate the display to any angle.

Variables

As with all these effects, you must enter the text to be displayed into the effect itself. Your positioning character determines the font and size that will be used for the text in your effect. You can also control the rotation angle for the star and its enclosed text. The two variables are listed in the front of the text effect, as follows:

(**TEXT!**) /Str **030** /Ang save . . .

You must observe the range and format rules for the variables strictly. If you don't, the effect may not print.

Str   The Str variable contains the string that you want to display. The bold characters in the example show you what can be changed in the effect file. When you change this variable, be sure that both the beginning and ending parentheses remain in the file. They are both essential. Note that the parentheses are not in bold.

The string variable can contain up to 100 characters. If you exceed 100 characters, you might find that the effect will not print, or will not print correctly.

Ang   The text and the star are displayed at an angle, which is defined by the Ang variable. The angle is measured counterclockwise from a horizontal line, so that 45 degrees rotates the effect and the text up to the right, for example, while 315 degrees rotates it down to the right. The values of Ang are degrees, with 0 being the way text is normally displayed and proceeding counterclockwise to 360, which is the same as 0.

The Ang variable may range from 000 to 360 degrees. You always need to use three digits for the angle, even if you are using smaller values (for example, 045 and not 45). If you don't, the effect may not print. Although you may use larger angles, any such values will be translated into the equivalent angle between 000 and 360. For example, 405 degrees is the same as 45 degrees, since 405 degrees is 360 degrees plus 45 degrees.

Size and Position

This effect is centered on the point immediately after the positioning character. The entire effect is rotated around this center by the rotation angle specified in the Ang variable. Figure 9-3 shows you some examples of the regular star rotated to various angles. The text inside the star is the angle used for rotation for that star. The text is displayed in the point size, style, and font determined by the positioning character. The starburst itself fits the width of the text string as displayed in the given font, so that longer strings result in larger starbursts.

The regular star has nine points of equal size spaced at 40-degree intervals around the perimeter. This means that if you use a multiple of 40 degrees as a rotation angle, you will see no effective change in the star, although the string of text will rotate.

Once the size of the text is set, the star is drawn around it. The starburst is scaled to the length of the text in all dimensions and has a diameter somewhat larger than the text string. Therefore, you must leave adequate room around the starburst effect to ensure that it does not overwrite other items on the page.

In these circumstances, it can be difficult to judge the distance to allow around your text. To set it the way you want, you may have to make some tests using different spacing in your document. This effect has three knots because it contains variables, and it may require test prints to set it exactly the way you want it.

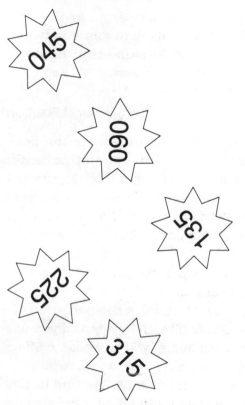

Figure 9-3. Rotation examples for regular starburst text

IRREGULAR STARBURST TEXT

Irregular starburst text

Description

If you look at advertising circulars and other types of displays, you will notice how eye-catching it is to place text inside a multi-pointed star and rotate the entire effect. The overall impression is that last-minute text was added to the page. The star in this effect has nine points of unequal length, spaced irregularly around the star.

You have already seen stars used as an outline for text. The regular and irregular stars discussed in Chapter 5 use text that is already on the page, so you can't rotate them. The star effects in this chapter include one line of text as a variable, so that you can rotate the display to any angle.

Variables

As with all these effects, you must enter the text to be displayed into the effect itself. Your positioning character determines the font and size that will be used for the text in your effect. You can also control the rotation angle for the star and its enclosed text. The two variables are listed in the front of the text effect, as follows:

```
(TEXT!) /Str 030 /Ang save . . .
```

You must observe the range and format rules for the variables strictly. If you don't, the effect may not print.

Str   The Str variable contains the string that you want to display. The bold characters in the example show you what can be changed in the effect file. When you change this variable, be sure that both the beginning and ending parentheses remain in the file. They are both essential. Note that the parentheses are not in bold.

The string variable can contain up to 100 characters. If you exceed 100 characters, you might find that the effect will not print, or will not print correctly.

Ang   The text and the star are displayed at an angle, which is defined by the Ang variable. The angle is measured counterclockwise from a horizontal line, so that 45 degrees rotates the effect and the text up to the right, for example, while 315 degrees rotates it down to the right. The values of Ang are degrees, with 0 being the way text is normally displayed and proceeding counterclock-wise to 360, which is the same as 0.

The Ang variable may range from 000 to 360 degrees. You always need to use three digits for the angle, even if you are using smaller values (for example, 045 and not 45). If you don't, the effect may not print. Although you may use larger angles, any such values will be translated into the equivalent angle between 000 and 360. For example, 405 degrees is the same as 45 degrees, since 405 degrees is 360 degrees plus 45 degrees.

Size and Position

This effect is centered on the point immediately after the positioning character. The entire effect is rotated around this center by the rotation angle specified in the Ang variable. Figure 9-4 shows you some examples of the irregular star rotated to various angles. The text inside the star is the angle used for rotation for that star. The text is displayed in the point size, style, and font determined by the positioning character. The starburst itself fits the width of the text string as displayed in the given font, so that longer strings result in larger starbursts.

The irregular star has nine points of unequal size spaced at irregular intervals around the perimeter of the star. Once the size of the text is set, the star is drawn around it. The starburst is scaled to the length of the text and has a diameter somewhat larger than the text string. Therefore, you must leave adequate room around the starburst to ensure that it does not overwrite other items on the page.

In these circumstances, it can be difficult to judge the distance to allow around your text. To set it the way you want, you may have to make some tests using different spacing in your document. This effect has three knots because it contains variables, and it may require test prints to set it exactly the way you want it.

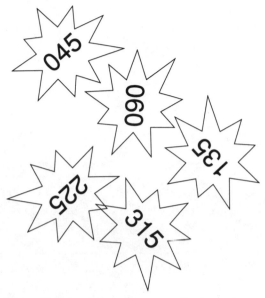

Figure 9-4 Rotation examples for irregular starburst text

10

Distorted

Text

THE SPECIAL TEXT EFFECTS IN THIS CHAPTER DISTORT OR color text in a variety of ways: by adding shadows to a line of text, by printing text as though you saw it in a mirror, by filling text with a fountain (even shading of light to dark), and so on. For all these effects, you must enter the words that are to be used into the effect itself. Therefore, you must know how to insert the text and how to place the effect correctly. The text used in these effects is restricted to a single line of not more than 100 characters.

Several of these effects use techniques that will not print if you select bit-mapped fonts for the effect. When an effect will not work with a bit-mapped font, that is clearly noted at the beginning of the effect. You should be careful not to use bit-mapped fonts in such effects.

BEHIND THE SCENES

If you have checked Font Substitution in the Page Setup . . . dialog box, then it may seem as if you can use bit-mapped fonts in some effects. What actually happens is that the PostScript fonts inside your printer substitute for the fonts that you have selected on the menu. For example, if you select Monaco as your font and have Font Substitution checked, then the printer will use Courier as the font when printing the effect. This makes it seem as if you are using a bit-mapped font, but actually you aren't. You can tell when you are using a true bit-mapped font by the dialog box that is displayed when you are printing, which tells you that a bit-mapped version of the font is being loaded into the printer.

INSERTING DISTORTED TEXT IN MICROSOFT WORD

1. Open your document. Insert a positioning character where you want to place the effect. The size of the positioning character determines the basic size of your distorted text.

2. Open the **xxxx**.w file, where **xxxx** represents the name of the desired effect. If only one line of text appears when you open the file, click on the Show Hidden Text box in the Preferences . . . selection of the Edit menu. Select and copy all

the text of the effect and place it at the beginning of the page that will contain the effect. Notice that the major part of the text in this file is in Word's PostScript style. (If you are unclear about how to use this style, review the instructions in Chapter 1.)

3. Cut the text at the end of the .w file that is *not* in the PostScript style from the end of the effect text. This is the second part of the effect.

4. Paste this text into your Word document immediately after (to the right of) the positioning character.

5. Enter the text that you want to use into the Str variable for your effect.

6. Select all of the text, and only the text, from the second part of the effect file that you pasted into your document. Change the font to the PostScript Escape font. This part of the effect text will disappear.

7. Be sure that the Print Hidden Text box in the Print dialog box is not checked. Print your document. The effect will print over the positioning character.

INSERTING DISTORTED TEXT IN OTHER WORD PROCESSING APPLICATIONS

1. Open your document. Insert a positioning character where you want to place the effect. The size and font of the positioning character determine the size and font used in your effect.

2. Open the effect file, and select and copy the effect text.

3. Paste the effect text into your document immediately after (to the right of) the positioning character.

4. Enter the text that you want to use into the Str variable for your effect.

5. Select the effect text, and only the effect text, up to the % that occurs inside the effect. The portion of the effect that contains the % character will appear as follows:

```
. . . save put } if % cf setfont . . .
```

The % is printed in bold in this line (although it is not bold in the file). Be sure that you have selected the text up to, but not including, the % and change it to the PostScript Escape font. This is the first part of the effect.

6. Select the remainder of the effect text, and only the effect text, after the %. Be sure that you have selected the text after, but not including, the % and change it to the PostScript Escape font. This is the second part of the effect. When you have finished, you should see only the positioning character followed by the % where your effect was.

7. Print your document in the ordinary way. The effect will print over the positioning character and will erase the % as it prints.

DROP SHADOW TEXT

shadow text

Description

This effect allows you to place a drop shadow behind a word or line of text. Both the text and the shadow can be rotated and the shadow can be any shade of gray. You might use this effect in flyers, circulars, and other advertising materials. In such situations, the shadow adds dramatic emphasis to a particular word or phrase.

Variables

As with all these effects, you must enter the string of text to be displayed into the effect itself. The positioning character that you choose determines the font and size that will be used for the text in your effect. You can also control the rotation angle of the text and the shadow features. The five variables are listed in the front of the text effect, as follows:

(**Text**) /Str **045** /Ang **–05** /Xoff **+05** /Yoff **0.50** /Gray save . . .

You must observe the range and format rules for the variables strictly. If you don't, the effect may not print.

Str   The Str variable contains the string that you want to display. When you change this variable, be sure that the beginning and ending parentheses remain in the file, since they are both essential. The bold characters in the example show you what can be changed in the effect file. Note that the parentheses are not bold.

The Str variable can contain up to 100 characters. If you exceed 100 characters, the effect might not print, or might not print correctly.

Ang   The text is displayed at an angle, defined in the Ang variable. The angle is measured counterclockwise from a horizontal line, so that 45 degrees slopes up to the right, for example. The values of Ang are degrees, with 0 being on the horizontal (the way the text is normally displayed) and proceeding counterclockwise to 360, which is the same as 0.

The Ang variable may range from 000 to 360 degrees. You must always use three digits for the angle, even if you are using smaller values (for example, 045, not 45). If you don't, the effect may not print. Although you may use larger angles, any such values will be transformed into the equivalent angle between 000 and 360.

For example, using 405 degrees is the equivalent of using 45 degrees, since 405 degrees is 360 degrees plus 45 degrees.

Xoff/Yoff   You place the shadow behind the text by setting the horizontal distance, called Xoff—an offset in the x, or horizontal, direction. In a similar fashion, the vertical distance for the shadow is called Yoff. Both distances are in points, a printer's measure. A point is $1/72$ inch. You can use either positive or negative values for both Xoff and Yoff.

Positive values of Xoff move the shadow to the right, while negative values move it to the left. Positive values of Yoff move the shadow down the page, and negative values move it up the page.

You must place plus or minus signs in front of the Xoff and Yoff variables, and you must use two digits, as shown. Acceptable values range from ±00 to ±99. Of course, +00 and −00 are identical and give you the same result: no offset in that direction.

Gray   The darkness of the shadow behind your text is set by a control named, reasonably enough, Gray. The values of Gray are percentages, with 1.00 being black and 0.01 being almost white. Although you can use a value of 0.00 (white), this may be some-what misleading since that value actually means that nothing is printed on the page. It doesn't cause white letters to print on colored paper, for example.

The Gray variable may range from 1.00 to .01. You always need to have a decimal point in the value and two digits after the decimal point, even if you are using exact tenths. For example, use .50 and not .5 as your value. Otherwise, the effect may not print.

Size and Position

Shadow text is sized in the same way as any other standard text effect. The positioning character determines the point size and the font for the text. The shadow size matches that of the text, as a shadow should. As shown in Figure 10-1, the position of the shadow and the amount of shadow that shows under the text is determined by the Xoff and Yoff variables.

The text is displayed beginning at the positioning character and continuing to the right. If you have used a rotation angle, the line of text rotates around the front of the line of text and then displays at the selected angle.

The four examples in Figure 10-1 show how changes in the offset values move the shadow effect around the text. As you can see, you can create variations in shadowing by changing the signs of the offset values.

Because the text string stretches to the right, you must allow room after the effect for the text to print correctly. Also, if you

This is 24-point text with offsets of -05 and +05. The shadow is .50 gray.

This is 24-point text with offsets of +05 and +05. The shadow is .50 gray.

This is 24-point text with offsets of -05 and -05. The shadow is .50 gray.

This is 24-point text with offsets of +05 and -05. The shadow is .50 gray.

Figure 10-1. Examples of the shadow text effect

have rotated the text, you may have to leave space above or below the effect for the text to print.

It can be very difficult to judge the distance that you want to offset the shadow behind your text. To set it the way you want, you may have to make some tests using different offsets in your document. Also, for rotated text, you may have to adjust the lines above or below the effect for correct positioning. This effect has two knots because it contains variables, and it may require test prints to set it the way you want it.

BEHIND THE SCENES

When you print text effects like this one, you may notice that sometimes the effect prints slowly and sometimes it prints quickly. Generally, the effect prints slowly the first time you use it and more quickly if you use it several times in a row—such as when you are making test prints. Because the first print can take a noticeable time, all the text effects have at least one hourglass. This is because the first time that you print the effect, the complete outline of all the characters must usually be drawn by the printer. On second and subsequent prints, the printer reuses the images that it made the first time, thus speeding up the process considerably. Therefore the second and subsequent prints that you make (assuming you make them one after another, without turning the printer off or running many other prints in between) will be much faster than the first.

Using the Effect

The examples in Figure 10-2 illustrate various angles of rotation. The top three examples use the same offset values with different orientations.

In Figure 10-2, you can also see variations in the darkness of the shadow. The last line shows you an interesting use of a 1.00 Gray (black) shadow. Here, the rotation is set to 90 degrees and the offsets are Xoff +00 and Yoff –19. Since this is 24-point type, the shadow is close to, but still distinct from, the text itself. The result, as you see, is a double line of the same text, with the shadow indistinguishable from the original text.

This is 24-point text rotated 20 degrees. The shadow is .20 gray.

This is 24-point text rotated 45 degrees. The shadow is .50 gray.

This is 24-point text rotated 90 degrees. The shadow is .70 gray.

This is 24-point text rotated 90 degrees. The shadow is 1.00 gray.

Figure 10-2.   Orientation and the shadow text effect

TIP

Normally, you will use relatively small values for the offsets. If you keep the offset values the same, the shadow will look most natural when it prints. However, if you want to create a special effect, you can use different values for the offsets to make the shadow appear distorted.

BACKLIT TEXT

backlit text

Description

The previous effect allowed you to place a shadow behind your text, giving the appearance of text lifted off of the page. The backlit text effect allows you to throw a shadow in any direction, as though you could move the light that is casting the shadow. This is an interesting and useful effect for specialty text.

Variables

As with all these efects, you must enter the string of text to be displayed into the effect itself. The positioning character determines the font and size of the text in your effect. You can also control the shadow features. The three variables are listed in the front of the text effect, as follows:

(**Text**) /Str **135** /Ang **0.50** /Gray save...

You must observe the range and format rules for the variables strictly. If you don't, the effect may not print.

Str   The Str variable contains the string that you want to display. When you change this variable, be sure that the beginning and ending parentheses remain in the file since they are both essential. The bold characters in the example show you what can be changed in the effect file. Note that the parentheses are not bold.

The Str variable can contain up to 100 characters. If you exceed 100 characters, the effect might not print, or might not print correctly.

Ang   The shadow is displayed at an angle, defined by the Ang variable. The angle is measured clockwise from a vertical line, so that 45 degrees places the shadow behind the text and up to the right, while 135 degrees places the shadow in front of the text and down to the right. The values of Ang are degrees, with 0 being directly behind the text (without a shadow) and proceeding clockwise to 360, which is the same as 0.

The Ang variable may range from 000 to 360 degrees. You must always use three digits for the angle, even if you are using smaller values (for example, 045, not 45). If you don't, the effect may not print. Although you may use larger angles, any such values will be transformed into the equivalent angle between 000 and 360. For example, using 405 degrees is the equivalent of using 045 degrees, since 405 degrees is 360 degrees plus 45 degrees.

Gray The darkness of the shadow behind your text is set by a control named, reasonably enough, Gray. The values of Gray are percentages, with 1.00 being black and 0.01 being almost white. Although you can use a value of 0.00 (white), this may be misleading since that value actually means that nothing is printed on the page. It doesn't cause white letters to print on colored paper, for example.

The Gray variable may range from 1.00 to .01. You always need to have a decimal point in the value and two digits after the decimal point, even if you are using exact tenths. For example, use .50 and not .5 as your value. Otherwise the effect may not print.

Size and Position

Backlit text is sized in the same way as any other standard text effect: The positioning character determines the point size and the font for the text. The shadow size is based on the size of the text and the angle of the light, as a shadow should be.

The text is displayed beginning at the positioning character and continuing to the right. Because the text string stretches to the right, you must allow room after the effect for the text to print correctly. Also, since the shadow takes additional space, you may have to leave room above or below the effect for the text to print.

It can be difficult to judge the angle that you want to use for the shadow with your text. To set it the way you want, you may have to make some tests using different offsets in your document. You may also have to adjust the lines above or below the effect for the correct positioning and spacing once you have set the shadow as you want it. This effect has three knots because it contains variables, and it may require several test prints to set it the way you want it.

Using the Effect

The examples in Figure 10-3 illustrate how the angle variable affects the printed result. The easiest way to think about the shadow angle and placement is to imagine a light directly in front of the text and slightly above it. This represents an angle of 000 degrees—the resulting shadow is directly behind the text. As the light source moves clockwise around the line of text, the shadow also moves. When the light is directly behind the text (at 180 degrees), the shadow falls in front of the text, and so on.

Figure 10-3 also shows you a variety of angles that you can use for the shadow. The effect text is 24-point Helvetica Bold, and the shadow darkness and angle for each example is as stated. The result, as you see, is an effect that is particularly attractive for display or headline text.

TIP

An angle of 000 places the shadow directly behind the text. The result is that you cannot see the shadow. If you want the shadow to show directly behind the text, use a small angle, like 010 degrees, as illustrated in Figure 10-3.

Text This is 24-point text with a .50 gray shadow at 010 degrees.

Text This is 24-point text with a .50 gray shadow at 045 degrees.

Text This is 24-point text with a .50 gray shadow at 180 degrees.

Text This is 24-point text with a .50 gray shadow at 225 degrees.

Text This is 24-point text with a .50 gray shadow at 315 degrees.

Figure 10-3.   Examples of the backlit text effect

FADED TEXT

faded text

Description

The faded text effect is essentially a fancy variant of shadowed text. As shown, it has a long shadow that changes from white to black over a short distance.

425

For this effect, you must not use bitmapped fonts. Bitmapped fonts cannot print in the outline format used here.

Variables

As with all these effects, you must enter the string of text to be displayed into the effect itself. The positioning character determines the font and size of the text in your effect. The variable is listed in the front of the text effect, as follows:

```
(Text) /Str save . . .
```

You must observe the range and format rules for the variable strictly. If you don't, the effect may not print.

Str   The Str variable contains the string that you want to display. When you change this variable, be sure that the beginning and ending parentheses remain in the file since they are both essential. The bold characters in the example show you what can be changed in the effect file. Note that the parentheses are not bold.

The Str variable can contain up to 100 characters. If you exceed 100 characters, the effect might not print, or might not print correctly.

Size and Position

Faded text is sized in the same way as any other standard text effect: The positioning character determines the point size and the font for the text, before the faded effect is in place. The faded shadow size is the same for all sizes of text. The shadow extends to the left and below the text by a fixed amount and matches the text in all dimensions. As illustrated in Figure 10-4, this creates somewhat different results as the point size of the text changes.

426

The first character of the text is placed over the positioning character. If you use the faded text effect with a small point size, be sure to allow enough room so that the faded shadow does not touch the text below and to the left of the effect.

Using the Effect

Although this effect looks something like the shadow text effect, it has no controls for shadow placement. Fading a shadow is quite complex and time-consuming, so you don't have options to adjust shadow placement or coloring. The examples in Figure 10-4 demonstrate how this affects the resulting output. As you can see, smaller point sizes have a faded effect that tails out a great distance, relative to the size of the text itself. On the other hand, on large point size text the faded background hardly differs from the basic shadow effect. The best results are generally obtained when the text is between 18 and 48 points, but you may want larger or smaller sizes for special purposes.

    This is an example of faded text at 12 points.

This is an example of faded text at 24 points.

This is an example of faded text at 60 points.

Figure 10-4.   Examples of the faded text effect

RAISED TEXT

raised text

Description

The raised text effect is a variant of shadowed text. It has a long, angled shadow that gives the impression of letters that are carved in three dimensions.

For this effect, you must not use bitmapped fonts. Bitmapped fonts cannot print in the outline format used here.

Variables

As with all these effects, you must enter the text to be displayed into the effect itself. The positioning character determines the font and size of the text in your effect. You can also control the position of the raised shadow and the color used for the face of the text (the shadow itself is always black). The four variables are listed in the front of the text effect, as follows:

```
(Text) /Str -05 /Xoff -05 /Yoff .00 /Gray save . . .
```

You must observe the range and format rules for the variables strictly. If you don't, the effect may not print.

Str   The Str variable contains the string that you want to display. When you change this variable, be sure that the beginning and ending parentheses remain in the file since they are both essential. The bold characters in the example show you what can be changed in the effect file. Note that the parentheses are not bold.

The Str variable can contain up to 100 characters. If you exceed 100 characters, the effect might not print, or might not print correctly.

Xoff/Yoff   You place the raised shadow behind the text by setting the horizontal distance, called Xoff—an offset in the x, or horizontal, direction. In a similar fashion, the vertical distance for the shadow is called Yoff. Both distances are in points, a printer's measure. A point is $^1/_{72}$ inch. You can use either positive or negative values for both Xoff and Yoff.

Positive values of Xoff move the shadow to the right, while negative values move it to the left. Positive values of Yoff move the shadow down the page, and negative values move it up the page.

You must place plus or minus signs in front of the Xoff and Yoff variables, and you must use two digits, as shown. Acceptable values range from ±00 to ±99. Of course, +00 and – 00 are identical, and give you the same result: no offset in that direction.

Gray   The darkness of the text is set by a control named, reasonably enough, Gray. The values of Gray are percentages, with 1.00 being black and 0.00 being white letters with a black outline. Although you can use a value of 0.00 (white) this may be somewhat misleading, since that value actually means that the letters are outlined in black with nothing printed inside them—it won't make white letters on colored paper, for example.

The Gray variable may range from 1.00 to .00. You always need to have a decimal point in the value and two digits after the decimal point, even if you are using exact tenths. For example, use .50 and not .5 as your value. Otherwise, the effect may not print.

Size and Position

Raised text is sized in the same way as any other standard text effect: The positioning character determines the point size and the font for the text, before the faded effect is in place. The raised shadow size is set by the offset variables in the effect and matches the text in all dimensions.

The first character of the text is placed over the positioning character. If you use the raised text effect with a small point size, be sure to allow enough room so that the raised shadow does not touch other text on adjoining lines.

Using the Effect

Although this effect resembles the faded text effect, it allows you to control the shadow placement. Creating the raised shadow is quite complex and time-consuming. Under any circumstances, this effect takes a long time to print—notice the three hourglasses. The examples in Figure 10-5 demonstrate how the text size and

This is an example of raised text at 24 points.

This is an example of raised text at 48 points.

This is an example of raised text at 60 points.

Figure 10-5. Examples of the raised text effect

shadow positioning affect the resulting output. As you can see, in general, larger point sizes produce a better effect than smaller ones. However, on large point sizes the printing time is significant. I suggest you test this effect once or twice with larger point sizes before using it in your documents.

MIRROR TEXT

mirror text

Description

The mirror text effect prints the text as though you saw it in a mirror. In fact, if you hold the output up to a mirror, you will be able to read it like ordinary text. In the same way, if you print it on a transparent medium, it will read correctly when viewed through the medium.

Variables

As with all these effects, you must enter the text to be displayed into the effect itself. The positioning character determines the font and size of the text in your effect. The variable is listed in the front of the text effect, as follows:

```
(Text) /Str save . . .
```

You must observe the range and format rules for the variable strictly. If you don't, the effect may not print.

Str The Str variable contains the string that you want to display. When you change this variable, be sure that both the beginning and ending parentheses remain in the file since they are essential.

The bold characters in the example show you what can be changed in the effect file. Note that the parentheses are not bold.

The Str variable can contain up to 100 characters in length. If you exceed 100 characters, the effect might not print, or might not print correctly.

Size and Position

Mirror text is sized in the same way as any other standard text effect: the positioning character determines the point size and the font for the text. The text itself is positioned where the text would normally appear, although backward, with the last charac-ter of the line over the positioning character.

Using the Effect

This effect prints the text that you insert in the string in mirror fashion, as you see in Figure 10-6. This effect is useful for trans-fers or transparencies.

ƎƆИA⅃UᗺMA

If you see this in your rear view mirror, you
immediately understand why some things
require mirror text.

Figure 10-6. Example of the mirror text effect

MOVIETITLE TEXT

movietitle text

Description

The movietitle text effect distorts the text so that it appears to be receding from the reader. This is the classic movie effect where a text scrolls away from the viewer. You can't make the text scroll, but you can print a single line in this style. This effect is effective and eye-catching.

Variables

As with all these effects, you must enter the string of text to be displayed into the effect itself. The positioning character determines the font and size of the text in your effect. The variable is listed in the front of the text effect, as follows:

(**Movie Title Text**) /Str save...

You must observe the range and format rules for the variable strictly. If you don't, the effect may not print.

Str   The Str variable contains the string that you want to display. When you change this variable, be sure that the beginning and ending parentheses remain in the file since they are both essential. The bold characters in the example show you what can be changed in the effect file. Note that the parentheses are not bold.

The string variable can contain up to 100 characters. If you exceed 100 characters, the effect might not print, or might not print correctly.

433

Size and Position

Movietitle text is sized in the same way as any other standard text effect: The positioning character determines the point size and the font for the text. The text itself is centered over the positioning character, unlike the other text effects in this chapter. This allows you to center several lines of text, one after another. If you keep the positioning characters at the same place on each line, the resulting text will all be centered on those characters.

Using the Effect

The examples in Figure 10-7 show you several different fonts and text lengths with the movietitle text effect. Because the effect distorts the text toward the center of the line, longer lines of text appear more curved than short ones. A single, short word hardly looks distorted at all. You will generally get the best results with short phrases of text. This effect can be used in a variety of display situations, such as advertising headlines, notices, and so on.

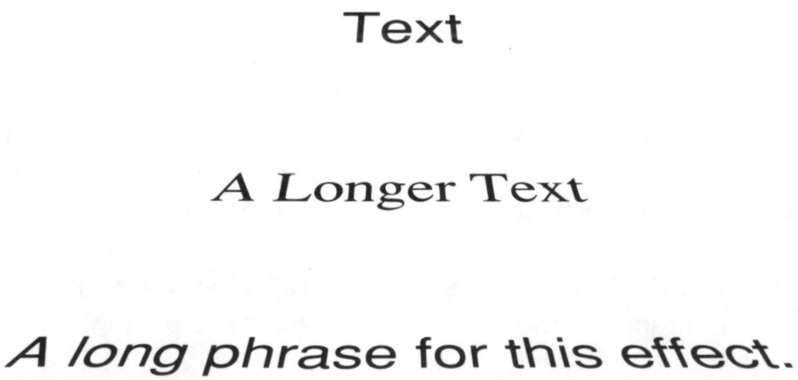

Text

A Longer Text

A long phrase for this effect.

Figure 10-7. Examples of the movietitle text effect

inline text

Description

The inline text effect is a fancy form of outline text. In this case, the text is outlined in black, outlined again in white, and then filled with black. This makes quite an effective and eye-catching display font.

For this effect, you must not use bitmapped fonts. Bitmapped fonts cannot print in the outline format used here.

Variables

As with all these effects, you must enter the text to be displayed into the effect itself. The positioning character determines the font and size of the text in your effect. The variable is listed in the front of the text effect, as follows:

(**Text**) /Str save . . .

You must observe the range and format rules for the variable strictly. If you don't, the effect may not print.

Str   The Str variable contains the string that you want to display. When you change this variable, be sure that the beginning and ending parentheses remain in the file since they are both essential. The bold characters in the example show you what can be changed in the effect file. Note that the parentheses are not bold.

The Str variable can contain up to 100 characters. If you exceed 100 characters, the effect might not print, or might not print correctly.

Size and Position

Inline text is sized in the same way as any other standard text effect: The positioning character determines the point size and the font for the text. The first character of the text is placed over the positioning character.

Using the Effect

The examples in Figure 10-8 show you several different fonts with the inline effect. Because the effect requires extra room to create the inline fill for the text, it is best to use sans-serif fonts or bold versions of fonts to provide enough room for the effect to work. This effect can be used in a variety of display situations, such as advertising headlines, notices, and so on.

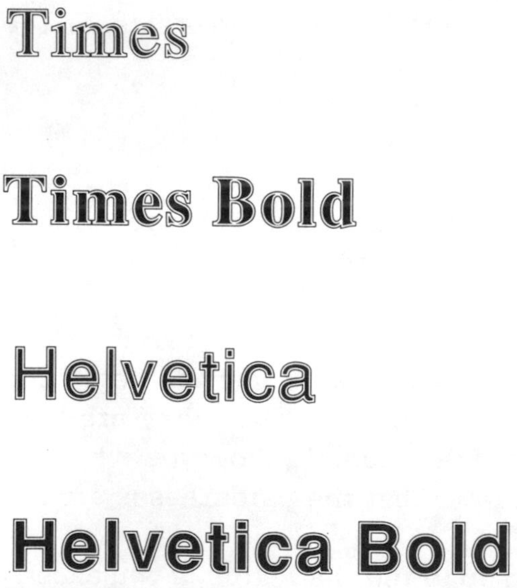

Times

Times Bold

Helvetica

Helvetica Bold

Figure 10-8. Examples of the inline text effect

half&half text

Description

The half&half text effect is a fancy form of filled text. In this case, half of the text is outlined and filled with white, then the other half is filled with black. This creates an interesting and unusual display font.

For this effect, you must not use bitmapped fonts. Bitmapped fonts cannot print in the outline format used here.

Variables

As with all these effects, you must enter the string of text to be displayed into the effect itself. The positioning character determines the font and size of the text in your effect. You can also control which half of the text is black and which one is white. The variables are listed in the front of the text effect, as follows:

(**Text**) /Str [**0 1**] /TBColor save . . .

You must observe the range and format rules for the variable strictly. If you don't, the effect may not print.

Str The Str variable contains the string that you want to display. When you change this variable, be sure that the beginning and ending parentheses remain in the file since they are both essential. The bold characters in the example show you what can be changed in the effect file. Note that the parentheses are not bold.

The Str variable can contain up to 100 characters. If you exceed 100 characters, the effect might not print, or might not print correctly.

TBColor   The name, TBColor, is intended to help you remember how the variable is used. The variable consists of two numbers, 0 or 1, enclosed within brackets. This arrangement is called an *array*. The numbers control whether the top or the bottom of the text is black or outlined. The first number controls the top half, and the second number controls the bottom half.

As you see, this order corresponds to the initials in the variable's name. The 0 means outline, and the 1 means fill. Therefore, the default settings [0 1] mean that the top half of the text is outlined, while the bottom is black. Conversely, if you want the top black and the bottom outlined, use [1 0].

You can only use the values 0 or 1 in this array. Any other numbers will result in errors. You must provide one number for each half and have no more than two numbers.

Size and Position

Half&half text is sized in the same way as any other standard text effect: The positioning character determines the point size and the font for the text. The first character of the line of text is placed over the positioning character.

Using the Effect

The examples in Figure 10-9 show you several different fonts with the half&half text effect and both settings of the TBColor variable. Sans-serif fonts or bold versions of fonts give the best results with this effect, although any font that is not bitmapped can be used. The coloring is done for each letter individually. Therefore, mixing upper- and lowercase letters does not produce a satisfactory effect, as the mid-line where the color changes varies from one letter to the next. You will find that using all capital letters, as shown in the example, produces a more even and satisfactory effect. This effect can be used in a variety of display situations, such as advertising headlines, notices, and so on.

HELVETICA

HELV BOLD

TIMES

TIMES BOLD

Figure 10-9. Examples of the half&half text effect

FOUNTAIN FILL TEXT

fountain fill text

Description

The fountain fill text effect is a fancy form of filled text. The text is outlined in black and filled with gradually increasing color, ranging from white at the top to black at the bottom. This creates an interesting and unusual display font.

For this effect, you must not use bitmapped fonts. Bitmapped fonts cannot print in the outline format used here.

Variables

As with all these effects, you must enter the string of text to be displayed into the effect itself. The positioning character determines the font and size of the text in your effect. The variable is listed in the front of the text effect, as follows:

(**Text**) /Str save . . .

You must observe the range and format rules for the variable strictly. If you don't, the effect may not print.

Str   The Str variable contains the string that you want to display. When you change this variable, be sure that the beginning and ending parentheses remain in the file since they are both essential. The bold characters in the example show you what can be changed in the effect file. Note that the parentheses are not bold.

The Str variable can contain up to 100 characters. If you exceed 100 characters, the effect might not print, or might not print correctly.

Size and Position

Fountain fill text is sized in the same way as any other standard text effect: The positioning character determines the point size and the font for the text. The first character of the text is placed over the positioning character.

Using the Effect

The examples in Figure 10-10 show you several different fonts with the fountain fill effect. Because the effect requires extra room to create the fountain fill for the text, it is best to use sans-serif fonts or bold versions of fonts to provide enough room for the

HELVETICA

Helv Bold

Times

TIMES BOLD

Figure 10-10. Examples of the fountain fill text effect

effect to work. The shading is done for the entire line of text as a unit, so that mixing upper- and lowercase letters produces different shading than all uppercase text. Remember to test any text that you intend to use with this effect to ensure that the fountain fill appears even. This effect can be used in a variety of display situations, such as advertising headlines, notices, and so on.

Appendixes

APPENDIX A: IF IT DOESN'T PRINT

THIS APPENDIX WILL HELP YOU FIGURE OUT WHAT TO DO IF your effect doesn't print. Chapter 1 provides a basic approach to handling effects that will not print. But if you have the time and interest in tracking down the problem, you can use the techniques in this section to find out what is causing the error and, often, how to correct it. You do not need to read this appendix to use the effects. If you follow the directions in the text, the effects will work correctly without any further effort on your part.

This appendix is not very technical, but you may find that some of the discussion is clearer and easier to follow if you are familiar with the issues and concepts presented in Appendix B. If you do not understand any part of this discussion, read Appendix B and then return to this section. This appendix assumes that you are familiar with your application software and the Macintosh operating system. If some terms or concepts are not familiar to you (like capturing files, for example), read the *Macintosh User's Guide* for your system software and the manuals that came with your application.

HOW TO FIND AN ERROR

A variety of things can go wrong when you insert an effect in your document. In most circumstances, of course, the effect prints successfully. However, as you use more effects—and possibly make additions or changes to them—you may occasionally have difficulty printing an effect.

The most common symptom is that the effect page doesn't print. If you are watching your printer, you will usually see the processing indicator light go on for a short time, then revert to the idle display. On a LaserWriter II, the green processing light begins blinking (indicating that the page is being processed) and then returns to a steady green (indicating that the printer is done processing and waiting for a new job), but no page is printed.

Since some effects are quite complex, some pages may process for some time. In that case, the green light on the LaserWriter II will continue to blink. As long as you have a processing indication, be patient and wait for the output. If you are using manual feed, you may notice a short interval (one to five seconds) between the time the printer stops processing and the manual feed indicator light comes on. This is normal and does not indicate a problem with the effect. If you are using an older LaserWriter, or some other PostScript output device, review the standard operation of the device so you can tell when it's processing a page and when it's idle. For every device, in my experience, there is some external indicator, such as a light, display, or counter, that indicates when the device is processing. Although the indicators on your system may be different, the process is identical to that described for the LaserWriter II: First the device shows that it is processing, and then it returns to idle without producing any output.

The most likely cause of a printing problem is a PostScript error in your document. This can occur if you incorrectly modify the effect text. Since all the effects have been tested repeatedly, the first step to correcting an error is to reload the effect and replace it in your document. Print a test page with no changes to any of the effect variables. In most cases, the effect will print correctly. Adjust the variables to suit your requirements and print again. This procedure will usually correct the problem. If you continue to have problems or have made other changes in the effects, the following discussion will help you understand the sources of PostScript errors and will give you some additional tricks for finding and correcting them.

TYPES OF ERRORS

Correcting errors in the effects requires that you save your output as a PostScript file instead of printing it. In System 7 you can do this by selecting the radio button labeled Disk File. Then print only the page that contains your effect, using the From and To options in the Print dialog box. If you are running an older version of the system, hold down the Command and the F keys together while you click on OK to print. Either action saves your document page to disk and allows you to review the document in detail. The file name is PostScript0 (or any number from 0 to 9, depending on how many times you have done this), and the file generally will be located in the Spool Folder or in the folder where you store the application itself. You can open this file with any application that allows you to open ordinary text files. All of the word processing applications used in this book allow you to open text files such as this.

Open the PostScript file and look for the effect text. If you are using Microsoft Word, look for the second part of the effect, not the first. Once you have found the effect text, you can examine several things to see if there is any visible error.

Length

If you are not using Microsoft Word, look to see whether the lines of the effect program have broken in the middle of a word. The effect text must break between words to work correctly. Look at the beginning of each line of the effect text to see if it begins with only part of a word. You can do this by comparing the words in the effect text to the output that you have saved in your file.

You can retune the effect by finding the line where the break has occurred. This is usually easy to see as the first word of the line will be only a partial word. Place additional spaces on the line so that the break comes between words and not in the middle of one.

If you have added information to the effect or changed any variables without observing the limits and other variable restrictions, then you may have caused the effect text to go out of alignment and to break a word or command, thus causing a PostScript error. Suspect this error if you have made any changes in the variables or the effect text.

To see if this is the error, convert your effect text into a visible font and review the variables. Be sure that you have not altered any variables beyond the limits given in this book. If you are uncertain about the changes you made, see if the effect prints with the default variables. If it does, then most likely your variable changes caused the problem. However, if the defaults don't work, then the problem is probably somewhere else in the conversion process or in the application of the effect.

Conversion

Another common source of errors is converting more or less than the effect text into the PostScript Escape font. This usually happens when you try to change text adjacent to the effect text and accidentally select a portion of the effect as well. You should change the effect into a visible font, such as 9-point Monaco, before making any alterations to the surrounding text or the positioning character. This ensures that you don't select some of the effect text as well.

This type of error is quite easy to correct. Change the effect text and all the text around it into a visible font. Then select only the effect text and convert it into the PostScript Escape font again.

Spacing

If you place one effect after another, the second effect may run into the first one, especially if you've already changed the first text into the PostScript Escape font. When this happens, neither effect will print, because the last word of the first effect and the first word of the second effect run together.

The correction is to change all of the effect text into a visible font and then check to see that there are one or more spaces between all of the words in each effect and between the effects themselves.

String Variables

String variables present one of the most difficult areas when working with effects. Each line of an effect is limited to 255 characters. Since strings vary so much in length, the effects in which they appear must be handled differently. This was described in Chapter 1 under the discussion of the rotated text effect. For Microsoft Word, there is little concern, because the effects are already in two segments. For all other applications, however, the effect must be split into two at the % marker after the variable information block.

The presence of a string variable in the effect text requires special handling to place the string into the effect correctly, regardless of its length. Although the effect block structure, described in Appendix B, remains generally the same, the actual code is different for string effects, allowing the string to be defined for the effect code that follows it.

If you have a string effect that does not print, try changing the string variable to a single, fairly short word. The effects usually use the word Text as a variable. If the effect prints with the short word, then you have either used a string that is too long or you have an invalid character (perhaps a nonprinting character) in the string. Check the length, then re-enter the string variable and try the effect again.

Error Reporters

If you create documents with a variety of effects, or if you use page layout or other advanced printing applications with your LaserWriter, then you will find that having a PostScript error reporter for your printer is a sensible and time-saving investment. The best commercial error reporter that I know (if I do say so myself, since I wrote it) is the PinPoint Error Reporter™. This program can identify and debug all types of errors and comes with a complete error dictionary that allows you to identify and fix a wide variety of PostScript errors. If you have an effect that will not print, PinPoint will enable you to identify the type of error and its location in your document. PinPoint is available from the Cheshire Group, 321 South Main Street, Suite 36, Sebastopol CA 95472. Write for information on pricing and availability.

APPENDIX B: WORKING WITH THE EFFECTS

THIS APPENDIX EXPLAINS SOME OF THE INNER WORKINGS of the effects presented in this book for readers with an interest in the technical background and actual code structure of the effects. You do not need to read this appendix to use the effects. If you follow the directions in the text, the effects will work correctly without any further effort on your part.

Although you do not need to know the PostScript language to understand this appendix, you will find some of the discussion easier to follow if you have some familiarity with it. In such a short space as this appendix, it is not possible to explain fully the PostScript techniques used in the effects. Therefore, at some points I have assumed that the reader is familiar with basic PostScript concepts and programming issues.

HOW THE EFFECTS WORK

As you know from Chapter 1, these effects are small PostScript programs that you paste into your documents. The crucial factor in using these effects is that your application must use the standard Macintosh printing system. In this section, you will learn what components are used in this process and how the process works.

To begin with, you need to understand how a typical Macintosh application prints. Let us suppose that you are working in a word processing application. You create a document by using menu items and by entering text—and possibly some graphics—onto your computer screen. When you are ready to print your information, you use the Chooser to select an output device, and then you select Print from the File menu (assuming your application follows the Macintosh human interface guidelines) and print. Normally, you don't think anything more about it.

When you click OK in the Print dialog box, several things begin to happen. First your application calls the Macintosh Toolbox print routines, collectively known as the Printing Manager, and sends it the text that you have on the screen. This is done in essentially the same way that information is displayed on the screen; all the same positioning and font information is sent to the Printing Manager.

When printing starts, the Printing Manager checks to see that there is a printer chosen through the Chooser. This selection tells the Printing Manager what type of printer you are using and selects a translation program, called a *device driver,* that changes the information on your screen into the correct commands for printing. If your application uses the standard Macintosh printing facilities and you select a LaserWriter or compatible printer, the device driver is named LaserWriter. When the data to be printed is sent to the Printing Manager, it calls the LaserWriter driver to convert the data into PostScript, which is the language that your printer uses.

When you print, the LaserWriter driver changes the font names from the ones you see on your Font menu to those used in PostScript, which are somewhat different. Then the driver changes the text into PostScript format and sends these commands to the printer. This translation offers a singular opportunity for sending PostScript code directly to the printer. If the font selected on the Font menu is named PostScript Escape, then the text in that font is not converted into PostScript commands. Instead, the text is sent directly to the printer without being changed at all. This feature allows us to insert the effects into any document and print them.

This process, of course, is somewhat complex. To begin with, the application is trying to print the document exactly as you see it on the screen. If anything shows on the screen, then the application adjusts the printed text to match. This is why the PostScript Escape font is "invisible"—that is, it has no associated display and no width or height for any of the characters. The application does not see any text in the PostScript Escape font and so doesn't try to move other text around on the screen (and, therefore, on the printed page) to compensate for it.

Because PostScript is a complete programming language, you can create effects that interact in a limited way with the text on the page, even though the commands that generate the printed text are produced by the LaserWriter driver in conjunction with your application. Using these techniques, the effect programs look at the current font and the current position on the page, which you have set with the positioning character, and determine how to place and size the effect.

Effect Structure

A typical effect program is divided into a series of blocks. Figure B-1 shows the structure using the shadow checkbox effect broken into blocks.

The effect starts with the variable information that it requires. This appears in the form of PostScript variables. If the effect does not require variable information, then this block is not present. A standard header block comes next. This block creates a special dictionary for each effect and places the variable information into the dictionary. This is followed by the definitions of all of the support procedures required for the effect. Since every effect must erase the positioning character, there is always at least one support procedure: erase. Many effects have additional support procedures such as the one shown here, QDRect, which draw all or part of the effect.

After the variables and support procedures are defined, the next block contains the effect procedure itself. This typically has a name that reflects, to some degree, what the effect does. After the effect is defined, the next block is an effect setup block. This block verifies that the font and size, which you set with the positioning character, have passed correctly into the effect program. This block also saves the font size in both the x and y dimensions for use in the effect program. The effect setup block erases the positioning character from the page—if you used a printing character, this ensures that it doesn't print on the page. The erase function also checks that the position on the page has passed correctly into the effect.

variable information
block

```
-03 /Xoff
+03 /Yoff
1.00 /Gray
```

header block

```
8 dict begin
exch neg 1 add def
2 {exch def} repeat
```

support procedure
 definitions

```
/QDRect
{...
}
bind def
/erase
{...
}
bind def
```

effect definition

```
/shchkbox
{...
}
def
```

effect setup

```
{
  currentfont /ScaleMatrix get
  dup 0 get exch 3 get
}
stopped
{ 12 -12 } if
/Yh exch def
/Xh exch def
erase
```

effect

```
shchkbox
```

cleanup

```
end
```

Figure B-1. Typical effect broken into blocks

After all this setup, the effect itself is executed by a single call to the effect procedure defined earlier. The effect cleans up after itself by releasing the dictionary used for the effect definitions and, in some effects, by performing other cleanup tasks as well.

Once you understand how the effects are constructed, you can see that a lot of the code is shared between effects. In particular, the support procedures are often the same for a number of effects. Much of the header and setup code is also the same or similar from one effect to the next. Obviously, the more alike two effects are, the more likely they are to share code blocks.

EFFECT FORMATS

Two formats are used for the effects in this book: the one used by Microsoft Word and the one used by all other applications. The following sections describe the features of each of these formats and explain how they work with the effect programs.

Microsoft Word

The Word effect files are constructed in two parts: one large part contains the effect, and a second, smaller part contains one single line of PostScript code that invokes the effect. As explained in Chapter 1, this construction is required because Word automatically inserts a line return after 255 characters, no matter what font those characters are in. For this reason, Word effects must be placed into your document in two sections: the first one in the PostScript style at the beginning of the page, and the second in the PostScript Escape font at the point where you want the effect to print.

In terms of the block structure shown in Figure B-1, the first section of the Word format contains a single procedure block that includes all the blocks except the variable information. This section begins and ends with special code that allows the effect to work within the Word PostScript style. This adds some PostScript code to your document that must be accounted for in the effect processing. The second section of the effect sets up the effect, contains the variable information block, invokes the first block, and cleans up when the effect is complete.

All code in Word's PostScript style is automatically placed at the start of the page, no matter where it is physically located on that page. For this reason, the effect code must be set up to save the effect information while the page is being processed. This is why you can insert the first section of the effect only once on a page and then reuse it several times. However, since some cleanup and special processing occurs as each page prints, you cannot be certain that the effect definitions and other information will be preserved correctly from one page to the next. Therefore, it is best—and usually required—that you insert the first section of the effect on each page where you are going to use it.

Other Applications

The effect programs for other applications consist of one file inserted into your document at the point where the effect is to print. These files consist of all the effect program text—that is, all the blocks outlined in Figure B-1—in one lump. These are simple text files with no special formatting or font characters. They can be read and used by any application that will read and write text files. An effect file contains one long line of text, with one or more spaces between each word. This ensures that the text does not move any other information on the page when you paste it into the document.

Remember that the application itself does not know that the effect text is in PostScript. The conversion to PostScript code is done by the LaserWriter device driver when the document is printed. So the application sees and records all of the effect text as part of the document page. If the effect text contained any line returns, then the application would, automatically, move all subsequent text down a line. This would not matter for the effect code, but it would matter for the normal text that follows the effect. Therefore, it is important that the effect text have no carriage returns or line feeds imbedded in it.

The fact that the effect program files are one long string of text is important when you are debugging your document. The text of the effect is broken up into strings of 255 characters when it is inserted into the document, prior to printing. This conversion occurs whether or not the text is in the middle of a word or number. Since the PostScript language requires that all names and other information not contain any spaces or line returns, the effect text must be tuned so that these forced breaks occur only between words. Each effect in this book has been tuned in this way.

APPENDIX C: QUICK REFERENCE

CHAPTER 2: CHECKBOXES:

Position	*Centered on end point of positioning character*
Gray	Darkness of shadow Must use decimal point; two digits following Range: .01 to 1.00 (Black)
Wid	Percentage of height of positioning character Range: 10–999
XOff	Horizontal distance for shadow + moves shadow right, – moves left Must use two digits and sign Range: ±00–±99
YOff	Vertical distance for shadow + moves shadow down, – moves up Must use two digits and sign Range ±00–±99

CHAPTER 3: BULLETS

Position   *Centered on end point of positioning character*

Gray   Darkness of effect
Must use decimal point; two digits following
Range: .01 to 1.00 (Black)

Num   Number to insert
Single digits may be preceded by a space
Range: 0–99

Pct   Ratio: bullet diameter to font size of positioning character
Range: 10–999

Ps   Controls vertical placement of effect
Center of effect same position as
center of capital X in given font size
Range 1–99

XOff   Horizontal distance for shadow
+ moves shadow right, – moves left
Must use two digits and sign
Range: ±00–±99

YOff   Vertical distance for shadow
+ moves shadow down, – moves up
Must use two digits and sign
Range: ±00–±99

CHAPTER 4: BUTTONS

Position   *Centered on end point of positioning character*

Num   Number to insert
            Single digits may be preceded by a space
            Range: 0–99

Pct   Ratio: button diameter to font size of positioning character
            Range: 10–999

Ps   Controls vertical placement of effect
            Center of effect same position as center of
                capital X in given font size
            Range 1–99

TRBLSideColor
            Top, Right, Bottom, Left, SideColors
            Must be four numbers in array
            0 = Clear side
            1 = 50 percent gray side

Wid   Percentage of height of positioning character
            Range: 10–999

CHAPTER 5: BOXED TEXT | TEXT |

Position   *Where positioning character placed*

Gray   Darkness of shadow
Must use decimal point; two digits following
Range .01 to 1.00 (Black)

Hgt   Width of box drawn around text as percentage
of text point size
Range: 10–999

Line 1   Inner line point size
Range 0–9

Line 2   Outer line point size
Range 0–9

Maj   Number of large division lines in ruler
Lines spaced evenly along ruler length
Range 0–9

Min   Number of small lines within larger ruler divisions
Spaced equally inside large divisions
Range 0–9

Pct   Diameter of star drawn around text
Range: 10–999

Space   Distance between lines in points
Range: 0–9

Wid   Percentage of positioning character
Range: 10–999

XOff   Horizontal distance for shadow
+ moves shadow right, – moves left
Must use two digits and sign
Range: ±00– ±99

YOff   Vertical distance for shadow
+ moves shadow down, – moves up
Must use two digits and sign
Range ±00–±99

459

CHAPTER 6: BACKGROUND TEXT

Position *Where positioning character placed*

Ang Measured counterclockwise from horizontal
    Range: 0–360

Gray Darkness of text
    Must use decimal point; two digits following
    Range: .01 to 1.00 (Black)

Str   Text to be printed
    Maximum 100 characters

Xpos Horizontal location of text in inches
    Measured from left of page
    Use decimal point, two digits following
    Range: 0.00–99.00

Ypos Vertical location of text in inches
    Measured from top of page
    Use decimal point, two digits following
    Range: 0.00–99.00

CHAPTER 7: CHECKMARKS

Position   *Tip of checkmark at positioning character endpoint*

Gray   Darkness of checkmark
Must use decimal point; two digits following
Range: .00 (White) to 1.00 (Black)

Pct   Ratio: checkmark to font size of positioning character
Range: 10–999

XOff   Only used in combined effects
Set horizontal distance in points
+ moves checkmark right, – moves left
Must use two digits and sign
Range: ±00–±99

YOff   Only used in combined effects
Vertical distance for shadow
+ moves shadow down, – moves up
Must use two digits and sign
Range. ±00–±99

CHAPTER 8: ARROWS

Position   *Arrowhead on positioning character*

Ang   Specifies rotation angle
000 makes arrow begin at base of
    positioning character
Must use three digits
Range 000–360

Gray   Darkness of arrow
Must use decimal point, two digits following
.00 will produce white arrow with black outline
Range .00 to 1.00 (Black)

Len   Length of arrow in points
Positioning character establishes default
    minimum size of arrow
Must use two digits
Range 00–99

Pct   Ratio size of arrow to positioning character
Overall size of arrow as percentage of font size
Range 10–999

Shadow   Percentage of gray for shadow
Must use decimal point; two digits following
Range .01–1.00 (black)

XOff   Horizontal distance for shadow
+ moves shadow right, –moves left
In combined effects moves arrowhead right or left
Must use two digits and sign
Range ±00– ±99

YOff   Vertical distance for shadow
+ moves shadow down, – moves up
In combined effects moves arrowhead up or down
Must use two digits and sign
Range: ±00– ±99

CHAPTER 9: TEXT AND SHAPES

Position   *Arrowhead on Positioning character, others centered on point after positioning character*

Ang   Rotation angle; measured
                counterclockwise from horizontal
           Must use three digits
           Range: 000–360

Str   Text to be printed
           Maximum 100 characters

TRBLSideColor
           Top, Right, Bottom, Left, Sidecolor
           Must be four numbers in array
           0 = Clear side
           1 = 50 percent gray side

Movie Title | # CHAPTER 10: DISTORTED TEXT

Position   *Movietitle text centers on positioning character; others start on positioning character and extend right; mirror text extends left*

Ang   Rotation angle; measured counterclockwise
from horizontal line
Range 0–360

Gray   Darkness of shadow
Must use decimal point; two digits following
Range .01 to 1.00 (Black)

Str   Text to be printed
Maximum 100 characters

TBColor   Top, Bottom Color
Must be two numbers in array
0 = Outline
1= Black

TRBLSideColor
    Top, Right, Bottom, Left, SideColors
Must be four numbers in array
0 = Clear side
1 = 50 percent gray side

XOff   Horizontal distance for shadow
+ moves shadow right, – moves left
Must use two digits and sign
Range: ±00– ±99

YOff   Vertical distance for shadow
+ moves shadow down, – moves up
Must use two digits and sign
Range ±00– ±99

Index